From Here To... Obscurity

The sensational inside story of the pioneer of
the music video and top showbiz agent

– JON ROSEMAN –

From Here To...Obscurity

First published in the UK 2010
ISBN 978-184426-833-7
© Bambam Publishing Limited 2010

A catalogue reference for this book is available from the British Library.

Cover design by Simon Drake, with thanks to Lerone Clarke and Maria Bates

Printed and bound in the UK by Print On Demand Worldwide

Become a fan of 'From Here to... Obscurity' on www.facebook.com

Contents

INTRODUCTION

In truth I'd known the game was up weeks, maybe months earlier, but on the 27th April 2009, I called a meeting in my solicitors' boardroom. Geraldine, Vanessa and Fiona made the short journey from the Agency's office in Queen Anne Street to the lawyers' office in Upper Berkeley Street, near Marble Arch in Central London. I'd also invited an administrator/ insolvency accountant.

I might have been a television insider, the godfather of the pop video and a presenters' agent for 40 years, but this was the most difficult business meeting of my life.

'The Roseman Organisation' could not continue for another day. It was insolvent. It owed several clients money it could not repay. I tried to say this to the girls. They had been given no prior warning. They were not happy. I couldn't blame them. I felt pretty wretched myself. Mercifully the accountant soon took over and summarised the position more clearly than I could. The girls all wanted to continue to help their clients. The accountant gently explained that the shareholder had agreed to appoint him and that he now ran the Agency - or rather he was responsible for collecting its assets and paying its debts in a specific order of priority. Only, as I had said to him earlier, there was a shortfall and certain clients would be owed monies. It was a nightmare that had brought me to the very brink of suicide weeks earlier.

In part, the loss over the years of several major clients, starting with the murdered Jill Dando and followed over the years by Natasha Kaplinsky, Fern Britton and finally Kate Garraway, and the failure to attract a sufficient number of high earning replacements, was the major cause of the Agency's drop in turnover. But there were other major factors – the near collapse of the corporate market led to the decline in lucrative speaking opportunities and engagements for the clients the Agency retained and still attracted. The serious problems at ITV, and to a lesser extent throughout the British television generally from about 2007, made job retention for presenters difficult. Attempts to negotiate pay increases (and thus improved rates of commission), were fewer and further between.

Finally, I was reluctant to make the sort of cuts I should have accepted and also to sack good staff and relocate out of central London. I always clung to the hope that the Agency's credibility would be totally undermined if it had to downsize drastically.

Within three months I had left England for a sort of self-imposed exile to try to recover from this latest in a series of personal and financial setbacks that had punctuated my life and more than offset the highs and successes.

I decided that I would try and put this disaster in context and that the only way to do so was to write this autobiography. I hate self-pity. If you find any, you can stop reading. But I do want to explain, before I forget the detail, how and why I came to leave the country, the Agency and my family and friends. I couldn't have survived without the extraordinary support of Danielle Sterrie, my partner since the death of my wife Pearl in 1992. This book is dedicated to them both. It is the very least I could do. And it will never be enough.

AUTHOR'S NOTE

B ooks are not written in a vacuum. Whether you sell one book or a million, an author's work will have an effect on someone – even if it's only regret for having bought it in the first place! Writing an autobiography can be a dangerous pastime, particularly if you've led a life that some people might describe as 'colourful'. Mine possessed all the colours of the rainbow – plus some shades yet to be discovered.

Apart from legal problems with libel and the new interpretations in England of privacy, my major concern was that I was opening up some of the most intimate aspects of my life to my four children. But, the eldest is now thirty-one, the youngest, twenty-six, so 'children' they no longer are.

I can't say they were completely unaware of many of the things their father got up to, having heard versions of the stories over innumerable Sunday lunches. But some of the excesses, while not necessarily upsetting or shocking them, (since having me for a dad would have put paid to most of that anyway), nevertheless wouldn't have made this book an altogether, comfortable read for them. After all, they have friends who may now read about their father's exploits. I can't say I'm overly proud of some of the things I did. Indeed, there are some events that I'm completely ashamed of – particularly in the final pages.

To my children I can only say how proud I am of them and that I love them all so very deeply.

There are some people I'd like to thank for their help and support over the years, and particularly in this last one – though a few might not care to be mentioned!

In no particular order: my late and lovely wife Pearl, Ian Bloom whose advice and friendship over many years has been invaluable to me, Nick and Sally Pollard whose friendship has known no bounds, Seamus Lyte, Barry Kernon whose sound advice I rarely followed, Jonathan Shalit, John Knowles, Jan and Rees, Katie, Sean and Jane, Simon Drake a most resolute friend. Caroline Righton – so special, Bosh, Peter Willis, Lerone my surrogate son, the BBC's Nigel and Simon, which makes them sound like an odd couple, they're not. Cookie who's loved me long time, Les (aka lesbian), Jack who lent us his beautiful house in Cyprus, Jane and Tim, Wendy, Bev, Elena, Andreas and Costa for so many memorable times. Tom Kuhn, Liam and Ilaria, Julian and Penni, the wonderful and talented Steve Knightley and Phil Beer, Paul Simnock, Farmer Andrew, Martin and Nicos our friends in Cyprus for feeding us on too many occasions, our friend Simranjit for introducing me to Indian food. Lester, Steven Smith, Richard Jeffs and not forgetting Sadie, Petronius, Mitzi, Doesty and Blanco. They know who they are. There are so many more names, but I'm not paid by the word! So to all those other supportive friends, I say thank you with all my heart.

Finally to the love of my life, Danielle. She has suffered more than most. Her love and support have been incalculable and I just don't have the words to express my feelings for her. She has always been so very special – and I mean that in the best of all possible ways!

Jon Roseman. Cyprus June 2010

FROM HERE TO... OBSCURITY

The door bell rang. It was eight o'clock on a January morning in 2007. I glanced out of the window and saw a clear blue sky. We were enjoying the warmest January on record. I'd been up for an hour, eaten breakfast, been through the tabloids and had just emerged from the shower. Wrapping a towel round my waist I traipsed downstairs. I opened the door to eight policemen. Six were in uniform.

One of the non-uniforms flashed a search warrant and intoned,

'Are you Jonathan Martin Roseman?'

I thought for a moment. It's not as if I had an early onset of Alzheimer's. I reviewed my options. After a nano-second or two, I decided to fess up.

'Yes!'

'This is a warrant to search your premises for the offence of obtaining property by deception under section 15 (1) Theft Act 1968 from Fern Britton a.k.a. Fern Vickery.' He then placed the warrant in my damp left hand and they all marched in. I stood by the front door, my wet towel clinging to my waist for dear life, thinking about **those *fucking*** photographs.

CHAPTER ONE
THE EARLY YEARS

When I was a kid growing up in Hove, the gentile neighbour of Brighton in East Sussex, I had few special talents. I was one of the fastest runners in the county for my age and I was an excellent actor. The renowned theatre critic, the late Jack Tinker, then starting out and writing for the Brighton Evening Argus reviewed a school play I was in and predicted 'great things' for me. Well, he was right – after a fashion. I spent my entire life acting. *Will the real Jon Roseman please stand up?*

No one moved.

I seemed to have an innate ability to attract people who just wanted to talk. I would sit upstairs on an empty bus coming home from school and someone would inevitably park themselves next to me and unload their life's problems. I would listen; say little, then getting off, say goodbye. It was something I became used to, thinking, as a child would, that this happened to everyone.

Perhaps these odd traits helped me through a career which would make San Antonio's *rattler* ride a mere merry-go–round. With more luck than judgment, I set up the first agency exclusively for television presenters and aided and abetted the founding of the music video, working with the biggest rock stars of the twentieth century. I enjoyed interminable arguments with the likes of Richard Branson and assorted moguls on both sides of the Atlantic, found time to bump in to a couple of Presidents, a bunch of movie icons and let's not forget the Mafia. I then managed to regally fuck it all up.

Brighton and Hove were seaside towns joined at the hip. Brighton had a reputation for The Royal Pavilion, a weekend retreat for the Prince Regent, the heyday of handbag confrontations between *mods* and *rockers* circa 1964, a second-rate soccer team that early in life I had given my heart to, dirty weekends and buckets full of anti-Semitism. Hove was a dead zone.

There were around four hundred boys at my school. Among these Neanderthals there was one dwarf, one lad who had an endocrine problem which meant that by the age of thirteen he was over six foot tall and five Jews. Sounds like the start of a bloody joke. We five Jews had to put up with the daily curse of *you fucking yid*. I never found out why Brighton was a hot bed of anti-Semitism. Sure there was a large Jewish population, but I was never able to get to the bottom of it. Perhaps it was the sea air and the stony beaches.

Now I'm not a brave man, nor was I a brave boy, but there was something about being called a *yid* that really pissed me off. It blinded me to my own built-in cowardice, and provoked me into battle. As a kid I was the size of a normal twelve year old. I was no budding judo champion or boxer. When I went into battle I wasn't able to choose my adversary. If they used the word *yid* I just went for them. Some were a lot larger and older than me and consequently I took a right beating. With boys of a similar age and size, I did ok. The real dilemma was the younger boys. I had to make a judgment call that if I hit them, I risked the accusation of bullying. I figured that as I was getting my arse kicked most days from older boys then fuck it! For good measure I also threw a protective blanket around the dwarf and the tall kid. When they were bullied I was there for them. I was kept pretty busy. I think this is when my politics began to surface.

My leanings to the left soon became apparent. I once exited the local library clutching Khrushchev's tome, *Socialism in Peaceful Coexistence with Capitalism*. I didn't know what I was going to do with it - use it as a door stop perhaps. I loved books. At thirteen, apart from God knows how many science fiction novels I'd got through, I stuffed myself with Dickens and Conrad, a bunch of French writers like Camus and Sartre, explored existentialism and immersed myself in Freud and Jung. I was a right little intellectual!

The fact that the other Jews stayed out of any confrontation and showed no interest in defending their birthright didn't concern me at all. I never asked for their support and never had any expectations that I would get it anyway. It didn't help that our respective parents refused to allow us to attend morning assembly on the grounds that hymns were sung and consequently such close proximity to Christianity would somehow endanger our very souls. This simple exclusion sent out the rather obvious signal that we were different. They might as well have tattooed on our foreheads, 'Hit me, I'm a Jew.'

I was the fourth youngest in a family of five. My elder brother Raphael (Ray) was the real athlete. In the 1960's he ran for England in the mile and was the first Jew anywhere in the world to break four minutes. Three sisters, Sandra, a nurse; Jane, a travel rep and Wendy well she was just Wendy. That's a little harsh; she worked as a sales rep for Gestetner.

Why my parents even had five children perplexes me to this day. If awards were given out to dysfunctional families we would have been tossed a couple of Oscars.

They had little or no time for any of us. Mostly we were left to our own devices. *Love* really was a four letter word in our house. My father was a commercial traveller selling greeting cards. When he left the army after the war, having been away for over four years, he set up his own company. I can't begin to imagine what my mother, Ray and Sandra must have felt when this man suddenly reappeared in their lives.

After some business success, his brother, who worked for him, ripped him off, leaving him bankrupt. This kind of activity seems to happen in a lot of Jewish families. We moved from a nice house in Balham, South London, to a small flat in Hove. I was three.

My father had a great fondness for his *Sam Browne* belt. The belt was army issue. He had served in India for much of the war. Unfortunately he had saved his belt as a souvenir. It was unfortunate because he often used it on our backsides for even the most minor of infractions. I was beaten for drawing a chalk hopscotch outline on the pavement. My father died a few years back. He managed to reach ninety five. My mother is still alive - depending on your definition of *alive*. She resides in a Jewish old people's home in Brighton. We're not sure how old she is, but when she dies, we're going to have her carbon dated.

I have few memories of my childhood and most of them are not that great. But there's one memory that's seared in to my cerebral cortex. Living next door to us in Hove was an elderly Jew. Tall and thin with grey hair and an aesthetic face. He lived alone, I think his wife had died some years before and I had no idea if he had any family. We would meet in the street every now and again and became very fond of each other. He was gentle and kind and full of good advice. All the stuff I didn't get at home. After a while I would spend time with him in his flat having tea. He seemed, at least to my childish years, very wise. We would sit in his study, him behind his desk covered with photographs, and me in a big Queen Anne chair opposite. Among the photographs on his desk he had one of those old silver tubular calendars. A tiny winder changed the date, month and year. I loved playing with that calendar. It seemed almost magical to me.

One day as I walked past his flat on my way back from school, I noticed an overflowing dustbin in his yard. I stopped and looked, wondering why there was so much stuff covering the ground and that's when I saw it. On the very top of the dustbin was the silver calendar mixed up with all the photographs from his desk. My friend had died and all his worldly possessions had ended up in a big, dented, grey dustbin. I think that single event may have coloured my whole life. I should have taken the calendar. Of course I should. But I didn't.

I have done my best over the years to repress all my childhood memories but a few bizarre ones have still managed to cling on for dear life. When I was around seven, my little sister, Wendy, needed to have her tonsils removed, but as she was hyper-excitable, my parents decided to have *my* tonsils removed as well to placate her fears. In retrospect that was the only shred of thoughtfulness I can recall them expressing for any of us.

I was taken to a London hospital for the minor procedure. Only it didn't turn out to be so minor. Complications turned a day or two into a two week stay. My father, who travelled to London on a daily basis, found time to visit me once. My mother also showed up on a solitary occasion.

My sister Jane delights in the story that aged four, when we lived in London, she had to take herself to school having to catch two buses. When she brought this up, many years later, my mother said simply, 'That's what you wanted to do!' I'm not sure how Social Services would view such behaviour today.

I had just started secondary school when we moved house. I'd heard my parents talking about it for weeks and I found it all rather exciting. The big day arrived and as usual I set off for school at eight o'clock. School was out at four and as I ran to the bus stop (I ran everywhere in those days) it suddenly hit me - they hadn't given me the address. It took me three hours to find them. I'd heard them talking about it being close to Hove fire station and I asked around for directions to the fire station and eventually found the pantechnicon parked directly opposite the home of our brave fire fighters. What's a little worrying was that I didn't find their memory lapse remotely disconcerting – and nor, apparently, did they.

I loved sport and apart from my prowess as an athlete, I boxed a little and played in goal for the schools' second eleven. In one fiercely fought boxing match I hit my opponent so hard that I broke my thumb in three places though I didn't know it at the time. The following day, Saturday, I had a football match. As was usual in our household, I had to leg it to the game some four miles away. No lift was offered and rarely was the bus fare forthcoming. Being young and fit running four miles before playing was not an issue.

As soon as I made my first save it was all over. The pain was excruciating. I made my way back home and found my mother and showed her my hand with its accompanying swollen thumb. 'It could be broken,' she mused, 'perhaps you should go to the hospital.' I walked the mile and a half to Hove General Hospital only to find the X–ray department closed on Saturday. The nearest hospital was the Royal Sussex in Brighton some three miles away. After the usual four hour wait I was x–rayed, and the fracture was put in plaster and I wandered back home. It never occurred to me then that even the most preoccupied parent would have either given me a lift or provided the bus fare for my excursion.

We were all made to attend synagogue. Ray and I were both bamitzvahed. It's customary for family and friends to give the bamitzvah boy money as a gift so he had a little nest egg that he could turn to when he hit eighteen or so. My loving parents had me endorse all the cheques I was given and banked them. I never saw a penny.

We were not an orthodox Jewish family and certainly not brought up immersed in Jewish history or tradition. So where my rather eccentric support for Judaism came from I don't know. Perhaps it was from reading Leon Uris's, *Exodus* (1958). The book tells the heroic story of how some European Jews who had survived the war fought their way into Palestine. I read it when I was twelve. Looking back now I really think that bloody Uris book cost me a thousand bruises!

I left school and college with qualifications that would have been a disappointment to Lindsay Lohan. Sure I'd read a lot, having now added to my leftie studies, astronomy (still a passion), Greek and Roman history and stuff on particle physics, but all this made little difference to my ability to pass exams.

By now, 1964, I had a girlfriend, Pearl. We had met at the Brighton Art College's Friday night club. It was less a club, more a very large basement with a bar. I was with a friend when we spied these two great looking girls. I rather fancied Pearl's friend, but my mate got there first! Pearl was studying fashion design and was a brilliant illustrator. She was petite and wore the shortest skirts. She showed a great pair of legs and had long thick red hair and had a temper to match. Her father owned a small factory in the East End making rubber washers. They were comfortably middle-class.

I looked and dressed like the archetypal student. Long black curly hair, the must-have wispy beard, brown corduroy trousers and oversized sweaters. I was medium height and had an oval face which set off my prominent aquiline nose to perfection! I'd inherited from some very distant ancestor a boxer's physique; the broad shoulders metaphorically would come in useful as the years slid by. Pearl and I started to date and fell in love. She was eighteen and I was a few months younger.

CHAPTER TWO
AMYL NITRATE, THE SWINGING SIXTIES AND PEARL

I'd always wanted to be a writer. For me, it was less a burning desire, more a question of inevitability. It's only taken sixty odd years. I long comforted myself in the belief that the great French writer André Gide didn't put pen to paper till his late fifties. I now know this to be complete bollocks! But in the summer of 1968, I travelled up to London from Brighton with a few pounds in my pocket, ready to pickaxe the golden pavements. I planned to get a job, any job, and write.

I had a crazy drug fuelled artist friend called Charlie Zuber who I'd met at Pearl's art college. He was now living in London and offered me a place to stay. His place. Charlie was pencil thin and short with long straggly brown hair, hazel eyes that hinted at a touch of insanity and wore clothes that were better suited to an Indian peasant. He'd studied Fine Art. Pearl told me he was very talented but Art and I were complete strangers.

It seemed to me he only had one ambition - to try out every illegal substance known to mankind. He lived in Finchley, a reasonably nice area of North London, having dropped out of his course. Charlie, however, had managed to find the only bed-sit in an area that could have been twinned with sixties Beirut. The room was home to my friend and a bunch of rather hungry rats. Rather than sleep on the floor I chose to sleep across two chairs in the vain hope that the distance from floor to chair would give me some defence from being partially consumed by undiscriminating rodents.

Charlie loved drugs. I could recognise cannabis and grass but some of the other stuff he did was unknown to me and probably most qualified pharmacologists. It was however the smell of poppers, amyl nitrate, that always comes to mind when I think of Charlie. They became part of the drug culture of the seventies and were supposed to enhance sexual pleasure. He got there first. But why he would break one open and inhale it as we walked along the street was a complete mystery. Sexual gratification and the Finchley High Road had no obvious sexual connection that I could see. At this point in my life I didn't do drugs. I had to wait till I was twenty-eight and my second trip to America before I was formally introduced.

Until I got a job, I couldn't afford the rail fare back to Brighton so I had to rely on Pearl using her allowance to visit me most Saturdays. She'd purchase a cheap return ticket and I'd meet her at Victoria Station and we'd catch the tube and go in search of the swinging sixties. This was the time of Harold Wilson and his sad 'I'm Backing Britain' campaign, of Vietnam and student protests. I loved it all, apart from the Wilson bit. Pearl and I would sit in cafes along the King's Road listening to the Beatles' Sergeant Pepper album or Jimi Hendrix blaring out of the café speakers. If truth be told I didn't really get Hendrix. I had always been more of an opera person, something that was not shared by my red headed girlfriend. Pearl and I searched the King's Road for the swinging sixties as we'd read that it was the epicentre of all things cool. We never found it.

CHAPTER THREE
LONDON WEEKEND TELEVISION AND THE EIGHTEENTH FLOOR

I needed to make some money. I needed to work. I studied the employment adverts in the London Evening News and thus began my writing career in earnest. I posted off job applications to half of London. I was called for only two interviews. One at British American Tobacco (BAT), the other at a new television station, London Weekend (LWT).

BAT was located on the Embankment near Westminster Bridge. Wearing my only pair of dark trousers, my father's cast off fawn jacket, so large that it almost concealed my hands, and one of Charlie's shirts with my old school tie, I met their Head of Personnel. The office was quite impressive, at least to me, probably because the only other office I'd ever visited was my headmaster's for the occasional caning. After the usual cursory greeting he asked if I smoked and offered me one from his packet. I had started smoking when I was twelve. As I was broke I took one with grateful thanks. 'That's good,' he smiled, 'can't work here if you don't smoke!'. Those were funny old non PC days. I didn't get the job.

My next interview took me to a building called Station House, the administrative base of LWT. It was located on the North Circular road close to Wembley. It was without doubt a truly god forsaken spot. It stood almost alone amid the noise and smell of a busy dual carriageway. It was a cold grey building that had twenty stories and tiny windows conjuring up visions of the worst nightmares of the old Soviet regime.

I took the lift to the eighteenth floor and was interviewed for the position of junior cost planner in the programme management department. What that meant to me was up there with the secrets of the universe or how Fearne Cotton ever found work.

I got the job!

It was 1969. London Weekend Television was borne out of the breakup of Rediffusion. Now there would be two separate companies broadcasting to London. Thames and LWT. LWT ran from Fridays at seven o'clock in the evening to close down on Sundays. Thames had the lion's share of the week. My salary was £950 a year. Those were the days of trendy £6 suits and rents of tiny flats at £13 per week.

My job was to estimate the costs of television programmes on a weekly basis. If the company waited for the real costs via the accounts department it would have taken months. There were two other cost planners. The more experienced one dealt with drama; the other handled light entertainment (LE) and sport. My remit was children's programmes and current affairs. All these estimates were amalgamated into one document so the Controller of Programmes could see where the money was going and, crucially, how much he had left to spend. Initially, all this was way beyond me.

As the months rolled by, Pearl moved to Clapham in south London and I was sharing a flat in Hampstead Garden Suburb which I'd spotted advertised in the Evening News. She joined a company that required her to visit all the major European fashion shows, memorise all the cat walk designs and scurry back to London where she reproduced what she had seen. Her work was sent to Japanese and American manufacturers (nowadays, it would be sent to China). They then made up cheap copies and put them in the high street shops. All probably highly illegal but very well paid.

I soon got a handle on my work and learnt exactly how much programmes cost and why. Producers with new scripts would hand them over to me, so I could cost them out over the weekend before they were submitted. Usually I was rewarded for these unofficial efforts with a bottle of something.

The top floor of this hideous building contained the canteen and bar. The bar was a wondrous place. All the stars of the shows would often hang out there. Some drinking in such quantities that would put Oliver Reed to shame. Frank Muir, the Head of Entertainment, always needed a few drinks before decamping to the BBC for his radio quiz programme, *My Word*. He told me he wouldn't be able to do it without a little Dutch courage. On the other hand, Tommy Cooper went way beyond a few. I'm not sure if I ever saw him sober. And I saw him a lot. The TV stars of yesteryear queued at the bar with the rest of us. Barry Evans, the star of the *Doctor In The House* series, John Alderton and Derek Guyler from *Please Sir* and Reg Varney a mega star of *On The Buses*. Reg was taking home a thousand pounds a week - more than I earned in a year. They were all very approachable, particularly after a few drinks. The nature of stardom today is very different. While TV audiences back then were huge, (eighteen million was a prime time average), egos weren't. No retinues of hangers on to feed them bullshit - only beer and nuts in a bar where they were safe from the tabloid gossip columnists.

The studios where the programmes were filmed were located a mile up the road in Wembley. I often dropped by and experienced firsthand how programmes were actually made. It was a revelation. The sets always appeared ten times bigger on the telly than they did in the studio. In those early days everything was in black and white.

The coming of colour threw LWT into confusion. How much more would it cost? Would extra staff be required? Cameras would have to be changed and all the monitors dumped and colour ones purchased. The technology cluttering up the control rooms would have to be re-examined and augmented. In fact the changeover was relatively smooth and the programme costs didn't rise significantly, much to everyone's surprise.

CHAPTER FOUR
DAVID FROST AND GUESTS

After I'd been there ten months the bosses were looking for a unit manager for the *Frost Programmes.* A unit manager was a hands on administrator. Booking facilities, liaising with all the other departments that contributed to the making of the programmes, keeping a tight eye on all the costs, and generally being the fall guy when the producer fucked up were the main requirements.

Frost, being a founding father of the station, had three shows. *Frost on Friday, Saturday and Sunday.* Friday was an interview show, Saturdays and Sundays more light entertainment and satire. I was doing ok, work-wise, at the time but was certainly nothing special. I was astounded to be offered the job. I later 'found' a confidential memo that basically said, *'...we'll have to give it to Roseman as we've left it too late to find anyone suitable'.* Can't get a better recommendation than that!

My job had additional responsibilities as the three programmes were so varied. I had to ensure that all the guests got to the studio on time, check the team's expenses, sort out all the travel, not just for the guests, but for the team as well, liaise with agents for guests' special requirements and deal with the American secret service when required!

David was being paid £5,500 per programme or £16,500 per week. My salary had moved to £2,000 per year as a result of this promotion. I knew my place. On top of Frost's LWT money, the Westinghouse Corporation in America were paying him God knows how many dollars for four other shows a week that were broadcast from Manhattan.

David would arrive at around ten o'clock every Friday morning having flown in overnight from New York. The team had worked all week getting the shows together and rarely bothered the great man while he laboured away in the Big Apple. He would walk in to the conference room where we were all gathered, some thirty or so of us, a mound of traditional bacon butties a centre piece on the huge table and take his seat at one end.

The producer was a totally ineffectual man who has long since passed on. The fact that even I appreciated his limitations, having only been in the business for ten months, says a lot about him. On more than one occasion David would listen to the plans for the shows and say simply, 'I don't think that's a great idea,' The team were then forced to dump all the work they'd done over the previous four days leaving eight hours to find guests for that night's programme.

On one of his Friday shows, we had the ex-President's wife, Lady Bird Johnson, and her younger daughter, Lady Bird Nugent. The previous morning, the telephone had rung in my rented flat in Westbourne Grove, Notting Hill Gate. I had just moved in there with Pearl. Her parents would never have approved of us living together and on their rare visits all remnants of my life had to be hastily removed. The call was from the American Embassy. Would I meet several members of their staff at the studios in an hour? As the Beatles song says, 'got up, got out of bed, dragged a comb across my head,' (I had curly hair in those days) and shot over to Wembley. I met three nice guys who turned out to be secret service agents. They were all dressed in identical black suits and brilliant white shirts. They wanted to know the 'route' the ex- President's wife would be taking from reception to her dressing room and how she would get to the studio and then back to her dressing room and then back to the limo. One of the men, let's call him Chuck, did all the talking. He was all business but very polite. I think he knew he was dealing with a *schmuck*.

David never met any of his guests when they arrived. He would amble over to their dressing rooms to introduce himself just before the show started. It went out live at nine o'clock. It was the producer's job to greet them in reception, when they arrived, shake a hand or two and guide them to their respective dressing rooms.

An hour or so before the arrival of the ex-President's wife, I was allocated to sit with the three secret service guys in reception and when her arrival was imminent, make the producer aware so he could do the glad-handing. The secret service didn't do sitting. They wandered the large reception area like lions searching for prey or went out in to the street looking keenly around no doubt searching for hidden assassins concealing themselves behind the occasional lamp post. I found all this activity great fun. What would my old anti-Semitic buddies back home in Brighton think of me now, all scrunched up with the American secret service? After watching the three men doing their job for a while, I asked Chuck how long before the ex-President's wife would show. He looked at me, then spoke to his wrist and said,' Now!'

At that moment, a dozen police motor cyclists roared up outside the front doors of the studio followed by a fleet of police cars and a half a dozen blacked out limos. I was transfixed. This couldn't be for real. I'd been transported to Hollywood and had become an extra in some terrible B movie. I should have called the producer, but all my reflexes had been put on hold. The doors swung open. More secret services poured in to the reception area followed by Lady Bird Johnson and her daughter Lucy Baines Nugent. Any movement became impossible for me. I tried but the signal from brain to legs had been temporarily interrupted. Suddenly Chuck was introducing me and I'm shaking hands with a woman whose husband was, until recently, the most powerful man in the Western World. Chuck must have noticed my plight as he put a reassuring hand on my shoulder and turning me toward the direction of the dressing room said something like, 'Mam, Jon will show you to your dressing room.' I managed the short journey up two flights of stairs and fifteen feet of corridor and opened the door. The way she thanked me made me feel that I had just done some great service for the American people. I liked her!

Working on the Frost shows made a young man grow up fast. Standing, unable to move, every time you met a President or his wife was not an option. The first President to cross my threshold was Julius Nyerere of Tanzania. This time I was ready! He and Woody Allen were on the same programme. Nyerere's security were called the ten foot men. Not because they were particularly tall, but because they would never stray more than ten feet from their charge. When David had finished the interview, there was a commercial break. I had to escort the President from the studio to the green room (where the booze and sandwiches were) or out to his car(s). He suddenly gripped my arm tightly and for a terrifying moment I thought I had become embroiled in some unforgivable diplomatic incident.

'David will be interviewing Woody Allen, yes?' he whispered in my ear. I nodded. 'Then I must stay. Big fan of Woody Allen'.

He wanted to sit in the studio to watch the interview. Sounds simple. However the programme goes out live in front of an audience of perhaps four hundred people. The studio is packed. I had two minutes to remove the entire front row, some forty people to accommodate the president and his 'ten foot' men before we went on air. A man has to do what a man has to do.

Pearl's career was flourishing and there was even talk of marriage. We were now living together. Her parents would still not have approved of the arrangement and I was still having to eradicate my existence whenever they visited, which wasn't often, but nonetheless a little wearisome. I began to call it Operation Anne Frank.

Many years later, Dan (about who much more later) and I had a very good friend who lived in Amsterdam, Rineke, who has since sadly died. She was a remarkable woman. One day when we visited her she insisted on taking us on a canal tour of her beautiful city. As we passed Anne Frank's house, she pointed it out. Thinking of that little girl hidden away all those years ago deeply unsettled me. I mentioned this to Rineke.

'Me too,' she said. 'One day I was walking near the house and a German couple, on holiday, asked if I knew the way, I told them that they didn't have any problem finding it last time!' I guess there is still no love lost been the Dutch and the Germans.

We had, by now, become part of the LWT social scene. We invited people to our tiny lowly rented flat and they invited us to their very upmarket abodes.

Pearl's friends were fascinated by my work. Who wouldn't be? Presidents, film and TV stars all passed through my young life. For the record I never actually had any friendships with these people. They were merely luxury yachts that passed in the night.

It was November 1970. David wanted to interview Jerry Rubin. Rubin was a major player in the Yippies. The Yippies were an anarchist movement founded in 1968. The name referred to the Youth International Party. Think the sixties, anti-establishment, multiply by the first number you think of and you get the picture. Rubin wasn't the kind of man who would baulk at using the "fuck" word on television, and as the show was live, a lot of thought was given to what would happen if he started swearing and wouldn't stop. The only precaution the powers that be could come up with was to provide another studio in case Rubin went on an obscene rant. That way the other guest, the social commentator Robert Ardrey, could be interviewed, albeit without an audience, but more importantly without a bunch of anarchists screaming profanities into the ether.

The evening arrived and David began the interview. For a while the signs looked good. Then, without warning, Rubin called out to the audience for his friends to join him. Thirty or forty young men and women suddenly jumped up and made their way down to the front of the studio. The men pulled off their hats revealing long flowing hair and sat down at the feet of Frost and their leader.

We'd been hijacked!

I was standing off camera watching this incredible scene. For an incredible scene it surely was.

Unprecedented in British television history. David, the ultimate pro, did his best to contain this flood of humanity. The language everyone feared began to envelop the airways. One or two Yippies pulled out water pistols and began aiming them at David, the camera crew and even me. Control was inevitably lost and the director went to a commercial break. Frost and guest left for the stand-by studio leaving me and two elderly commissionaires to deal with the expulsion of the uninvited interlopers. They were very accommodating. Seeing their chance for further network exposure had vanished, they all left in an orderly fashion.

Whenever Pearl worked abroad, stealing designs from some foreign catwalk or other, she would call me at the end of the evening at my office after I had finished the show to say goodnight which was normally around eleven. That night she was frantic. She couldn't get through to the studio. It had been inundated with so many calls of complaint that the switchboard had ceased to operate.

The following day the entire programme team was ordered before the Programme Controller, Stella Richman, who angrily waved newspapers at the assembled gathering carrying front page headlines condemning the programme and LWT for transmitting it. All the papers claimed it was a publicity stunt and that the executives who authorised it should be fired. Fortunately, I was so far down the food chain that her ire had no effect on me.

On the Monday morning following the debacle, I was rung up by one of the Controller of Programmes' secretaries and ordered to meet some people in the studio reception within the hour. I wasn't deemed relevant enough to be told who or what they were.

It was the only time, to my knowledge, that I had to deal with Special Branch. I had to escort four rather overweight and badly dressed men in to an edit suite where the entire programme was played back for their edification. They would instruct the editor on occasions to freeze frame pictures, all close ups of the Yippie intruders, so they could take photographs of them. The seventies were such a fun time!

I knew it was time to move on after one particular programme. David gave a very poor interview to someone he should have shredded. After the show I wandered down the dismally grey painted corridor on my way to the green room and the remains of a few curled up sandwiches when the great man popped his head out of his dressing room. 'Hey Jon, how do you think it went tonight?'

Did I tell him the truth?

'Not one of your best,' I finally replied. We looked at each other for a few moments.

'Seriously,' he said. 'What did you *really* think?' Another pause.

'Great David.' I managed to say. He smiled.

Fuck! I was becoming one of them.

The experiences I endured on the Frost programmes were unique. Those kinds of programmes would never be made again.

CHAPTER FIVE
BARRY TOOK, SIMON DEE AND RUPERT MURDOCH

I'd frequently bump into Barry Took in the LWT bar and we hit it off. Barry was one of the finest comedy writers of his generation. From writing *Round The Horne* and *Rowan and Martin's Laugh-In* to putting together the *Monty Python* team. So when he asked me to be the unit manager of *The Simon Dee Show* I accepted. One show a week had to be easier than three. But, looking back, frying pan and fire come to mind.

Poor old Simon. He had been seduced away from the BBC where he hosted a hugely successful chat show, *Dee Time*, to present *The Simon Dee Show* for LWT. But it turned into a disaster on so many levels.

For a start, Simon wasn't that bright. To say he believed in his own publicity is like saying Simon Cowell isn't shy and retiring. Tito Burns, then head of variety at LWT, had made him promises that could never be fulfilled. Tito had apparently told him he could have a major say in the selection of the show's guests. Now if you are David Frost and you sit on the LWT board, ok. But if you smoke a lot of dope and believe in your own hype, then dream on. Simon was the Jonathan Ross of the early seventies in terms of television persona. There are no other similarities. Jonathan is a clever lad. Three years at Shrewsbury notwithstanding, Simon was not.

Tito didn't stay too long at LWT. He wasn't a corporate kind of man. He'd run his own thing for far too long and didn't take kindly to attending meetings he hadn't called.

But he'd left us with the problem called Simon Dee.

Dee's shows were a lesson in making car crash television. The first producer, Brian Izzard, did have a lot of talent. After a couple of months though, he'd had enough and moved on. We had no credible producer and no credible programmes lined up. But we had thirteen more live shows to make on Saturday evenings when 15 million viewers tuned in.

Dee lived the sixties dream. Unfortunately it was early 1970. David Frost was not his biggest fan. Dee's show followed his on Saturday nights and there are only so many credible guests to go round. Barry Took, in common with just about everyone else in television, was not a founder member of the Simon Dee Appreciation Society either. So after Izzard left, he appointed LWT's only female camera operator to produce the remainder of the series.

Bimbi Harris had been one of the first camera 'men' and had worked in television before cameras were on dollies. In the good old days, it could take a rope and two shire horses to shift a studio camera. Technological advances meant you could now move one with your little finger. She wasn't even five foot tall but could still haul one of those old cameras. Such skills did not, however, make her a great producer.

She had been taken off producing *Police 5*, a five minute filler hosted by Shaw Taylor asking for the public's help in finding a few villains. It was the forerunner of Crimewatch. Prior to that, she had worked on some low-budget children's programmes. Not a great track record to take over a major prime time live chat show series.

The Simon Dee Show! was similar to every other chat show, before and since. Bring on one guest, go to a commercial break, guest leaves, reel in the next one, often a singer, singer sings, interview said singer. Finally, bring them all on together and it's a wrap. And all in front of a studio audience of some three hundred and fifty people.

The first of many disasters was when Bimbi decided that it would be a great idea to pair Shirley Bassey and Eartha Kitt on the same programme. Both were hugely successful forty years ago. Unfortunately, they were not best friends. The other guest was Terry Thomas, a British film star of the late fifties and sixties. Though a fine actor, he mostly played the same part – the definitive English cad. His trademarks were a large gap in his front teeth and a long cigarette holder.

Ms Kitt was the first on for an interview and a song. It went well. Then Terry did his thing and I did what I normally did on show night. I kept the guests happy. I escorted them to and from their dressing rooms. I made sure they had plenty to drink.

Having heard the rumours about Bassey and Kitt, I did my best to keep them apart. It was after Bassey's interview that the multiple pile up happened. Bassey sang *two* songs. The producer might as well have stuck a rusty knife into Eartha Kitt's heart.

After the commercial break, I had to take Kitt and Thomas back in front of the cameras for the show's dénouement. I was still only twenty-two and I had been transported to celebrity hell. I had three minutes to persuade Kitt to return to the stage. She was really, really angry. 'How could they do this to me?' she wailed. 'How could they give that ***** *two* songs?' I didn't know. I didn't care. It was my job just to get her back. I can't now recall how I did it. Mercifully, it's a memory long lost. Then I had to stand at the side of the set with Terry and wait for the show to resume recording before he re-appeared and joined Bassey, Kitt and Dee on the sofa.

It was Bimbi's bright idea that Terry should bring on a silver tray with champagne as a pastiche of one of his famous butler roles. This pathetic proposal had only been explained to him while Bassey was banging out her second number ten minutes earlier. Live filming resumed. I lifted the tray from a side table and tried to hand it to him. Terry Thomas promptly burst into tears. This was becoming a truly memorable night.

'It's so demeaning,' he began to sob. 'I can't do it. Oh my god!!' I was pretty sure that I hadn't asked him to strip naked. It was just a silver tray after all.

My first thought was that we were only separated from the studio audience by about fifteen feet and his mini-breakdown would soon be picked up by members of the public.

'Come on Terry,' I cajoled,' you're just presenting your world famous image to your fans.'

'No, Jon, I mean it. I can't do it.' Ignoring his protestations, I placed the tray in his hands and gently nudged him toward Dee and co. As he gathered pace, he turned on his famous swagger and changed back in to the star he was.

This kind of disaster wasn't a weekly occurrence. After all, the St John's Ambulance Brigade needed some time off. Towards the end of the series, celebrity guests were starting to steer clear, so 'real' people with a story to tell became, briefly, the order of the day. They were desperate times. A hairdresser from Wales, Monty someone, contacted a researcher claiming he could cut a girl's full length hair into a page boy bob in two minutes. Blindfolded!

He came to the studio with two models, one for the rehearsal and the other for the show. The starter's gun fired. He started cutting. It was mayhem. After nearly three minutes, we had to stop him. It was a total disaster. The girl looked in a mirror and became hysterical. She had been scalped.

I sat with her and did my best to calm her down. I promised to send her to Vidal Sassoon to sort it out. Not just to his salon, but to the man himself. Monty, who had been pacing up and down in the green room, demanded to know if we were going to pay his expenses. I took another look at the sobbing model and told him he had three minutes to leave the building or security would help him on his way. We tended to avoid those kind of items after that.

Towards the end of the series, a petulant Simon Dee suddenly announced that he wouldn't do the next show. Barry Took asked me to call in Pete Murray (remember, this was nearly 40 years ago!). Pete agreed and was our stand-by presenter. Someone, somewhere, must have got through to Simon, because he did turn up on Saturday and did present the show. At Barry's request, I sent Pete a crate of champagne.

But it was George Lazenby's appearance that became the proverbial nail. Invited on to talk about his one and only starring role as James Bond in *On Her Majesty's*

Secret Service, a year or so after its release, he pulled a bunch of papers from his inside jacket pocket, waved them at the studio audience and then launched into a monologue of conspiracy theories surrounding the assassination of President Kennedy.

Dee didn't have the skills to stop him. He sat transfixed, fear of the unknown leaking through his eyes, sweat running down his forehead, his mouth open. The mute button had been activated. Lazenby's diatribe continued unabated for five minutes before the director was forced to cut it off. This was so far beyond a normal motorway disaster; it was the television equivalent of 9/11. Dee was finished. When his series ended, he never worked in television again.

As Barry Took and I got on so well he invited me to be the manager of the entire light entertainment department. Two months later he was gone. Not to be replaced. I was boss-less. Worse was to follow.

Rupert Murdoch had recently purchased a chunk of LWT shares and was now spending time 'fixing' all LWT's problems. He fired nearly every senior executive! The controller of programmes, Stella Richman, was given an hour to leave the building, Humphrey Burton the head of Drama Arts and Music and others too numerous to mention all got the Australian's boot.

Stella's daughter, nicknamed Cookie, was working at the company and we became good mates. She is still one of my closest friends. Through our friendship I got to know Stella, often visiting their beautiful London home in Maida Vale. It was very unusual for someone like me in such a lowly position to have a relationship with a Controller. She was the first female controller in the history of TV as well as becoming the first female independent producer going on to make stunning award winning dramas.

Finally the broadcasting authority decided Murdoch couldn't own a controlling interest in a TV company and run a bunch of newspapers. Something had to give. He went, leaving a ship with no rudder and a huge hole amidships.

CHAPTER SIX
JOHN BIRT, WEEKEND WORLD AND GUNS

I had now worked at LWT for just over three years. It was 1972. I had had to contend with some very difficult situations and most importantly hadn't written a single word of *the* novel/screenplay/poem etc. I had become so caught up in the TV business that I had not given any thought to where I was going. I figured I was a stowaway on a boat to nowhere land and was praying no one would ask me for my ticket. I was now twenty-four and being paid a reasonable whack and meeting 'exciting' people, so I figured the book could wait a while.

As unit manager of light entertainment, I worked from a tiny open plan office. The entire department was divided by small screens. Only the most senior controllers had a room with a door. My office sat next to the new Head of Programmes, Rex Firkin. He was a good man, and an award winning drama producer. However what he knew about LE was close to zero. He thought *I* knew about light entertainment and had decided to rely on me completely for guidance.

Everyone in the department was a stranger to him. The fact that I had only been doing the job for two months was of no concern to him whatsoever. He was used to dealing with Stella Ashley the late, great unit manager of drama who was a fantastic operator. I was being asked to make contributions to things that were totally beyond me. It was the darkest period of my LWT life.

Just after his appointment I'd gone home early, thinking seriously that I'd call an end to my short lived TV career. I didn't go in for three days and no one called me to find out where I was or why I wasn't at work. I discussed the situation with Pearl and told her I was in no position to play at being some kind of *de facto* head of light entertainment. I'd had enough of it all. Frankly, I was scared of being put in such a ridiculous position after such a short time in the business. The phone rang. It was Rex Firkin. Pearl handed me the phone. I expected to be fired on the spot for pissing off without permission.

'Sorry to call you at home,' Rex said, relaxed and truly apologetic, 'but we need to talk about future LE programmes. You know I've got no idea about them. When do you think you'll be popping back?' I stared at the phone and wasn't sure who I felt more sorry for, him or me.

'Monday,' I said.

'Grand,' he said, 'See you at nine.'

I put the phone down and wondered what to do. If he had no idea I had even less to offer. I went out and bought the Radio and TV Times. In those days they listed all the programme production credits. I studied them carefully to brief myself on who was doing what and where and prepared for a meeting that I had absolutely no right to attend.

He was really pleased to see me and went straight to it. For my part I began reeling out names of people for upcoming projects in such an authoritative manner that Rex obviously felt he was dealing with a skilled and experienced junior exec and not some schmuck who had just gleaned a bunch of info from the TV guides.

One day, after suffering the job for about eight months, I was chatting with Rex in his office and noticed a memo on his desk. I had become a past master at reading memos upside-down. It was a note from John Birt outlining a current affairs series for a Sunday transmission which would later become Weekend World (WW).

Having had my fill of LE, I decided to go and see Birt to find out more about the new series. When I first spied the man he had shoulder length hair and wore a blue shiny satin jacket. He had recently left Granada TV where he'd edited World In Action. This was one of the great current affairs series of all time. Frost had brought him in to work on his programmes, having finally given up on the old producer who'd left to run Oracle.

Tucked up in a small corner office on the seventeenth floor was the myth that was John Birt. Corner offices were important; they were the ones with windows, albeit widows that would only open twelve inches. I once asked someone why the windows only opened a fraction, to be told it was to stop people from jumping out. LWT could be a difficult place, but such precautions did seem a tad over the top. That is 'till two months into working for Birt, a young, very troubled and emaciated secretary, managed to squeeze herself through an eighteenth floor window and jump to her death.

My meeting with the new whiz-kid of British television didn't start off too well.

'I recognise you,' he said,' you're the guy who's always in the bar.' I have had my moments, but I thought this a little presumptuous. He went on to lecture me about his ambitions for the proposed new series and told me the kind of people he intended to hire and how this new Sunday slot would accommodate a live two hour programme that had never been done before. I tried to keep focus as he spoke, but as he didn't stop for nearly forty-five minutes, I began to fear I may slip in to a coma.

Finally he said, 'So you want to know if I'd like you to be the unit manager?'

'No that's not quite right,' I replied,' I wanted to see if it was something *I'd* like to do.'

This set the tone for our relationship.

I never had the ambition to work in television and couldn't have cared less if either he hired me or someone else fired me. I was in my early twenties and I had my whole life ahead of me. In those halcyon days there was so much choice for an averagely intelligent youth with some kind of personality.

Everyone who fell into Birt's orbit felt they had something to prove. Often it was his approval they craved. For me it meant more money and not having to deal with the likes of alcoholic producer/directors and crazy LE writers and performers. The number of times I returned to my pokey LE office to find Graham Chapman (of Monty Python fame) and his lunatic cohorts had turned it upside down yet again was enough already.

I shouldn't dismiss the whole experience in LE as negative. One major effect it had on me was that being Jewish or gay was never an issue. After my experiences at school, this was a revelation. Not the gay thing though!

The only other time in my life, apart from school, I had experienced anti-Semitism was strangely enough at a lunch at Pearl's parents house. They'd invited two of their friends as well as Pearl and I. Like her parents, their friends had been married for ever and they'd all known each other for over thirty years. As the conversation round the dining table picked, up I soon gathered that he was a banker in the city. When the soup was being served, Pearl's father and the banker were involved in some discussion about interest rates and loans. The banker mumbled something about the real problem being the Jews. His wife gave him a rather obvious kick under the table. It was odd having lunch in this large detached house in Hove, with ostensibly normal middle class people, for the ugly face of casual anti-Semitism suddenly to reveal itself.

Apart from Graham Chapman's predilection for turning my office around, he was great fun, if you like your fun packaged and delivered by a maniac. At that time he was drinking ludicrously heavily, eight pints of lager every lunch time. One day I made a grave error of judgement and joined him and a couple of other writers for a quick drink. It lasted seven hours. Graham and co. were contracted to write for the hugely successful LWT Doctor series. The writers were a who's who of television. John Cleese, Barry Cryer, Graham Garden and Bill Oddie all worked on the series.

By five in the afternoon, I couldn't feel my legs. I don't usually drink lager, but by this time I wasn't sure what I was drinking. I had a vague nagging memory that Pearl and I were having some friends round for dinner but that particular thought kept fading with each drink. I found myself at around seven o'clock sharing a minicab with Graham and a couple of the writers hurtling down the North Circular Road.

I recall Graham screaming that he wanted to walk and he tried to open the car door as we hit eighty miles an hour. He was hauled back in as I passed in and out of consciousness. We all ended up at Graham's flat somewhere in West London. The drinking continued on apace, but I just dumped myself on a sofa, lent forward, head in hands and wondered not only where I was but, by then, who I was. I gradually raised my head and witnessed my first gay kiss. Graham and the minicab driver were hard at it. Somehow I managed to find my way home and stagger up the stairs to our flat. Pearl was rightly pissed off. Our friends had been there for an hour. I told her that I needed to go to the bedroom for a minute. I woke up ten hours later.

I worked on the first two series of WW and that was sufficient. The company had recently moved to a purpose built building on the Embankment near Waterloo. Looking across the Thames, I could see the Savoy hotel and further east, St Paul's. The team was mostly magnificent. They included the late Mary Holland whose knowledge of the Irish troubles was without parallel, Christopher Hitchens, now a regular contributor to Vanity Fair, John Fielding who broke the thalidomide scandal through his work on the Sunday Times Insight column and David Elstein, a producer /director, and sometime Chief Executive of Channel 5, a man later dubbed "two brains" by the press. There were, of course, a couple of real arseholes, but someone had to make up the middle ground.

Birt ruled with an iron rod. Birt was never wrong. Birt would have proffered the solution of the Unified Field Theory to anyone who asked. Only no one ever did. Among my myriad of functions one was to get people from A to B. That A could be Vietnam and B could be Egypt/Syria/Jordan/Israel/ at the start of the Yom Kippur war. All water off a duck's back, if you had my experience.

Wrong!

We were not a news organisation. We were not ITN or the BBC. Pearl didn't even allow me to book our Spanish holiday for fear we'd end up in Reykjavik.

When the Yom Kippur war started in October 1973, WW was left so far at the starting gate that the horse had long since bolted and was selling in cans at Tesco's. Birt wanted to know why? How come none of his people were on a plane to just about anywhere in the Middle East? Why Jon? Why?

My first thought was 'fuck you sunshine.' Six weeks ago I was telling Graham Chapman to leave my desk alone, now I'm supposed to absorb the logistics, as if by magic, of how to ship a bunch of journalists two thousand miles across the world into a major war zone.

I should have known better. I'd been at the sharp end of current affairs for nearly two months! After all this wasn't rocket science. Actually, from the Israeli point of view at the time, it probably was. Anyway I left for Heathrow where I hung out for two days sleeping on any available bench while I sorted it out. I finally managed to get all the bastards to their respective destinations.

With only access to the men's room washbasin in Terminal 2 and with little sleep in forty eight hours, I wasn't feeling or looking that great after my stay at hotel Heathrow and I had only managed to speak to Pearl once. At that time Paddington bear cuddly toys were doing great business and I bought one as a gift for her to say sorry for not having called more often. I made my way back to LWT and wandered in to the WW production office around noon to a few desultory cheers carrying the rather large bear in a brown paper bag, it's yellow boots sticking out the end like a bizarre scene from the movie Don't Look Now.

Birt stepped out of his office, saw me and shouted, 'Where the fuck have you been?' I wasn't in the mood to entertain a meaningless conversation.

'I'll tell you where I've fucking been,' I said, 'I've been at fucking Heathrow airport as you fucking well know!' I then hurled Paddington bear at him with a force that would have done the great shot putter Geoff Capes proud. Before the bear connected with our esteemed leader the paper bag split apart and Paddington's yellow boots detached themselves and flew across the office in different directions. Birt about turned and fled back to his office. Neither of us ever spoke about the 'Paddington Incident' as it became known.

I did admire some of the team on occasions. While war zones were a rarity, they were sometimes sent, albeit voluntarily, to some dangerous places. Northern Ireland, at the time, was not a place for those faint of heart. It was bloody dangerous and although Mary Holland was extremely well connected with 'the other side', nobody else was.

One day I was sitting in on a meeting with Birt and Nick Elliott, his deputy, attempting to pretend I wasn't there. Whenever Birt called me to join these meetings it usually meant trouble, particularly for me. Both men went way back. They were at Oxford together and were very close friends. As the years rolled by their friendship would turn full circle, particularly after Birt's divorce. I liked Nick. He was funny and brilliant in that mad professor way. He went on to run ITV's drama for many years.

Birt wanted to do the entire programme from a studio in Belfast. The 'troubles' were regularly visited by WW but the story that led him to want to make the entire programme from there was heartbreaking. Two kids, aged around sixteen and seventeen, who lived in St Leonard's Street, a tiny place off Dee Street in East Belfast, had nipped down to the off licence for their parents and on their return had walked into some shooting in their little road. They hid round the side of a building until things went quiet. One of them popped his head round the corner just to check everything was safe. He was shot through the head and died instantly.

For those of us back in England, death and bombs in Northern Ireland seemed to be a common occurrence. Birt felt that we were getting a little inured to it all. There had never been any shooting in St Leonard's Street or indeed anywhere else in the neighbourhood before and apart from the family being devastated, so was the whole street. Birt wanted to put the entire street in a studio to talk about what the 'troubles' meant to them.

He looked over at Nick and said he wanted him to produce the piece which would make up the entire programme. Now Nick, as Birt's deputy, had managed to avoid being sent to any areas of conflict and in his view, Northern Ireland was right up there with Vietnam. He returned Birt's gaze and began to argue why someone else, anyone else, would be better suited to produce the programme than he was. Birt cut him short and made it clear he was going. Nick looked helplessly around and suddenly pointed at me, 'If I'm going so is he!'

It wasn't my job. Why me? I'm not supposed to be bombed or shot at. I'm Jewish!

As we arrived at Belfast airport there was a bomb scare. They tended to take those things particularly seriously in those days. We were held up for an hour and armed soldiers littered the entire airport. I wasn't happy. We finally sped off for the Europa Hotel. Access could only be gained through armed sentries and the entire building was surrounded by concrete blocks and sand bags. Not the sort of place you'd take the girl friend for a dirty weekend.

We were there two days and while you could palpably feel the tension in various parts of the city things went pretty smoothly for us. After the programme I went ahead of Nick to our car which was waiting outside the studio to take us back to the airport. As I bent over to put my overnight bag in the boot I felt a sharp object pushed into my back.

'Don't move and place your hands on your head,' a thin Brummie voice commanded. Fuck! This was it. My first thought was to shout, 'I'm Jewish!' but to be honest, I was so scared I only just managed to stop emptying my bowels. The fact that it was a Brummie accent should at least have told me I wasn't dealing with the IRA. But fear does strange things to a man. It also did strange things to me. I was still wondering how by not moving I could place my hands on my head when he ordered, 'Move to the wall.' I moved to the wall. 'Place your hands on the wall.' I placed my hands on the wall.

I was then frisked mercilessly. 'Turn round with your hands on your head.' I turned round with my hands on my head. It was a soldier, barely seventeen years old with acne strewn across his face. His finger was on the trigger of the biggest gun I'd ever seen and I thought if he sneezed I would be cut in half and sent home in several body bags.

'I'm press,' I declared. Having watched a lot of movies I decided to emulate a scene I'd viewed many times. 'I have my press pass in my jacket.' I slowly, ever so slowly, opened my jacket and delicately put a couple of fingers in my inside pocket and removed my wallet containing said press pass. I handed it over. He studied it for a long moment, returned it, grinned, and went on his way. I closed the boot, slid in to the back seat and began shaking. Nick jumped in a few minutes later and sat next to me. 'Well Jon, I thought that went very well,' he said, 'no trouble at all.' None at all I thought.

CHAPTER SEVEN
MARRIAGE, A COUP AND THE MYSTERIOUS PASSPORT

In the middle of series two I married Pearl in Hove, Sussex on the 31st August 1973 at the church of The Good Shepherd. A church!! It didn't best please my parents but I was beyond competing in any pleasing stakes for them. They didn't attend the wedding. Most of the WW team did. Uninvited! Bless them. We had a small reception at the Grand Hotel in Brighton and the Weekend Worlders demolished a substantial part of the hotel's wine cellar. I know this as I had to authorise their expenses when I got back from my two day honeymoon. My best man, Pat Jennings, (not the Spurs and Arsenal goalkeeper – the other Pat Jennings) lent us his Rolls Royce and chauffeur as a wedding gift and we sped down to Cornwall and a great award winning restaurant called The Horn A Plenty. A couple of days later I was kept busy trying to hide two thousand pounds of the Grand's champagne in the budget.

Running the day-to-day affairs of a team of sixty people, many of whom were spread out on assignments in Vietnam, the USA, Ireland and the Middle East, though not all at the same time, was now not a problem for me. If I fucked up then nobody, least of all me, was going to be remotely surprised. The army coup in Portugal in 1974 did however give me a decent work out.

The call went out in the office that General Antonio de Spinola had kicked out the Portuguese Prime Minister Marcello Caetano. Everyone seemed to take this bit of news with great seriousness. Some members of the team began rushing about, doing what, I've no idea. Me, well if I was half way through a sandwich, I

34

wouldn't have stopped munching. This 'incredible' event meant nothing to me. Within an hour it took over my life for a week.

Birt wanted to dispatch reporters and a film crew to Lisbon immediately. So did the rest of the world's media. I'd been bitten very badly over the Yom Kippur war and had no wish to repeat the process. As the months had rolled by I had a contacts book that would have been the envy of any national paper's news editor.

Two weeks before the General had made his move I had to get a researcher on a one o'clock plane to Washington. Not a great problem I hear you cry. It wouldn't have been if the idiot hadn't mailed his passport to the American Embassy to get a visa and was still waiting for its return. He stood in front of my desk at eight-thirty that morning sobbing in fear of what Mr Birt would do to him if he didn't make the flight.

After checking with a contact in the American Embassy to confirm that it had been posted to him I wasted half an hour calling up various post office sorting offices across London to see if they could locate the precious passport. I might as well have lit incense, crossed my legs and chanted Hari Krishna for all the good that did. Now I had managed a few minor miracles in the time I'd worked on WW, but even I was surprised at the success of my efforts over the next few hours. I had contacts at the Passport Office and a man on the inside at the Embassy. I sent the researcher to *Petit France*, near Victoria, the address of the Passport Office in those days, via a photo booth at a tube station.

His passport was issued by ten-thirty and visa by eleven thirty and he was on the Washington plane at one. Birt had vaguely heard that there was some problem and asked me, after our hero had left for America, if everything was OK. I told him all was fine. The myth was born. The feat soon got round the office and then around LWT. I never spoke about it, I merely let it travel, osmosis like, into hearts and minds of others. I was becoming a legend in my own lunch time!

I was enjoying the work but it wasn't my future. I had no idea what my future should be though writing every now and then reared its back legs in my direction. I guess I was waiting for a sign.

Meantime back at the Portuguese revolution everyone who needed to be in Lisbon got to Lisbon. The crew shot some great stuff and we were confident that WW would be the first TV station to broadcast film of the coup. The advances in media technology have been so fast and furious over the last thirty-five years that it's almost impossible to remember a world without: faxes, computers, the internet, email and mobile phones, and most importantly, from television's point of view, easy access to satellites for transmission. The only way we would be first on the air with our pictures was to deliver them to LWT by hand. Getting footage out of a country locked in by the military was going to be tough.

In one of my many sorties into the Law Courts in the 1980's, my barrister made a submission to a high court judge stating that various documents had been faxed between the parties. The judge interrupted the proceedings to enquire of the barrister what a fax was. But this was the mid-seventies. When the General shut off all telephone communications with his country our only way of staying in touch with our team was via telex. I'm sure that anyone under the age of forty has no idea what a telex is or was. It was a huge machine like a typewriter that could communicate via a telephone line with a similar machine anywhere in the world. You'd type the message in your end and it would come out like magic the other end. I suppose it was like sending an email but without the need for machines that weighed ninety pounds.

I spent many a long night in the office trying to send telex messages to the team in Lisbon. The secretaries were very adept at using these contraptions. I wasn't. I spent hours asking the telex operator in the middle of the night for help. Yes there was a telex operator somewhere out there in hyperspace who could give advice!

One particular round of telexes comes to mind. It was a Thursday night around one –thirty in the morning. I was sitting alone in the office feeling thoroughly knackered and a not a little sorry for myself.

Since the coup I had lived and slept in that bloody place. This was my fourth day. Unlike the domestic arrangements at Heathrow, at least here I could get a shower in one of LWT's dressing rooms. I was 'speaking' to a researcher called Alan Patience. He of the passport fiasco.

'Alan,' I typed,' we really need to get you and the film back to London at the latest by Saturday night or we won't have time to edit the film or voice it.'

'There are no planes.' he moaned via the written word, 'The army have blocked everything...' Then, as if I cared, he wrote, 'I've been pretty ill over the last twelve hours.' The odd thing about Alan was that, in a previous life, he had been a priest. I wanted to suggest that he did a few Hail Marys and stop telling me his fucking problems. I had my own, the worst of which was getting the film back to England, followed closely by actually going home sometime in the next week or two.

'Sorry to hear you're not well,' I hammered out on the key board, 'but the main issue is getting our hands on the film.'

No response for five minutes. Then..'This is operator from hotel. Mr Patience be back in minute. He gone to be sick.' Oh happy days!

My problem really was how to get the film back in time. There was no one I could go to for advice and anyway by now my reputation as a fixer was such that they'd just assume I'd be able to handle it. Walking and water fluttered through my mind. I found a map of Portugal and adjoining countries (mostly Spain in fact) and studied it, much the same way as Eisenhower must have done while searching for possible D day landing sites in Northern France. I found 'it' after an hour or so. Badajoz!

Badajoz was on the Spanish border with Portugal. There was an old military airfield that had lain unused for years. I waited a few hours till the sun rose and began ringing round a bunch of private jet hire firms. I needed to know a) if the old airfield could still take a jet and b) how much this jolly jaunt was going to cost the budget. The answers were a) Yes and b) £2,500. That was a shit load of money in 1974 and a gigantic slice of the budget. It wasn't my call. It was Birt's.

When he arrived just before nine I gave him the news.

'But can they get to Badajoz in time?' he wanted to know. 'It must be at least three hundred miles. Will the military let them cross the border in to Spain?' And so on and on and on...All great meaningful questions of which after yet another sleepless night I couldn't care fucking less about. Why he thought I could possibly know the answers to any of his questions was utterly beyond me. Besides, I was sure I was beginning to black out.

Finally the decision was made. Put the jet on hold and see if the director could make it out of Portugal without being machined gunned to death. Actually he couldn't get to Badajoz but made it to Madrid and caught a scheduled flight. We got the film on air and saved £2,500. My life was complete!

WW was a very tight operation. The close proximity of so many people working together creates some unlikely relationships. Perhaps 'relationships' is a step too far. Shagging was the name of the game. Personally I took no part. You would say that wouldn't you I hear a voice from the back of the hall. Compared to the time I later spent in America, WW's shaggings were a disgrace to the whole concept of the word.

The programme's working week was Tuesday to Sunday. Saturday night was an all nighter for the editorial team which included Birt and to a certain extent Peter Jay, the programme's first presenter. Jay, once economics editor of the The Times, later became British Ambassador to the United States. He was for some years described as the cleverest man in Britain.

With great apologies to Simon Cowell, who is in danger of becoming a serial simile in this book, Jay's ego makes Cowell's look like a gnat's bite. This was a man who would die on the cross and utter the immortal line 'why have I forsaken myself.'

Lots of film for the programme came in late Saturday and had to be edited and voiced over - hence the late nights. Various senior editorial people slept over in artists' dressing rooms when they'd finished work around three or four in the morning. Unless I was working on an ongoing project I was out of the office by ten most Saturday nights.

CHAPTER EIGHT
SHAGGING AND A NEW HOME

Pearl and I were now renting in North Kensington, close to Queens Club, the *other* tennis venue. We now had three cats and a busy social life. As my work on WW gathered pace and my friendships with the team developed we would frequently entertain in our flat. Often the journalists would stop off on their way from Heathrow when they returned from a foreign trip for a few drinks before going on to their respective homes. After a few months, it became a ritual for a lot of them. Unwind with Roseman and back home to the wife and kids.

I would leave for the studio every Sunday at around seven o'clock and drive our ancient Triumph Vitesse to LWT. Walking in to my office one Sunday, I saw some of the secretaries, about seven of them, huddled in a corner whispering earnestly to one another.

'What's up?' I asked heading for my desk. The whispering stopped and they said their good mornings to me and drifted away. I had personally hired all of them and felt a huge responsibility for their welfare. Later I took one of them aside and asked what was going on. After a moment or two she said, 'Every Sunday when we come in, as you know, we have to wake up John and Peter. The fact is Jon, whoever wakes them is supposed to shag them! That's what we were talking about.'

I don't remember that being on their job description when I hired them. We talked about the situation for a while. Apparently most of the girls didn't mind this somewhat onerous task and no coercion was involved, though that didn't make the situation any more palatable. I figured there wasn't much I could do about it.

The shagging did get to ridiculous proportions. I was a big soccer fan in those days and LWT used to broadcast The Big Match. This meant that live feeds of the games were sent down the line to the studio. As a consequence, I could access all the games live in certain senior executive's offices. As the programme production offices were on the same floor as the boardroom, I'd often disappear for an hour or so at three o'clock on a Saturday afternoon to watch some of the games. The boardroom had it all. Six large TV's and a liquor cabinet!

On one occasion I opened the door intending to watch an Arsenal/Spurs derby only to come face to face with one of the programme's most senior executives (guesses can be sent to my website, www. laws of libel.com) screwing the living daylights out of one of the secretaries on the boardroom table.

The second series was coming to an end and so was I.

Pearl and I bought a little terraced house in Wimbledon. To be more specific Wimbledon Chase. The very cheap end of Wimbledon. She'd given up her work as a fashion spy and took a less exposed role in the local library. Leaving LWT at the back end of 1974 and starting up as an agent having just lumbered myself with a mortgage was utterly insane. I have no idea why I did it, I'd decided on the spur of some moment to become an agent. Just like Paul's sudden conversion on his way to Damascus. He'd seen the light and heard the voices. I hadn't heard any voices, though it would have probably been best if I had. Then at least someone could have had me committed. It was, without question, one of the single biggest mistakes of my life.

CHAPTER NINE
AN AGENT IS BORN AND MINICABBING

The Roseman Agency was born in 1975. I had no money and no savings. I took out a second mortgage and signed up my first clients. Two came from WW plus the great TV investigative journalist Roger Cook, though at the time and for several years more, Roger was still doing radio. After a month I was broke. I took out a third mortgage. After four months I was broke again. My minute coterie of clients didn't pay for the stamps let alone the mortgage. I needed to earn some money fast. I became a minicab driver.

My clients had no idea I had to drive a cab. They were all under the impression that they had signed up with some whiz kid who was going to make them rich. This kind of subterfuge was to become my life's undoing. In order to survive and grow, I needed to convey an image of success. Success means money. Sure there were times when I had money, lots of it, but it was spent all too quickly and never on assets that would see me right in my golden years. A line from Thom Gunn's poem *On The Move* has always been a centrepiece of my life. *'You're always nearer by not keeping still'.*

As an agent I needed an office and stationery. The letterhead boasted a phone number with seven lines. I had one line. The office was the spare bedroom. I would amble in to the 'office' in the morning, naked with a cup of tea and try to make a living. After I was forced to drive a cab, I needed a device to answer my home phone when I was on the road. In those weird and crazy days answer phones were at the top end of technology and to rent one that you could access from a pay phone was incredibly expensive. Options? I didn't have any. I rented one. I had to use a bleeper device and after dialling my number place the device by the phone and bleep accordingly. It then played back my messages, though most days it was just *a* message. Being an agent who knew nothing about agenting and who didn't have any contacts was proving a tad difficult.

My minicabbing was a disaster. I had to rent a car, our little Triumph not being suitable. Then I had to pay a special insurance in order to carry members of the public and finally cough up money to the cab firm for the radio. I needed to earn £100 per week before I saw a penny. In the six months I worked for the firm I don't think I ever made enough to cover my costs. Being the worst minicab driver in the history of minicabbing didn't help. If you got lost *all* the time a) the petrol killed you b) the cab controller wasn't minded to give you any decent jobs and c) the abuse from pissed off passengers could get a little wearing.

I worked for a firm called Meadway Cars based in Golders Green. Why I chose a company the other side of London from where I lived is another Rosemanic mystery. I would pick up a fare, listen to their destination and always ask if they knew the best way. I could have been speaking Urdu for the good that did. I then proceeded to get lost.

One pick up I made in Golders Green wanted Clapham in south west London. I lived in south west Londonish. I knew the back doubles to that part of the city. My passenger remarked on how impressed he was with my knowledge of London, adding that most mini cab drivers were crap. I was hot! Having navigated my way through Chelsea I headed for Clapham. Could I find it? No fucking way! No tom tom's in those heady days. For that matter there were no internet and no mobile phones. I think the world was perhaps a more comfortable peaceful place back then.

I lived in fear that I may, by malicious chance, be sent to transport one of my clients and then my cover really would be blown. I never comforted myself by calculating the odds of picking up one of four people in a population of seven million!

I worked six days a week, seventeen hours a day, bleeped a lot and never made a penny. I had also managed to acquire a couple of new clients and still couldn't pay the electric bill.

Then Music Videos exploded into my life.

CHAPTER TEN

BOHEMIAN RHAPSODY, MIKE OLDFIELD, AND CLIFF RICHARD 10cc

Bruce Gowers was one of the finest TV directors of his generation. I had known him from my days at LWT. He was a cameraman; some say the best in England, a production manager then finally a director/producer. Apart from his fantastic talent, he was also one of the nicest guys you could ever hope to meet. Always calm, softly spoken and a complete professional. His ability to deal with talent was legendary. On one occasion he was directing Liza Minnelli in a big special for LWT. During rehearsals he left the gallery (that's where the director and his team work) to come down to the studio to speak to the diva. Those who heard the conversation were incredulous. He quietly suggested that if she performed a particular number differently, it would look so much better. It took a lot of guts to have a conversation like that with a legend. Though none of that star shit was ever an issue with Bruce. He wasn't trying to score points or show who was in charge, he just *knew* what worked. It was totally instinctive. Some weeks later he received a letter from her thanking him for his advice and saying she'd incorporated his suggestions into her live stage performances.

The clarion call of I love rock and roll may as well have been ring a ring o' roses as far as I was concerned. Sure there were a few bands I liked. The Beatles, America, Simon and Garfunkel even Emerson Lake and Palmer at a push, but I was really into opera and classical music. So when I got the call from Bruce about some band called Queen, it was no surprise that I hadn't heard of them.

Bruce had been directing commercials at a studio called Trillion based in Soho, London. They were cheap video tape commercials produced in a tiny basement. Trillion owned a sound recording studio, Trident, situated just round the corner from their studio. As a result of a chance meeting between the band and Roy Thomas-Baker, a producer at Trident, a company was formed to manage Queen. The band was rehearsing for a huge UK tour and needed to video their new single, *Bohemian Rhapsody*. The tour would prevent the band being available to do television. Trillion were familiar with Gower's work so they asked him to direct the video. This simple request was to change the face of the music business.

It's probably incomprehensible to anyone born after the age of MTV to understand the contribution the video "Bohemian Rhapsody" made to the world of music. American TV networks had no interest in rock and roll. Occasional blips like the Beatles appearing on the Johnny Carson show were about as much as Middle America could take. There were a couple of late night syndicated shows that were band oriented, but that was about it. There was no US equivalent of Top Of The Pops (TOTP).

TOTP was the Holy Grail. If the band/artist got to perform on TOTP they were guaranteed to move up the charts. Radio on both sides of the Atlantic was, and always had been, the only way to promote records. But in England there was the added shove that only TOTP could provide.

Videos, as we know them today, didn't really exist in early/mid 1970's Britain. Sure a couple of films of a band strolling or staggering about in some forest clearing, their song playing in the background like some surreal backdrop to a silent film, came and went, but TOTP always liked to have the band in the studio. If they couldn't make it, then Pan's People, six sexy lissom, usually half–undressed, girls would gyrate to the song instead. A record company would have almost to provide a doctor's note for a band's no show before the BBC would allow a film of them performing instead. The BBC would brook no argument on this policy.

The collision of Gower's and Queen's mutual genius coming together with a song that ran over seven minutes and took the number one spot for nine weeks was a miracle of serendipity. Since the band was on tour, they had the legitimate excuse of not being available for TOTP and apparently the song wasn't conducive for Flick Colby, the Pan's People choreographer, to come up with a routine for her girls, so they'd run out of options: they simply had to play the video which made up a quarter of the show.

The video cost around two thousand pounds to make. The band was rehearsing for their tour in a large studio at Shepperton Film Studios just outside South West London. They had built a stage and had installed a huge lighting rig. It drastically reduced the video's cost. The visual effects on the video were created in the days before there were special effects. There was no digital technology either. Electronic editing was still a little down the line so it meant tape editing was performed in the same way as film editing – i.e. with a razor blade.

Gower's provided the 'howl round' effect of the moving faces by playing the pictures on a small studio monitor and shooting the screen while panning the camera. Simple, but enduringly effective. Although Queen became, of course, a massive worldwide band, right up there with the Stones and U2 as an outfit that could, and did, fill football stadia several times over whenever they toured, back in 1975, and before the video was released, they weren't yet Premier League players.

None of the four, Freddie Mercury, Brian May, John Deacon or Roger Taylor made any suggestions for the video. It was all down to Bruce's vision. He always possessed an innate understanding of the union between music and pictures. He had become the first director to achieve the making of a commercial for a song that didn't require the expense of buying air time. The video, rightly, has long since attained an iconic status.

About a month later, Gowers and I sat down over three or four bottles of red wine and discussed how we might exploit the success. Of course neither of us was aware of the power of his creation or how far-reaching the effect this seven minute video would have. As we hit the third bottle, I came up with a ground breaking idea. Why don't I contact all the record companies and see if they would like to make music videos!! The only problem for me was I didn't know any record companies or how to contact them. Simple solution. The public library. Pearl, who had been working in our local library, helped me find what I needed.

I did some copious research. It must have taken all of one hour. There were a lot of record companies back then, from huge multinationals like Warner's and CBS to smaller entities like Virgin and Chrysalis, and added to these were an enormous number of small independent record labels. When the record companies became too large, they set up various labels that specialised in a particular music genre. These were run by people who had a *special* feel for that genre. The hope was that the bands would believe that they weren't just talking to men in suits who were taking the corporate penny, but credible, caring guys who believed in them and their music. Who would buy that today? To me it was never going to matter. I would just be making videos.

The second video we made was Mike Oldfield's *In Dulci Jubilo*. Richard Branson rang me on a Tuesday morning. I recall the day of the week clearly as he wanted us to shoot Oldfield's track on Wednesday for transmission on TOTP for Thursday. It was already number two in the charts and Branson thought a great video would heave it to number one. He'd just started his fledgling Virgin record company, courtesy of Oldfield's *Tubular Bells*. You have to hand it to the young man; he could always spot the main chance Even though he'd just been done by HM Custom and Excise for a couple of hundred thousand pounds for avoiding VAT payments on imported records, he became unstoppable.

At that time, Oldfield was the classic rock and roll recluse. Alone he wanted to be. Alone he surely was. He refused to leave his Oxfordshire mansion. So the video was shot as an outside broadcast (OB) like the Grand National. We headed up the A40 with an OB truck and a few cameras. We shot the loony in multiple split screens in a process known as editech. *In Dulci Jubilo* is an orchestral track. No vocals. Recluse didn't do vocals. Take a blank screen and shoot man playing the whole track on guitar and place picture, say, in top right of frame. Roll the tape back, chose another instrument, play entire track again, insert in the bottom right frame, and so on, until all the screen is made up of Oldfield's playing every bloody instrument known to mankind. After ten hours we headed back to London with the finished video and it went straight to the BBC studios for the attention of Robin Nash, the then big boss of TOTP, for the following day's transmission. The video was shown. But the track never did make it to number one.

My role in the early days was one of marketing and producing. *Marketing* meant getting in the work. *Producing* was having to second-guess Gowers' requirements as a director. This was pretty difficult as the genius tended to make it all up as he went along.

We churned out a lot of rubbish and the occasional one you might want to write home about. It was next to impossible to make a good video out of a rubbish song, though that happened sometimes. *Good Morning Judge* by 10cc comes to mind. Using a similar technique for *In Dulca Jubilo*, 10cc's Goldman and Stewart appeared simultaneously on screen as judge, defendant and the entire twelve man jury. Whenever the video was shown, the song crept up the charts. Proof, if proof is needed, that a good 'commercial' can help shift the product.

We were asked to make a video of Cliff Richard's *Miss You Nights*. A clichéd ballad in my view but I loved it! It was videoed at Trillion's tiny basement studio in Soho. The budget was about fifteen hundred pounds. It was all shot on one camera which meant that Cliff had to mime the song dozens of times. He was, as he always appeared to be, a lovely man and totally professional. My abiding memory is walking into his dressing room and being confronted by the hairiest back this side of Transylvania.

CHAPTER ELEVEN
A REAL OFFICE AND ROD STEWART'S MANAGER

I had now left my front bedroom office and moved to a basement in Langham Street close to the BBC in Portland Place. The office had a tiny reception, a good sized room about fourteen by fifteen which was my abode, and a tiny back office. I now had a secretary. Things were changing. Now I was forced to wear clothes to the office.

It was mid-1976. I was about to get the big call. *Jon Roseman Productions Limited* was up and running and the work was pouring in. We had, as yet, no competition. It wouldn't be long before all that would change. Everyone with a Polaroid would soon be boarding the gravy train. But that was still a year or so away.

My phone rang in my new office, furniture courtesy of Habitat.

'Hi, is that Jon Roseman?' I didn't owe money in those days, so I confirmed my identity.

'Can you come to Los Angeles next week to shoot some film of Rod Stewart?'

Who was this guy?

'I'm sorry but who am I speaking to.' I could be sooo polite.

'This is Billy Gaff, Rod's manager, I'm calling from LA.' I realised he didn't mean Luton Airport.

'Hi Billy,' I said. 'Sure we can come over. When can you get us the song?'

'*Songs*,' he said. 'Three songs from his new album.'

'Ok. When can you get us the songs?'

'Small problem Jon. Tom Dowd, the producer, has gone missing and they're not quite finished. But the record company want the film in a couple of weeks and they love your work,'

'But we can't come up with any ideas, let alone a budget, if we can't listen to the tracks.'

'No problem about that. Just get over here ASAP. Call Wendy Watkiss at Warner Brothers records in London. She'll arrange the flights and hotel. See ya!' The line disconnects and I'm left staring into crazy void land.

The way we worked was simple but very risky. A record or management company contacted me. They would send over the track(s) and give us some idea of the budget. That could be anywhere between £3,000 and £20,000. We'd listen to the mulch and come up with ideas. Then we'd meet the band/singer and manager or record company person(s), discuss said ideas, agree the concept and budget and do the work.

The problem was, and it could be a very big problem, if things went wrong, and it wasn't the artist's fault, and the budget was blown, we had to eat the overage. In fifteen years of doing this ego oriented rubbish, it was NEVER the artist's fault. They, of course, were never too stoned or too drunk to perform and always turned up on time ready to give of their best. Yeah, right!

Back in the days of LWT, working out a budget was an accurate science. Pop videos were less of a science, more of a mud at wall scenario. It was usually the editing process that hurt us. In those days, a two machine edit was £200 per hour. That enabled you to do straight cuts. If you wanted to dissolve, mix in pictures, that was three machines. £300 an hour. The average edit was normally around ten hours. This *average,* usually depended on how much alcohol was consumed. As the years rolled by, drugs became the main issue.

Booking crews, studios, set design, make up, etc. were fixed costs - unless overtime reared its ugly head. After discussions with the crew, fees were agreed. If they screwed up, it was down to them. If the artist did, I had to try and squeeze additional money out of the record company. This was never easy. On top of those costs, were fees for the director and producer and an overall mark up, normally ten percent, to cover the company's on-going costs, secretarial, accountancy, phones and so on. There was very little room for screwing up. On the one hand, I wanted to give the director as much artistic freedom as possible: on the other, I didn't want to lose money. As Gowers wasn't a great planner, I was always working on the edge of fear.

I called him about doing Stewart. He was very excited and desperate to work in America. He was, however, in the middle of a major LWT entertainment series and could only set aside three days. Three very specific days. I called Wendy Watkiss at Warner Bros and asked her to check the dates with Billy Gaff.

'Jon there will be no problem with those dates.' She was so full of confidence it seemed heartless to push her.

'Ok, but I really would like to double check it, if that's alright.'

'Jon, it will be fine,' she insisted. 'I'll arrange tickets and the hotel for you for the day after tomorrow. Bye bye!'

I wasn't comfortable with any of this, but there wasn't a lot I could do about it. I arranged a visa - no big deal in those days and anyway I still had pretty good contacts at the Embassy. I instructed my secretary on what client stuff she might have to deal with while I was away, but in any event, they did have phones in LA, and then I went home.

I had dinner with Pearl and stroked a few cats. She helped me pack. It was none too complicated. Jeans and T shirts were my uniform. She observed that I was very calm for a guy who was on his way to Los Angeles but who had never travelled further than Spain. She was right. I hadn't really thought any of it through. Shit! I was going to have to arrange crews, studios, production personnel and I knew absolutely no-one. No-one at all.

CHAPTER TWELVE
AMERICA AND THE REAL ROD STEWART

DAY ONE

I gazed out at the new world as the taxi sped down La Cienega to my hotel, The Continental Hyatt House on Sunset Strip. The sun shoved its way through a smog laden sky. I didn't know it then, but the hotel was the main stopover for every rock and roll band that came to America. Its nickname was The Continental Riot House. It was all so new, so different, so American. So utterly ridiculous that I was here at all. It was, to my twenty-eight year old brain, a vast movie set.

I checked in at the hotel around five in the afternoon. I handed the voucher, that Warner Brothers London had given me, to the receptionist. It got me a broom closet. The building occupied around twenty floors in the middle of Sunset Strip. It wasn't the Ritz, but I didn't give a bull's testicle. I never thought I'd ever make it to the States anyway and here I was about to embark, or so I thought, on some great adventure. If I knew now, what I didn't know then, I would have stayed in Wimbledon Chase. America was to become a very bad experience over the next seven years. If you're still reading, as my American experience unfolds, you may want to consider continuing whilst crouching behind a sofa. I know I wanted to *write* it from behind a sofa.

I went straight to bed, jet lagged with my nervous system switched to *defcon 1*. Sleep was difficult and I woke at six. I showered, got dressed and took a wander. It was the first time I'd been abroad on a business trip. I strolled past shops that sold merchandise that I'd only been aware of from US imported TV and movies. It was the sidewalk newspaper vending machines that got me. They were pure Americana!

Back at the hotel I ordered breakfast. The menu was dominated by steak. Well, when in LA....I ordered a charbroiled New York steak. When I turned the menu over I saw the breakfast list. I'd ordered from the lunch menu.

To work. I had two numbers, Gaff's and someone called Chuck Dyson from Warner Bros. I decided Gaff would be my very first call on American soil. It was ten o'clock. Answering machine. Left message. Called Chuck. Was told he would be out all day. Waited an hour. Called Gaff. A lisping young male voice answered. He put the manager on.

'Hi Jon, welcome to LA. Your first time?'

'Yes it is.' I said. Was I coming across as a complete wanker?

'Great!' his tone was hearty. I wasn't sure what was so great about it. 'Come on over.' He gave me the address and I took a cab over to his vast house on Doheny Drive, ten minutes from the hotel. I rang the bell and was welcomed in to the opulent hall by a young fey lad. Chandeliers hung from the all the ceilings, at least in the rooms I visited. Antique furniture, original paintings. Being Rod's manager certainly seemed to be a profitable operation.

Billy, five foot five, very dapper and very gay, greeted me and offered coffee. As we settled in his lounge I asked about the tracks.

'Here's the thing Jon, no-one can find Dowd. Till we find the bastard, we can't finish the album.'

'So what am I supposed to do?'

'Look, Jon, Warner's are picking up the tab, so enjoy. You'll be the first to know when we find him.'

I decided to walk back to the hotel. I couldn't just do nothing. I took the executive decision to find myself a production manager and introduce myself to the video facilities available in LA. But before I could execute anything that cost money, I needed to speak to Chuck Dyson at Warner's. No Dyson today, so I took a cab and did some exploring.

LA was hot and humid with a veil of smog hiding the Hollywood Hills. I noticed LA's smog as I'd flown in. It created the uncomfortable humidity problem endemic to the city. One of the few bands I was a big fan of was America. While not huge in the UK, they enjoyed massive success in their own country with hits like 'A Horse With No Name' and 'Ventura Highway'. I felt a particular affinity to them as they'd all met in England as sons of US air force personnel. More than that, they played some of their first gigs in Brighton at the Norfolk Pub, my local, although back then I'd never heard of them. I met them once many years later when they guested on *The Russell Harty Show* for LWT.

I liked Russell and nearly signed him as one of my first clients, but my inability to tell the difference between Burgundy and Claret at lunch with him was to be my undoing. We first met when he was an associate producer on 'Aquarius', one of the longest running Arts programmes on British TV. He was one of life's great raconteurs. We'd been talking about the BBC and the kind of people they tended to employ. All very well spoken and public school back then. He told me that when King Olaf of Norway turned up at the BBC reception in Portland Place, West London for an interview with *The World At One*, the receptionist was in the process of painting her nails. She was rather annoyed to be disturbed and looked up, asking him rather perfunctorily, who he was and what he wanted.

'I'm King Olaf of Norway and I'm here to be interviewed by William Hardcastle.' With hardly a glance in his direction, the young woman dialled an extension being careful all the while not to disturb her nail varnish. After a moment or two she looked up and asked, 'Was that Denmark or Norway?'

I'd hired one of the hotel's limos for a quick tour of LA. The driver kept up a running commentary of where we were and places of interest to a backdrop of the radio blaring out MOR rock. As we turned onto Ventura Highway, America suddenly emanated from the radio with the hit song of the same name. I thought this may be a good omen. But after a mile or two driving down the highway, I did wonder why anyone would write a song about it.

DAY TWO

Called Dyson. Got through. He suggested we meet. I took off for Burbank. It billed itself as the media capital of the world. It's about twelve miles north of downtown LA. Dyson's office was spacious and minimalist. I sat down and he began.

'This whole thing is Gaff's idea. Warner's aren't comfortable with this video shit.' So much for Gaff's, "the record company loves your work!" 'We've told him that if he wants you to make anything, he's going to have to pay for most of it out of sales.' If Warner's weren't comfortable then I, as sure as God and the green apple thing, wasn't either. What was going on here?

'So who exactly do I speak to about money?' said deeply worried producer.

'Warner's will pick up the costs and, as I said, we'll just take it back from the album sales. So have you any ideas on what you're gonna do?' He sat back in his leather chair and made a steeple with his fingers.

'None. Haven't heard anything yet. Apparently the tracks aren't finished.

'Yeah, I heard Dowd had gone missing. That's going to cost.' I figured that it wasn't going to cost Warner's.

'I need to hire a production manager. Who shall I tell him to invoice?'

'Me.' He stood up. 'Good luck,' he said, gripping my hand.

I yellow paged a production manager. That's how I found Arnie Davidson. Mid-twenties, jeans, T shirt, medium height, thinning blond hair and laid back to the degree of horizontal. He'd been around TV and movies for about five years and persuaded me he could help me out. We visited various video facilities and studios so I could get some idea of costs. Compared to London they were forty per cent cheaper. Their OB trucks were a marvel. It left Trillion's looking like a steam driven caravan.

DAY THREE

I called Bruce to let him know what I knew which was sod all. I tried Gaff who told me that the boy wonder still hadn't surfaced. I took myself off to the movies. It then occurred to me that Warner's was not just a record company but a film studio as well. Perhaps visiting their studio lot would be a good idea. They might have a spare set we could use. One call to the studios put that idea to death. Warner Studios wanted nothing to do with Warner Records. Ho hum! Years later Warner Records would end up with a TV/film division and the Studio would have a music company!

I called Chuck to tell him what the Studio had said and his reaction shocked me. He was very pissed off. How dare I call the film studios and who the hell did I think I was? I was beginning to wonder that myself. I didn't need this, so I hung up on the dear boy. At that precise moment the red message light on my hotel phone began to blink. I called down to reception and received shock number two.

'Mr Roseman, your bill has reached a thousand dollars and you need to speak to our deputy manager.'

'I think there's some mistake,' I said, ' Warner's are covering the cost of my stay here.'

'Err, no sir. They are covering the room and breakfast only. Your phone calls, meals and bar are not included.' That must have been one hell of a lot transatlantic calls I'd racked up.

I called the airport to find out the time of the next plane to London. Then called Reception and told them I was checking out, and finally called Gaff and told him I'd had enough of Chuck and Warner's and was off.

I hit reception forty-five minutes later and went through the check out procedure. As we were going through the bill, the hotel's manager hurried over to the desk.

'Mr Roseman! Mr Roseman! There's been a very big mistake.' he panted the words out.

'How so?'

'Warner Brother's have called and confirmed that they are picking up the entire bill for your stay.'

'The *entire* bill?' I asked one eye on their very expensive in-house shop.

'Yes sir.'

'Excellent. I'd like an upgrade please. I'll be in the bar.' Dom Pérignon was about seventy five bucks a bottle. Did I care? No. Warner's were paying. Good old Billy.

DAY FOUR

Dowd appeared from God knows where to finish the record. I asked Gaff, at least to let me have the lyrics, which might go some way to provide inspiration for the video. They arrived. I got them over to Gowers. We talked endlessly over the phone about what can or can't be done, bearing in mind we have no budget yet. We agreed to book a studio with a four man camera crew to cover two of the songs and one of those super high tech OB trucks for a day to go we knew not where.

I dragged in Arnie and we hit the phones. I wanted to see if Chuck had a spare office I could use, but since Gaff had 'spoken' to him, he had mysteriously become unavailable. Arnie pencilled in make-up, set dressers, the studio, OB etc. I added it all up. Nearly seventy-five thousand dollars. That's how you can get burnt in the pop video business. You do a budget based on pure make believe.

DAY FIVE

Went to see Gaff. Worried no finished tracks. His mantra as always is,' Don't worry, Warner's are paying.' I was beginning to wonder if he was aware that the costs of all this, my hotel bill included, were coming out of his and Rod's end. On the other hand, taking in his palatial residence, I guessed they both could afford it.

DAY SIX

The music tracks arrived. Dowd had been told to finish the tracks we needed for the video first. Very kind of him. I mean I'd only been in LA for a week.

DAY SEVEN

Asked Gaff if I could meet the Man himself to chat over a few things. Told that's not really possible at the moment. Explain it's important to get his feedback. Told that ain't gonna happen at the present time. Start to think bad thoughts. Still, Bruce is coming in tomorrow late afternoon and I need to confirm everything. Gaff gives me the OK to shoot on days nine and ten. Call Arnie. We are up and running. Tell Arnie to call a meeting of all production personnel to the Hyatt house bar for tomorrow early evening to meet Bruce.

DAY EIGHT

Bruce now in hotel shower, jet lagged and wiped out from his busy LWT schedule. I offer no sympathy after what I've just been through. He spends an hour listening to the tracks. He has some thoughts. We talk about them, both knowing everything will have changed in the next five minutes.

We hit the Hyatt bar at seven thirty. Arnie has assembled the entire team of about twenty three people. I introduce Gowers. They love him immediately. Unlike the ego oriented directors they are used to, Bruce is a whirlwind of fresh air. I get the drinks in. After all, Warner's are paying!

It was nearly ten to eight when I got the call. I'd let the switchboard know where I was and the barman shouts my name. I picked up the receiver. It was Billy Gaff.

'Hi Jon.' The voice a little distant.

'How's it going? Got Bruce here, just going over things with the crew for tomorrow.'

'About tomorrow Jon.' A pause. A very long pause. 'Rod's changed his mind.' *My* mind is now racing. If we have to extend the shoot another day that could be another thirty thousand dollars.

'Any extension could be expensive,' I say.

'No Jon, that's not it. He doesn't want to make any videos. It's all off.' I knew for sure it wasn't April the first and besides it was well after midday.

'I want to ask you if this is a joke but I think I know the answer.'

'Sorry Jon but that's it. Don't worry, Warner's are paying. Thanks for everything. Bye!'

I gaze across the bar. Bruce is holding court. I wonder how I'm going to tell them. There is only one way. In English.

I walk over as my boy is explaining what he has in mind. Nothing he says bears any resemblance to what we had talked about in his room.

'Sorry to interrupt, but I'm afraid it's all off!' Pregnant elephant pause. Then laughter.

'You English,' grins Arnie, 'You English and your Monty Python humour.

'No,' I say trying to find some gravitas, 'No! I'm not joking. That was Billy Gaff, Rod's manager. I'm serious. Rod doesn't want to do it.' The message seeps in. Bruce is a little light headed, what with jet lag and Jack Daniels. I give him *the* look. 'Shit!' It's all he can come up with. Taking control I tell them I'll take them all out for a Chinese. We leave the hotel and head for the most expensive place Arnie can think of. After all Warner's are paying. I let the switchboard know where we're going and we proceed to Mr Chows.

It was one o'clock when the *maître d'* called my name. Telephone call for Mr Roseman. It was Billy.

'Hi Jon. Just spoke to Rod, he's changed his mind. Good news we're back on.' Turning round and looking at Bruce and the crew, I couldn't really see it as good news. They were pissed out of their minds and ordering more sake. Just waking tomorrow would be an issue for most of them.

I ambled back to the vast round table and stood behind Bruce. It took a while for me to shut them all up. 'Guys that was Billy Gaff. We're back on!' They all looked at each other, some with eyes that still seemed to serve a useful purpose. It was left to Arnie to break the silence.

'You English with your Monty Python humour,' he managed to slur.

'Listen up people. This is not a drill. This is the real deal. You all know where we're supposed to be tomorrow morning.' I glance at my watch. ' Actually *this* morning. Now fuck of all of you and get some sleep.' The party broke up. I got Gowers back to his room and told him I'd wake him at seven.

DAY NINE

The studio was situated on Fountain Avenue off Sunset Boulevard. Bruce gets to work setting up the lighting, camera angles and generally making it up as he goes along. Ten thirty no Rod. I call Billy who tells me he's definitely on his way. Twelve o'clock, no Rod. Gaff confirms that he should be there momentarily. One thirty, I call again.

'Jon, he got lost,' says the manager. Sure he did. The trouble was if I pinched myself I'd still be here.

'So what time should we expect him? We start to get into overtime in six hours.' Why I'm even having this conversation is beyond me.

'I'll call you back,' he says. I can't wait.

I didn't have to wait long. Fifteen minutes later the call comes. It's all off. I tell him that we've just blown nearly forty thousand dollars, but manage to hang up before he could give me the Warner's mantra for the fifteenth time.

Forlornly Bruce and I go back to the hotel. He hits his bed I hit the hotel's shop and rack up seventeen hundred dollars. Well, after all, Warner's are.................

DAY TEN

Bruce and I decide we've got a fabulous state of the art OB truck for the day so we might as well use it. Bruce and truck sped down to Malibu looking for locations we both knew we wouldn't need. I stay by the phone in case I get *the* call. I get *the* call.

'Is that Jon?' a husky voice mumbles.

'Uh huh.'

'This is Rod. Sorry about the mix up. Can you film at my place?' At this point I'd have shot in an abattoir.

'No problem.' I say. He gave me the address and I waited for Bruce to call in.

An hour later I turn up at chez Stewart's. If Gaff's house was big, this was vast. An estate in Beachwood Canyon. Tennis courts, swimming pools and a gate house. Rod's live in PR man greets me like a long lost friend and I'm given the tour. It was the air conditioned cloakroom that sorted out the men from the boys. It was air conditioned because back in those very non PC days, it was full of fur coats. Some of them belonged to a woman, who as we passed through the kitchen, was bent over a plate of cereal looking decidedly early morning. It was Britt Ekland.

The grounds covered a couple of acres of what was probably prime real estate. Bruce arrived with the truck and crew and we got to work. This situation wasn't new to Gowers. Normally, no director wants to make it up as he goes along. Good ideas take time to refine. Not for the Bruce. He revelled in uncertainty.

As Rod strolled up a long stone pathway in his grounds miming to *Only Women Bleed*, he pulled me to one side.

'This isn't going to look like Top Of The Pops is it Jon?' His concern, not unnaturally, was is it going to look naff? My view was that if it turned out to be remotely transmittable, we had a result. What the idiot expected, after what he'd put us all through, was way beyond me.

We moved to his beautiful living room for *Tonight's The Night*. It was an art deco wonderland. The crew set up cameras and lights Britt looked on with a mix of fear and anger. "Fear" because of the potential damage that could be done to the priceless art deco collection. "Anger" on account of a vast number of strangers tramping round her house uninvited. At least uninvited by her.

At one o'clock precisely, one of Rod's aides whispered something in his ear. He beckoned to Bruce and I to follow him. We were shown into what most people would call the library. There were a lot of books, all I'm reasonably certain unread, at least by Rod and Britt. The far wall of this huge room was divided into six panels. His flunky pulled one of them open to reveal that it was a cavernous refrigerated unit that contained racks of Dom Pérignon that stretched fifteen feet across and to a depth of four feet. Apparently it was Dom Pérignon time. I looked at a beautiful Georgian time piece and started to calculate the overtime this little excursion in to Rod's unreal world would cost. Well, he was paying one way or another. He could always sell a row or two of the vintage champagne. We supped from a couple of fluted glasses and discussed the socio-economic situation in China and went back to the shoot.

Tonight's The Night would feature Rod singing to a beautiful blonde woman whose face would never be revealed. It was of course Britt Ekland. After the tenth take, I heard Britt tell Rod that his performance was crap and to listen to her advice. After all as she put it, 'I'm the film star and you're just a singer.'

Minutes later, a huge HMI lamp we were using came crashing down missing Britt by inches and wiping out some priceless antique. Rod couldn't care. Britt turned puce. The day ended with Mr Stewart standing on an elaborate mirrored coffee table banging out some forgettable rock song as shards of mirrored glass headed in all directions.

The show was finally over. Warner's certainly got their bill. We wrapped and took the video back to London to edit.

CHAPTER THIRTEEN
THE ROLLING STONES

1976 was a busy year. Another Queen video, 'You're My Best Friend'. Genesis's 'Trick of the Tale', Ringo Starr and the Rolling Stones. While the music video was beginning to find a niche in the minds of record companies, many of the older bands, the dinosaurs, saw no value in them at all. I was about to travel down another road littered with anti-personnel mines. The Stones weren't easy.

The band would be performing in Kiel, as part of their West German tour. Their record company wanted three videos. The Stones couldn't care less. I was told to fly to Hamburg so I could see them perform and meet them before we took the autobahn to Kiel the following day. I tried to find a video facility house in Kiel but none existed, so I made contact with an OB unit in Hamburg. Bruce thought working with the Stones was a highlight of his life. To me they were like latter day premiership footballers, overpaid, unattractive guys who couldn't pull a hooker if it wasn't for the fame and cash.

For the first and only time, Bruce wanted to bring a camera crew over from London as he didn't feel comfortable with a German crew for such an important project. This would prove expensive and difficult. He wanted to work with familiar faces from Trillion. They were used to his 'shooting from the hip' style, but they were staff and not allowed to freelance. So we became embroiled in an absurd conspiracy to fly them over secretly to Germany. They didn't tell their bosses and moonlighted for us. When Trillion's board found out they were all fired. Bruce and I had to fight a vicious rearguard action to get them reinstated. This included threatening to take all our work elsewhere which was, by then, making an important contribution to Trillion's coffers.

I flew to Hamburg ahead of Bruce, who was up to his eyes as usual in his LWT work, and headed for the venue. I met the Stones' manager around seven, was given a pass to hang round my neck and placed next to the sound mixer to watch the performance. The sound man had prime position in the centre of the vast hall about thirty feet from the stage. He operated a mixer which would not have been out of place in any of the world's top studios. The band were due on at eight thirty. As ten o'clock came and went the audience of around ten thousand, was getting a little impatient. The sound man, grinning, told me this was normal and they probably wouldn't make an appearance till eleven. He was spot on!

I'm no expert when it comes to audio but even to my untrained ear I could tell the quality of the sound was terrible. Their fans no doubt felt they were so lucky simply to get tickets, so actually hearing them perform was secondary to just being in their presence. After the concert finished I was taken backstage to meet the legends. I'd never been a fan, but will admit to liking 'Ruby Tuesday'. Keith and Ronnie were friendly but to Mick and Charlie, I might as well have been a fly buzzing round horse manure.

I left for the hotel at around a quarter to two. We had all been booked into the most palatial hotel Hamburg had to offer. After I'd unloaded my stuff in the room I went for a tour. Keith and Ronnie were on the same floor. As I walked down the corridor I could hear the music pounding out from one of the rooms. I passed by an open door where the music was coming from. Ronnie saw me and invited me in for a drink. Jack Daniels was the nectar for these rock stars.

I stayed for a while. We didn't talk much as the decibels of the playback were so high. Keith was extolling the quality of the sound. I mentioned, in passing, that what they were listening to, a mix straight from the sound desk, was totally different from what their fans heard two hours earlier. This observation was met with a shrug. I went off to bed.

Bruce flew in that morning and we listened to the three tracks in the car as we left Hamburg. A month or so later we would return to take on Ringo. The single was *Fool To Cry* from their *Black And Blue* album. The plan was simple. We'd shoot it as fake/live using their stage and lighting. Stage lighting often isn't great for TV, so it's sometimes changed, though not so drastically as to upset the band's lighting crew. You touch their lighting at your peril. Mostly only the gels would be changed. They are the coloured plastic sheets that cover the lights.

"Fake/live" is what it says. The band mime in an auditorium on stage and the only thing that's missing, usually, is the audience. We checked into our splendid hotel in Kiel around eleven and geared ourselves up to meet Mick, a performer not known for his compliant nature.

We sat in Jagger's room while he reclined on his bed. Bruce as usual, was great with the talent and Jagger liked him immediately. What he thought of me I didn't care to think. He wasn't a friendly guy, his ego reached out to the stars. A phone call interrupts our little chat.

'Yeah what is it?' he mumbles.' What! Fuck it! What time did she get in?' he slams the receiver down. Bruce and I look at each other. We didn't like to ask!

'Fuck it,' the rock superstar says again. 'Bianca's just turned up.' So much for a happy marriage.

We agree to start at eight o'clock that night. The band's road crew, having left Hamburg late the night before, had already set up most of the lighting rig and the stage.

We arrived at the venue at around three to meet the Trillion crew. I watched as the maestro got to work with camera positions, chatted delicately with the Stones lighting director and briefed his vision mixer. All the cameras are linked to the OB truck via cables, and the pictures are recorded onto a video tape machine. Depending on the budget and the director's ideas, more than one machine can be used. That way you record everything that the camera 'sees'. In a live concert shoot, four or five or even more recording machines and cameras can be utilised. The only problem with 'slaving' a camera to a VT machine is the enormous cost of the edit. If you're shooting for two hours and slaved five cameras, that's ten hours of material to view and make decisions about. Very time consuming and so very expensive.

Eight o'clock came and went with no real expectation that Mick and co would be on time. By ten thirty I was concerned and pissed off. We were all getting a little tired. Finally at half past midnight they showed up. Our make up people worked tirelessly and an hour later we began shooting. It didn't take long for all the crew to realise we were dealing with some seriously wasted people. The Jack Daniels had been flowing freely since their arrival and I didn't need to see the results of a blood test to realise that other substances might have been at work. It was all becoming another rock and roll disaster.

By three o'clock the camera crew were so tired they could barely deliver a focused picture and all the while the band became more inept. They couldn't recognise their own chords and Jagger was so out of synch that he reminded me of a character from a badly dubbed Chinese kung fu movie.

When most artists mime, they can never get it right on the button, usually, they are out of synch consistently by just under a second. In the edit you can 'pull' the sound forward and match it up. It takes a real genius to mime so badly that no technology available either then or now could help save it. Jagger managed it. We did shoot the songs, but not before the morning light streamed through the windows and completely screwed up all the lighting effects. Bianca dancing like some stoned marionette in front of the stage did not help over much.

Back in London we reviewed the tapes. The results were unusable. £40,000 for nothing. The record company were understandably none too pleased. Nor was I. The only way to get anything out of it was to get Jagger back in to a studio in London and to record him singing live vocals which would be mixed in to the pictures we shot in Kiel. As he was playing keyboards and singing we had to find an identical keyboard to match the one in Germany. The big question for me was who was going to pay? The record company after much debate coughed up. If you ever get to see the video on YouTube, try and spot the difference between Jagger's mid shot/close ups and the German pictures. You won't.

CHAPTER FOURTEEN
MORE STONES

A few weeks later I got a call from David Elstein, a client and the editor of *This Week*, a very highly regarded current affairs programme for the now defunct Thames TV. We'd first met years earlier on *Weekend World*, and he'd since carved out a reputation as one of the great current affairs editors in British TV, though it was only by a stroke of luck that he got the job at all. He'd set himself a five year time limit to become an editor of a major current affairs series. He'd been producing strands for *This Week* for a number of years. By coincidence when that fifth year came around, three jobs came up simultaneously. *Weekend World*, *Panorama* and *This Week*. WW was spoken for internally. The BBC didn't want to hire anyone from outside the corporation and the Thames Board saw him as a leftie threat.

He was gutted. He saw his future blocked by the broadcasting establishment. He had recently set up The Association of Producers and Directors (ADP). This was a sort of trade union which existed to fight for the rights of its members to share financially in repeats of their programmes as well as arguing for a slice of overseas sales where applicable. The ACTT, which was the mainstream union for producers and directors, had never had the balls to campaign for these rights. The ADP was no friend of the broadcaster since they represented the threat of additional costs that neither the BBC nor the ITV regional companies were prepared to consider. If they hated the ADP, they hated Elstein even more.

We had lunch at Bianchi's, which was run by Elena Salvoni, London's premier *maître d'*. To this day I still think of her as my surrogate mum. I later named my daughter after her.

David was full of gloom. He had decided that as he'd missed out on the chance of running one of the mainstream current affairs programmes, he was going to give it all up and direct children's drama for Scottish television. I cautioned him not to be so hasty and to continue producing for *This Week*. I'm not given to premonitions, but within two weeks after the new editor took over the reins at *This Week*, his girlfriend returned to their home to find he'd committed suicide by hanging himself in the bathroom.

The Board needed to find a new editor fast. They turned to the best man for the job, David.

He had heard I'd been working with The Stones and was desperate to film a documentary of what he'd been led to believe was their last European tour. One of their very many last tours. Thames had been knocked back by everyone connected to the band. Could I help?

I still had Jagger's numbers as well those of his closest confidants. I set to work. One of the reporters on *This Week* was another client of mine, John Fielding. A brilliant very laid back journalist. When he was with The Sunday Times Insight team he helped break the Thalidomide scandal. John was perfect to report and interview for the doc. I persuaded Elstein that the only way it was going to work was if Bruce directed it and Fielding reported on it. He agreed. I then added that if I pulled it off my company would own the film and all the footage. He checked it out and called back and said we had a deal. Unbelievable!

It didn't take long for me to get everyone to agree. I persuaded Mick by telling him that *This Week* was an award winning prime time current affairs programme and the ideal vehicle to present a serious band like The Stones. All this, of course, was bollocks! But to a man with his ego, it was a no brainer.

We flew to Glasgow on what would be the start of a week's touring. I rented a car at the airport, and accompanied by Gowers and Fielding headed to our hotel. Bruce loved to drive so I sat in the back with Fielding in the passenger seat. Twenty minutes into the journey we were stopped by the police. Three scruffy men with beards in a rented car leaving the airport at a time of high IRA alerts wasn't a great combination.

Bruce wound down his window.

'Is this a rented car sir?' The policeman already knew the answer. Bruce nodded.

'We just rented it at the airport,' I chipped in.

'Can I see some identification?' We struggled in various pockets and produced our driving licenses.

'And where are you all off to?' I named the hotel.

'Your purpose in visiting Glasgow?' I explained about the documentary.

He looked dubiously at each one of us in turn.

Then to Bruce asked 'What do you do?'

'I'm the director.' Then to Fielding.

'I'm the reporter.' Then finally to me.

'I'm the producer.' He took that in for a moment.

'I know what a reporter does, and what a director does, but what's a producer do?' Before I could reply they both turned round to look at me as if to say, 'Yeah, what *does* a producer do?'

The Glasgow gig went well. Fielding interviewing all and everyone. Bruce capturing it all for posterity. I mostly hung out with the other hangers on and generally helped myself to the food and drink backstage. That's what a producer does!

The next day was a travel day to Reading with no gig until the following night. Mick wanted to go to London rather than spend a day in Glasgow and, God forbid, a day in Reading. The renting of a private plane was discussed but the cost was about £2,000. I heard them batting the topic around. It was £500 each. Finally they all agreed it wasn't worth the money. So much for the excesses of rock and roll.

Table tennis was a big thing with the Stones. Backstage, amid the canapés and Jack Daniels was a full size table tennis table. I stupidly challenged Bill Wyman to a series of games at ten pounds a game. Within thirty minutes I'm fifty smackers down. He laughed. I laughed. I said I'd had enough. He put his hand out and asked for the cash. Fifty quid was a lot in those days and I'd hoped he'd write it off as a bit of fun. He didn't.

It was in my interest, as the beneficial owner of the film, to get as much live footage as we could. The Stones, nobody's fools, were especially careful to restrict access to front of stage filming. The film finally went out two weeks later as *Stones On The Road*. After transmission, I asked for all the film to be delivered to me as per our contract. Our intention was to re-cut the documentary and replace most of the interviews with as much performance footage as we could cull which would make its potential sale more profitable.

After numerous calls the footage never arrived. In exasperation I contacted the Controller of Current Affairs, John Edwards, a man I knew well.

'Sorry about the delay,' he explained, 'but the ACTT (the all powerful technician union) refuses to hand it over. They don't see why an independent producer like you should make money on the back of their hard work'

'That's not my problem John, we have a deal.' Already I didn't like the way this was going.

'I'll speak to them again and call you back.

A few hours later he was true to his word.

'Perhaps we can do this another way. I'm afraid the union aren't budging.' Another way? 'What about if we offer you ten thousand pounds for you to rescind your rights.' Ten grand was a lot of money, but on the other hand my contacts in the international TV distribution business told me we could earn forty thousand or more in worldwide sales.

'I'd like to help you out here,' I said,' but that just isn't going to be enough.'

Over the next twenty four hours, the offer was increased in stages till it reached twenty thousand. I declined. Thames paid that exact sum into the union pension fund and two days later seventy cans of film were delivered to my little terrace house in Wimbledon. I hired a Steenbeck, a piece of equipment that was used for film editing. It was huge and took up most of the space in my tiny dining room. The seventy cans of film took up the rest of the space. Pearl was not happy. As each month rolled by, the stupidity of not taking the money became painfully evident.

We never saw a great return on the sales. We didn't have enough live performance in it to warrant the big bucks. After paying a year's rental on the Steenbeck, and distribution commission fees, I don't think we saw more than twelve grand. Not to worry, it was only a minor mistake compared to all the other ones I was to go on to make.

CHAPTER FIFTEEN
RINGO, RUSH, STEWART AGAIN AND THE BEE GEES

Ringo came in to our lives shortly after *Stones On The Road* was broadcast. We flew back to Hamburg and into the arms of the ex-Beatle and his bizarre manager, Count Dracula, as we called him. He looked and dressed the part to perfection. Ringo had some deal with Polydor Records. Being an untalented ex-Beatle can certainly empower you for years. There's always going to be some schmuck who's prepared to spend their money to be able to boast of an association with a Beatle. The track was *Hey Baby*. A worse track you could wait decades for. Thank the Lord we only had to make the video. Ringo, at best, was monosyllabic, at worst catatonic.

He had already worked out what he wanted to do. He would wear top hat and tails and meander up and down two huge white staircases lined with forty beautiful young models and warble the number. It was going to be just like the old days of *Sunday Night at The London Palladium!*

I contacted a couple of Hamburg's leading modelling agencies and we began the auditions. Ringo insisted on attending all the sessions. I didn't know it then, but while we were looking for girls who were the right height and had a modicum of rhythm he was looking for the ones he'd like to get a lot closer to. Memory tells me he actually dated one of the girls for a few months.

1977 was marked by the birth of my first born, Gideon, along with a nightmare trip to Canada and America. The agency client list was expanding. Jonathan Dimbleby, Carol Vorderman, Janet Street Porter (for the second time) and Emmy award winning film maker Frank Cvitanovich had joined. I had hired a unit manager from Thames Television, John Willcocks, to run my Agency.

Sitting in my Langham street office, pondering the day's big issue, like where I'd go for lunch, I took the first of three calls.

'Is that Jon Roseman Productions?' It was. 'This is Brian Taylor. I'm calling from Anthem Records in Canada. Rush have been recording in England and they've seen a lot of your work and think it's great.' Couldn't argue. 'We need you to come over to Toronto to film some videos for them. How's June seventh for you?' He left me his contact details and I tried to find out who Rush were. It turns out they were Canada's supergroup.

The second call.

'Jon, hi it's Billy, Billy Gaff.' I froze in fear, intoned a quick prayer and asked God to smite the man. It didn't work. 'How are you?' He asked.

'Fine Billy. How's it going with Rod?' Like I cared.

'That's why I'm calling. Any plans for June seventh? We need you guys to shoot three videos.' Was he serious? After the last experience I'd rather have my balls removed. On the other hand combining a trip to Canada round the same time as one to LA could make us a few bob on the air fares.

'Billy you may remember we had a couple of problems last time out.' It was like saying Custer had a few problems at Little Big Horn.

'Jon, Jon, Jon...' The voice was as soothing as Paul Mckenna's just before he makes you run round the stage thinking you're a chicken. 'That was then. Rod didn't have a handle on what you were trying to do. I promise it'll be fine this time.' I said I'd get back to him.

Later I decided to have lunch with a friend at Quaglino's. I came back to the office full of pasta and tanked up on Barolo.

The third call.

It was the Bee Gees management. Could we go to Miami for June seventh to video some tracks from their new album? Course we could. Though how we were going to be in Toronto, LA and Miami on the same day, I hadn't yet worked out. What was it with this date anyway? It turns out that record companies have particular release dates for certain times of the year which helped explain the connection. I worked out all the dates with Bruce who as usual would follow me over after I'd sorted everything out. Willcocks had been with me for a week when I waved goodbye and set off for Canada. He looked downright scared as I left the baby with him.

Toronto reminded me of an operating theatre. An antiseptic city. Clean, quiet and boring. Rush's management had me picked up at the airport in what looked like a forty foot limo and took me to a stadium, and I do mean a stadium. As we approached the vast arena we passed through tens of thousands of fans. This was one mighty band. I still hadn't heard any of their music and had first heard of them just two weeks ago. I'm treated as a VIP, and sipping a beer, I'm guided to the best seats in the house and wait to see and hear what we'll be dealing with.

I was blown away. Imagine standing next to a passenger jet as it takes off. The noise is tremendous. Now double it. What was incredible was that there were only three of them. After the gig I sat and chatted to the band. Such nice unassuming lads. I arranged the date for the shoot with their management. They were touring so they only had a few dates available. Every release of a new album means a long promotional tour. I had three days to set it all up. No problem. That is till I heard the tracks. One of them was eleven minutes long. Add that to the two other songs and we were being asked to make a half hour TV programme in a day.

We did it fake/live. There was no other way. But fake/live didn't make much use of Bruce's talents. He flew in and everything was shot in a very long day. Then, with the unedited video tapes in our suitcases, we flew south for Miami and the Bee Gees.

Now the boys Gibb were great blokes. For a group who had been at the top of their game for a decade they had a great sense of fun. The videos, *How Deep Is Your Love*, *Staying Alive* and *Night Fever* were all from the classic disco movie *Saturday Night Fever*. The trouble was no one saw fit to tell us about the movie. Would Bruce have shot the clips any differently? Unlikely.

We taped the tracks in a Miami studio and on location. Trying to tie Bruce down to specifics was impossible. He was actually deciding how he was going to shoot the tracks in the cab on the way to the studio. By this time I had given up on trying to second guess him. It was easier just to put my life in his hands. But he hadn't asked me to find out how sophisticated the studio's mixing desk was. He had assumed that the technology required for his ideas to work for two of the songs would be available. In just about any reasonable size facility he would have been right. Perhaps the tell-tale sign on the drinks dispensing machine in reception when we arrived should have been a giveaway. It read, *DO NOT USE MACHINE WHILE RECORDING IN PROGRESS AS THE SOUND OF THE CANS DROPPING CAN BE HEARD IN THE STUDIO.*

I'd never seen Bruce unsettled before. After five minutes with their technical people, he didn't look a happy man. We sat down over some coffee and I asked him what he was going to do. He emptied some more sugar in his plastic cup and stirred it reflectively. I watched as he forced the spoon through the sugar. Minutes passed and gradually his brow un-furrowed and he suddenly stood up and marched over to the control room saying nothing.

I wandered down to the band to let them know we'd soon be ready to rock and roll having no idea what miraculous thought process had engulfed the boy.

He flooded the stage with dry ice, back lit it, and the lads emerged, ghost like, through the mist, miming away. The image was strong but the videos we turned out were very poor. I wondered if Bruce and I should have a serious chat about his *modus operandi.* Without doubt he was a class act and I was merely his glorified gofer. But asking him to actually come up with a plan prior to the shoot would be like suggesting to Michelangelo that perhaps a gloss finish would be better than matt. I decided to take the coward's way out and said nothing.

We'd been in Miami for three days when I get the call from Rush's manager enquiring when they were going to get their videos. A very reasonable request. Neither of us had given it any thought. I prevaricate and tell them I'll get back to them. With the Bee Gees finished and edited we took off for LA with their videos tucked next to Rush's in our bags, under instruction that we should get them over to their management in LA.

Here we come Rod, ready or not. Probably not.

The first call I had when I checked in to my hotel room at the Hyatt was from Rush's people. Where the fuck are our videos? More prevarication was very difficult, but I managed it.

The Continental Riot House was not much fun second time around. Warners had wised up. There was no upgrade, no ability to pillage the in-house shop and no picking up bar bills. Arnie, my erstwhile production manager suggested I stay with him and his girlfriend Lisa. They had a large apartment with five bedrooms courtesy of Lisa's millionaire father. We got on well and I moved in for a week leaving Bruce, who loved hotels, at the Hyatt. They were a cool couple and they gave me a lot of space. She was also a production manager and it was agreed that they would share the load on the Stewart videos.

The Bee Gee's record company had paid all the bills as we went along. They had never given us a budget, and covered the cost of the studio in Miami directly. It was just our fees that needed to be dealt with. They'd never asked what they were and I'd never suggested what they could be. Very risky. If they loved what we'd done, hallelujah, the 'if not' was not a consideration.

I was asked to take a u-matic tape (an early VHS) of the Bee Gees shoot directly to Robert Stigwood, the big boss. Stigwood was enjoying huge success at this time having recently made the cover of *Time* magazine. The meeting was scheduled for eleven a.m. I drove down to the Paramount Studio lot on Melrose Avenue where he was producing 'Grease' his next blockbuster. Stigwood was a marketing genius. He spent as much on marketing as he had on the cost of the film. This was previously unheard of. But his blitzkrieg of advertising enticed vast audiences to watch his films.

I was directed to his opulent trailer. It was a typically hot, muggy LA day. Though the air con was working at full tilt, perspiration was running down my face and armpits as if I'd sprung a leak. It was nerves. What if he didn't like them? No chance. After twenty minutes he arrived with half a dozen assorted aids. Big smile and firm handshake.

'I've heard so much about you boys, can't wait to see what you've done.' He was a slight man with an infectious energy. I slammed the video in his player and waited at the back of the room for the verdict. After he'd viewed *How Deep is Your Love* he raised an arm and shouted to the other bodies, 'See! See! If you want talent you get it from England. Fucking fantastic!'

Relief surged through my veins like smack through an addict's.

I drove back to Bruce to give him the good news. We sat in the Hyatt bar and clinked a couple of Buds. I raised the subject of 'where do we go from here?' Kenny Everett an old friend of Bruce's wanted him to direct and produce his new series for Thames TV, but Bruce wasn't sure. Kenny was insane and it would be a lot of grief.

'Look mate,' I said,' we've been trundling round North America doing this shit and there's not a single company doing videos here. Let's open an office in LA. We'll clean up.' Bruce loved America. I could take it or leave it. It was only later that I had a drug affair with it. It was agreed I'd explore the opportunities.

One way we made a few extra bucks was by providing copies of the tapes of the videos we'd shot for the record and TV companies. We could earn up to another thousand pounds depending on the success of the record. When Stigwood's people didn't call me for any copies, I rang them only to be told he'd changed his mind, he thought the videos were crap, and he was flying over some director from Paris to re-shoot the lot. My first concern was, *were they going to pay our fees?* Bruce, on the other hand, was pissed off that his creative integrity had been questioned. I pointed out to him that if he actually spent more than a minute or two coming up with ideas, rather than continually going for the adrenaline buzz and making it up as he went along, it might save us both a little stress down the line. Not being told it was a disco based movie didn't help either.

Taking a deep breath, I sent in our invoice for twenty thousand dollars and before I could turn blue, the cheque arrived. Good ol' Stiggy!

CHAPTER SIXTEEN
FROST AGAIN, COCAINE AND THE MAFIA

Rather than impose an office atmosphere in Lisa and Arnie's apartment, I kept a room at the Riot House next to Bruce's. One afternoon while exploring the cable channel in my room vainly searching for adult programmes, I got a call from a worried John Willcocks, a serial worrier, saying that David Frost was looking for me. I knew he had a fantastic memory and could name your pet hamster ten years after you told him its name (this is not a joke, I've seen him do it), but what had I done to him all those years ago that warranted the call.

'Jon it's been a long time. Too long.' Too long for what? He was in New York. 'Do you think Bruce might be interested in directing my new series *Headliners* for NBC, here in the States?' Just a little I thought.

'When would you want him?'

'Could be anytime in the next two months.' I told him I'd check it out and get back to him.

I banged on Bruce's door. He let me in. I noticed he'd been able to find the channel I'd been searching for. When I told him about my conversation with Frost, his face turned into a big grin. He adored America. He wanted to live, work and die there. I still looked upon the States as a transient place. My feelings for it were always incomplete. Me, I loved the idiosyncrasies of England, the bloody weather and its pace. That said no-one should judge such a vast country by having only visited New York, Miami and LA. There were great swathes of the Mid West I'd never explored and to understand her you'd have to live there and travel extensively. Though most Americans tended not to leave their own State let alone travel abroad.

Bruce's instructions to me were, 'Make it happen.'

'What about Kenny?' I asked.

'Nothing's agreed.'

'Nothing's agreed with Frost either,' I reminded him. 'If you're not careful both jobs could slip away.'

'Why can't we negotiate both jobs and then pull out of one at the last minute?' I could see why he was a director and I was the agent. Attempting to do what he suggested could get an agent skewered on his own petard. I didn't mind taking a few risks. Actually I had always taken a lot of risks, but on the one hand I had Frost and on the other Everett and his Thames boss Philip Jones. Jones could fillet you and you wouldn't know he'd done it, until you tried to stand up. This was the man who stunned the BBC by stealing Morecambe and Wise. It would all have to wait until we returned to London.

On my third day of staying with Arnie and Lisa, I came out of the shower, bottom half concealed by fluffy towel, and walked past the living room. They had a few friends round and as I sashayed past they called out to me. Getting dressed wasn't an issue so I joined them in their beautifully furnished living room. They were all standing around a large polished oval rosewood dining table. Lisa beckoned me over and offered me a rolled up dollar bill. I stood there like the statue of David (the only difference being I was the one with the towel). Anyway, I didn't move because I didn't understand why anyone would pass me a rolled up dollar bill.

'Here,' she said pushing the note in my hand. 'It's very good.' What was very good? I remained motionless and confused. She stared at me for a moment not understanding. 'It's coke,' she explained. We now enjoyed a shared confusion. On the table was a large mirror with lines of white powder stretching across it. I had never seen the stuff before and I guess she'd never met anyone who hadn't seen the stuff before.

'I don't really do drugs.' I said. Eight years previously I'd had a few hits from a friend's joint, didn't like it and that was my entire experience of the swinging sixties. All her friends looked at me as though I was an extraterrestrial. They were staring at a twenty eight year old man, up to his neck in rock and roll, who had never done coke. I smiled, told them to enjoy, and went to get dressed. If only that was the end of the story. If only.

A day or so later Lisa finally persuaded me to give it a try. I liked it. I liked it a lot. Hello hell, here I come. I made the decision that while I enjoyed their company, living and working together was a step too far, so I decamped to the Sunset Marquis. It was a little more upmarket than The Riot House but still occupied by miscellaneous rock bands from around the globe.

Second time around Mr Stewart was so much easier to work with. At least he turned up this time. Apparently he had begun to realise that music videos were not such a waste of space after all.

At around this time Britt and Rod had split up after spending two years together. He moved out of his palace and rented another near Malibu, leaving Britt living alone in the house 'till 'matters' were settled. Bruce and I are sitting by the pool of his rented home, Rod's new blonde girlfriend sun-bathing close by, two bits of cloth clinging to her voluptuous body, talking about ideas for the videos.

'I want some football in one of them,' he says sipping his omnipresent Dom Pérignon. Bruce and I do the 'look'. 'I've got a load of great tapes of some Scottish games back at the house.' I have the urge to check the contents of his glass for hallucinogenic substances. We listen politely to his inane ramblings and agree to placate his insanity by at least looking at the tapes. Trouble was, as he said, they were back at the house. The house currently occupied by Britt. And Britt, he warned us, wouldn't take kindly to anyone dropping by and leafing through his video collection which was located in his magnificent art deco lounge.

Rod's idea was that as his PR man was still living at the lodge in his grounds he could let us in allowing us to search for the said tapes. All this when Britt was out of the house shopping. If she returned he'd signal for us to leg it! Marx Brothers eat your heart out. The 'us' became me. I made it to his lounge and begin to flick through his vast tape collection of Scottish games. After twenty minutes Britt returned. The warning signal never materialised and I was caught with my hand in the tape cupboard. She remembered me from *Tonight's The Night* so there was no need for LA's finest to come calling. I explained what it was all about and she laughed. 'That Rod is such a coward. Shall we have tea?' We did and I saw another side of the film star, a side I liked a lot.

Lisa and Arnie had a friend called Reed Wallace. Reed was *the* man. He knew everybody because he supplied coke to everybody. We liked each other instantly and remain friends to this day, notwithstanding the eleven year prison term he would serve some time much later for manslaughter. He shot a fellow dealer. He claimed it was self defence. He got a great kick out of my association with music videos and no doubt a lot of extra business, and he, in turn, introduced me to his life of beautiful girls, the mafia and Peruvian flake.

Roy's, a Chinese restaurant located on Sunset Strip, was Reed's eatery of choice. It was to a certain extent his local. He seemed very close to the *maître d'*. She was an oriental woman of an uncertain age - though it was certainly close to seventy. She looked like she had a "lift" or two but I think gravity had long since interceded. The restaurant's clientele fitted Reed's business perfectly. It wouldn't have surprised me if they all had his phone number. Whatever went on between Madame Ying Yang and Reed I didn't know and didn't want to know. I did however find the girl we were to use in Rod's *Hot Legs* video there.

Roy's was a restaurant with certain peculiarities other than Madame Ying Yang. The main one was that surrounding the large dining area was a series of private mirrored booths. The booths had room enough for eight people to dine, though dining was not generally what went on. The mirrors must have been supplied by the spy factory. They were two-way. No waitress would ever open a booth door without knocking and being invited in. Roy's girls didn't do clothes *per se*. I'm not talking completely naked, but you could certainly leave your imagination at home. Our waitress, Sheri, as in, 'Hi, I'm Sheri I'll be your waitress tonight,' enters our booth. Everyone's shovelling coke up their respective noses and I'm sipping a glass of Napa Valley's finest. At that time I still preferred a glass to a rolled bank note. The girl is stunning, her long legs just one of her great features. We order the food which no-one but me will eat and I come out with the ageless Hollywood line,

'Sheri, I'm making a music video and we're looking for a girl with beautiful legs.' I might as well have asked her for a blow job. She'd heard it all before and politely ignored me as she finished scribbling our orders.

'Actually he's not shitting you,' Lisa said in that pleasant formal west coast way. 'He's making a video with Rod Stewart. Jon is one of the world's biggest music video producers.' I wouldn't necessarily go that far but...Lisa handed her a business card and told her to call tomorrow.

We shot the video for Hot Legs starring Sheri on location at some beat up gas station outside Malibu. Bruce, because he's not into preparation, forgets to film one of the verses. Not sure anyone noticed.

The studio shoot for the other tracks is of Jaggeresque proportions. After every take, Rod disappears in to his dressing room to say "hi" to the marching powder. After a couple of hours, he's so wired it's another lost cause. You pays your money, you takes your choice. Warner's, thank God, paid the money.

By now I'm avoiding the calls from Rush's management. I tell Bruce the day after the Rod hoovering fest that he's going to cut Rush that day or I'm going to cut him. Thirty six hours later the finished video is on its way to Toronto. They love it. Delay is forgiven and bouquets all round.

I mention casually to Arnie and Lisa my idea of setting up in LA. They get very excited. They really enjoy working with us. American producers and directors weren't like us. We were funny and easy going with no pretensions. She said she'd have a word with her father, the millionaire, and ask his advice on our behalf.

I've now established a special relationship with Reed. We're not talking the kind of special relationship that exists between London and Washington. I start to use his product on a regular basis though not to the extent that I couldn't function. Bruce had also picked up the habit. By this time, I don't know anyone who wasn't using it. I had no idea how Reed obtained his product and didn't care to ask. One day while sitting in my LA office wondering, as usual where to lunch, he rang me.

'I need a favour,' he said, 'a big favour.'

'What do you need?'

'Some friends of mine are coming in from Miami. One has already arrived and he's been arrested at the airport.'

'Should I be asking why?'

'He was carrying some coke.'

'Oh!'

'If the others are stopped and questioned, would you say they've come over to see you about shooting some rock concerts?'

'Mmm.'

'They're not carrying anything, but they are known to be associated with the guy who's been arrested.' I thought for a moment. And I agreed. I must have been crazy. That evening I met Reed and his friends from Miami. There was Frank Marino, a six foot seven bundle of muscle and danger, and a large obese man, known as Joe 'the fat man' Perello. He was about five foot but must have weighed in at nearly seventeen stone. His neck was wider than my head and he wore six or seven heavy gold chains around it. More gold decorated his wrists. If ever Fort Knox was short of a bar or two they could always give the fat man a call.

One evening at Roy's, Reed and I are with a bunch of people, mostly beautiful young girls, when a waitress knocks on the door of the booth.

'Jon Roseman?' she asks. I nod.

'Rod Stewart and Kiki Dee are in the bar.' Why she's telling me this I have no idea. I smile.

'Sheri told me to let you know, as there aren't any booths available.' I might have had to work with the man, but at least I could choose who to spend my leisure time with.

'Come on Roseman, let's get wild with Rod,' says Reed all smiles and a little coked up.

'Ok if he wants to join us it's no problem,' I tell our waitress. Ten minutes later we're making room for Rod and Kiki. Surprisingly he is a lot of fun when he's not being Rod Stewart. Plenty of anecdotes about the business and a shared pleasure in the powder. Kiki sips mineral water and doesn't partake. It gets to about twelve thirty when Rod suggests we should go party at his manager's.

We pile in to a couple of limos and head to Gaff's place on Doheny. He opens the door to Rod who marches straight in with a, 'Hi manager!' Billy, in evening suit, is hosting an intimate dinner for ten fresh faced young men also attired in evening wear. Oddly he's not best pleased to have his house invaded by a bunch of strangers at that time of night or I guess anytime of night. Rod's attitude is 'without me you're nothing.' We all traipse in after Rod and hit Billy's champagne. Soon his pool is busy with naked bodies including my own. Party! Party!

By two thirty I've had enough. I call a cab and head back to my hotel. The fact I'm just wearing a towel and carrying my clothes over my arm doesn't faze the driver at all. Welcome to LA. As I stroll in to the hotel's foyer I'm greeted by what looks like a roadie who asks me if I want to go to a party. I'm just wearing a towel for Christ's sake.

I figure the night's still young and follow him to the lift which opens into a massive penthouse suite. The door is opened by an armed policeman and I find myself among seventy or so crazy people dancing, drinking and doing God knows what. More armed police sit around turning blind eyes to the proceedings. I end up sitting on a huge bed, still wearing a towel, with my clothes still draped over my arm. I'm offered a drink and some coke and try to work out what I'm doing there and why are there armed police? I never managed to answer either question and finally hit my own bed around five o'clock. Just another normal night in Hollyweird.

Bruce and I finish our work, say our goodbyes and head back to London and Everett and Frost. Couldn't wait.

CHAPTER SEVENTEEN
KENNY EVERETT AND MORE FROST

John Willcocks, who now occupied the tiny back office in Langham Street, was full of regrets at having left Thames TV. He didn't feel he was up to the job. He was a nondescript fellow. Melons had more personality. He was average height, average looks and he even had average hair. I spent half an hour convincing him he was London's answer to Mike Ovitz and he bought it.

I called Philip Jones.

'Good morning Philip, it's a pleasure to speak to you,' Oily doesn't come close. He knew I was Bruce's agent and was prepared for the first round.

'Morning to you. Kenny is very keen for Bruce to do his show and so am I. They're both great talents. Can't talk specifics at the moment as we're still working out the schedule. Why don't I call you when I know more?' Fine by me.

I wait a couple of days before calling Frost. We speak, he hasn't got anything to tell me either. Lisa calls me from America to tell me her father would love to help us set up in LA and when are we coming back? I'd no idea. I had to give it more thought. Setting up in the States would have a big impact on my family.

I finally got the call from Philip Jones. We were on. At least Bruce was. I called him.

'Philip wants to do a deal,' I said.

'Shit! What about Frost?'

'Haven't heard from him.'

'Shit! I'd rather do Frost.'

'I know but that's not looking good.'

'Call him,' he said rather plaintively. I called. He was out of town. I avoided Jones for a couple of days, but his messages were starting to get more brusque. I told Bruce that I should at the very least start negotiations. He knew it made sense. Just ask for ridiculous money, he told me. In those golden days, when TV companies were full of money, courtesy of huge advertising revenues, the top directors could pull in a thousand a week.

'Sorry to keep missing you Philip,' I lied, 'But I've been filming all over the place.' I doubt if Philip Jones would have given a flying fuck if I'd been in a coma.

'No problem Jon,' it was his turn to lie, 'What are we looking at here?' In other words how much do you want? I took a deep breath, the kind you'd need to stay under water for life.

'I was thinking £2,000 a week.' The pause was so long I thought he'd either hung up or died.

'Jon, did you say £2,000 a week?!' I could hear the exclamation mark.

'Yup,' I coughed.

'I'm not sure we can go that high. I'll get back to you as soon as I speak to our financial people.' He didn't sound happy and I suddenly needed to take an urgent leak.

Bruce was getting very nervous. He desperately wanted to go to New York and work with Frost but I couldn't get hold of the man. Two days passed before Jones called me back.

'You've given me a terrible headache with this one Jon. But Kenny is adamant he wants Bruce so we'll pay the money.' I was shocked. The money would make him the highest paid director in television. Normally I'd be digging out the bunting, but I knew how Bruce would react.

'Thanks Phillip. I'll let Bruce know.' I hung up. Did that mean I agreed the deal? Not necessarily. It meant what it said. But what did it say? I called Gowers.

'You're now the highest paid director in British television,' I told him sounding like I was reading out his obituary. 'Congratulations!'

'Jon, I don't want the bloody job.' I had already been converted. I said nothing, there being nothing to say.

'Are you still there?' he was genuinely upset.

'Yes.'

'So?'

'So?' I repeated.

'So I don't want it.'

'Listen, we don't have anything going with Frost. We asked for a ridiculous sum of money and he's agreed.'

'*You* asked for it.' Petulance.

'Bruce, I've had enough of this. What do you expect me to do, go back and say I know you've given me everything I've asked for but it's not enough?

'Ok, Ok you're right, you're right. I'll do it.' I called Jones and closed the deal.

A couple of days later I leave the office early and drive down to Sussex. We had recently moved from Wimbledon to Crawley Down in West Sussex. A lovely detached house in three acres. I didn't get to see much of it as I was beginning to spend more time in London and America. Pearl had settled in quickly and soon made friends with the locals. The house was called Stonecross and despite not being there much of the time it was a wonderful place. Selling it five years later was a huge mistake. But my life was a litany of mistakes so why make an exception?

Gideon is now eighteen months, and as I cuddle him I wonder if he knows who the hell I am. Pearl and I have dinner which was becoming a rare event and I go up for a bath at around ten thirty. I soak and think what's going to happen next? Grief that's what happens next. Pearl walks in to the bathroom with the telephone.

'It's David Frost,' she says handing it to me. You couldn't make it up.

'Hi David.'

'It's not too late is it?' For what I wonder.

'No, no it's fine.'

'Great news, we're ready to do a deal.' He sounded so happy.

I listened to the deal and my testicles drove up into my body.

The next morning I passed on the news to Gowers. Twice the money, four months in New York, all expenses paid.

'Fuck, fuck, fuck,' and then, 'what are you going to do?'

'What do you mean?'

'What are you going to do about Frost?'

'What do you mean?' I say again.

'You know what I fucking mean.' It was true I did know what he fucking meant.

'Listen Bruce, I'm not going to call Phillip. Ok?'

'No it's not ok. I'll go and see him myself.'

'I wouldn't advise it.'

'He'll understand. This is my big break in America.' I knew Phillip wouldn't understand. Phillip wouldn't give a fuck about America or Bruce's career.

I got to the office just before ten thirty the following day. Drank some coffee, met Willcocks, talked client stuff and he toddled off. Pushing Gowers out of my mind I sat and thought about where I'd go for lunch. There was a new Italian I'd heard about and I thought I'd give it a try.

Bruce limped in to my office an hour later looking as if he'd been mugged by an SAS unit.

'What happened,' I ventured. He could have done with a blood transfusion. He was shaking and his face was grey.

'He went mad. Said I was a shit and that he'd personally see to it that I never worked again.' I wasn't surprised. What did he really expect? This was not going to be good news for my agency either. Phillip would do all he could to put the boot into me as well.

CHAPTER EIGHTEEN
BUDGETS AND VIDEO SURGERY

Bruce and I flew to the States two weeks later. Me to LA, him to New York. I needed to set things up for us on the West Coast while he did his Frost thing. He'd made the decision to work in the States for as long as he could, get the green card and go for it big time. He's still there thirty years later.

Lisa's dad made his money in the rag trade. He was very helpful and guided me towards various lawyers and accountants. While I was grateful, there was still something about him that I found a little unsettling, I couldn't put my finger on it, so I let it go. After a week the production company was incorporated and I needed to get back to London.

At about this time Russell Mulcahy walked into my life. A freelance producer came to see me with Russell's show reel. It was low budget work, but wonderfully inventive. Would I like to meet him? By this time work was flooding in. There was no way Bruce could do it, particularly as he was committed to Frost for four months and so I was on the lookout for newcomers. Russell was an Australian director and cameraman. He'd worked as a news film editor at a Sydney TV station and still lived there. I said if he wanted to pay to come over, I'd definitely hire him.

Russell was an amazing talent. He went on to a successful movie career, directing *Highlander* and *Resident Evil*. His specialities were visual, normally violent extravaganzas. His videos included The Buggles, *Video Killed The Radio Star*, all the best of the Duran Duran videos and a bunch of Elton John's.

We met and I liked him immediately. Like Bruce, there was no ego to him. He was quiet and polite and great to share time with. He was delicate in looks with a mop of brown hair. He loved his movies and his drugs. My only criticism was that he rarely picked up a book. I think that his lack of reading set him back as a director, though his innate visual skills were groundbreaking.

But his timekeeping was always a problem for me. A shoot normally starts around seven in the morning for the director and I regularly had to send someone round to his tiny flat to haul him out of bed. I was never sure if it was drugs, alcohol or sex that kept him up most of the night.

David Mallet was now also signed to my production company. He was, at the same time, a supreme talent and yet a total prick. He was, other than Bruce, the maestro of the live concert. When Russell arrived in England, he was keen to work straight away. I didn't have anything immediately for him. Mallett was just going to start work on the Boomtown Rats, *I Don't Like Mondays.* I suggested that we use Russell to shoot the opening sequence. So his very first job was filming an anonymous house (the school) in the middle of nowhere in Wales.

Ex-Monkey Mickey Dolenz also joined me briefly. He was clever and innovative with a bizarre sense of humour. A likeable man with little ego which surprised me bearing in mind his success.

The company would soon be churning out videos and racking up huge losses. I flew out directors to America to handle our ever increasing workload. We were shooting anything that moved, including Ambrosia, April Wine, George Benson, Debbie Boone, Alicia Bridges, Shaun Cassidy, Alice Cooper, Journey, Rufus, Van Morrison, Peaches and Herb, Rose Royce, Sparks, Supertramp, Styx, The Tubes, Ron Wood, The Doobie Brothers, Al Jarreau, The Kinks, Van Halen and Prince.

I possessed no accounting skills whatsoever. Never have: never will. I rarely took advice in these matters and always thought that it would be alright on the night. Those nights came and went with increasing frequency and I was *never* alright. I lived in the eternal hope that just round the corner lay my salvation. What lay round the corner was reality. I was always a financial accident waiting to happen and happen they did - with scary regularity.

Video budgets were manifestly works of fiction. The producers I hired also had, like me, the accounting skills of a gutted rabbit. In those early days all the producers and directors wanted was to turn out great work whatever the cost. Great work meant more work and career enhancement. This could lead to commercials, possible TV shows or the Holy Grail, movies. They were in business for themselves and I was picking up the tab. Of course I could have enforced some serious accounting practises, but I was rarely there and if I was, I didn't find it exciting enough to deal with.

I'd been arguing for some time with record companies that they didn't always need to use the actual artist or band in the video particularly when, not to put too fine a point on it, said artist or band were not great to look at. This fell on deaf ears. One of the videos we did in the States fell right in to that category. I was surprised to get a phone call from RSO, Robert Stigwood's company, bearing in mind his feelings on the Bee Gees shoot. They had an artist, Samantha Sang, who had recorded *Emotion*, a song specially written for her by Barry and Robin Gibb. The Bee Gees sang backing vocals on the track. She was Australian, actually half aborigine. She wasn't the best looking girl on the block and when I met her in Chicago for the shoot I knew we were going to have to employ some serious video plastic surgery. The song was already destined to go top five so, thank God, the video wasn't going to be crucial to any success.

She turned up wearing a short top and hipster trousers. She was overweight and the outfit accentuated the fact. We pumped in gallons of dry ice followed by vast amounts of smoke. The smoke machine is oil based which meant her hair went lank every twenty minutes. It didn't seem to matter what we pumped into the studio, you could still see her! The edit was a nightmare. Finally we ended up stretching the picture to give her, at least the appearance, of being svelte. The video was one of the worst we'd ever done.

I tried to persuade the record company to let us shoot a story around a song by The Atlanta Rhythm Section without using the band, I lost. They were four very big lads and I'm not talking muscle here. Meeting such a band after seeing their pictures on album covers or posters can be a bit of a shock. Any resemblance to their photos is merely coincidental. The photographer could have spent days shooting them before coming up with a single useable picture.

As pop video producers we would sometimes spend just one day, sometimes two, to come up with four minutes of cut footage. A thirty second TV commercial could take up to two weeks or even longer to shoot, a luxury that was never going to be afforded to the likes of us. Given the amount of time and money our commercial brothers enjoyed, we could have turned the ugliest mother into a beautiful swan.

CHAPTER NINETEEN
HOBBS CHOICE AND FILM FESTIVALS

One of my clients at the time was a young Australian, Lyndall Hobbs. She had been a reporter on an early evening local TV programme for Thames Television and was the long-time girl friend of Michael White, a very successful theatrical impressario and film producer. He'd been behind *The Rocky Horror Picture Show* and *Monty Python And The Holy Grail*. Over dinner one night with the pair of them, the idea for a short film starring the lovely Lyndal somehow seeped in to our conversation in-between the fettuccine and crème brûlée. Lyndall would go to the Milan and Paris fashion shows, film the models on the catwalk and magically become one of them and then mixing to another location she'd be seen in the identical cat walk dress dancing á la Ginger Rogers with a gang of hunky men. Now I know this idea must seem up there with the likes of fly fishing for the blind, but it was 1978.

The more the two of them talked about it the more excited Michael became. For my part I just concentrated on the crème brûlée. Suddenly out of nowhere the impresario says, 'So what do you think Roseman are you in?' In what? 'I shouldn't think it will take more than £40,000 to make.' Now he's *tres* excited. 'We can probably get our hands on some Eady money.' His mind is racing. "Eady money" had nothing to do with Mr Justice David Eady QC, the leading defamation High Court judge. It was a government fund set up to help the British film industry.

Two days later, I've found myself committed to funding a third of this crap, with Michael coughing up the rest. I had no idea if I could afford such a significant outlay, but then that never stopped me before. We filmed over a period of two weeks and the edit began while I was in LA.

On my return Michael asked me to view the rough cut. That's as it sounds...a rough edit. I met him at the cutting rooms in Soho and while he loitered outside I watched fifty minutes of the worst film since the invention of celluloid. Lyndall had voiced a rough sound track to add to the disaster. She asked me excitedly what I thought. I told her I needed some time to think and her eyes started filling with tears. I left the suite and found Michael.

'It's fucking terrible,' I said. He shrugged. 'It'll have to be cut in half and we have to lose Lyndall's commentary.' He nodded in agreement. 'You'll have to tell her.'

'Can't you do it?' I guess as it was his girlfriend he didn't feel it was something that would necessarily end in kisses and cuddles.

'I really think it's your call.' I said.

'I don't think I can do it.' His face told me that he couldn't do it and it was going to be my job to play the bad cop. The very bad cop. I told her. She wasn't happy but she did as I asked.

We never saw a penny in profit and may have got some of our money back, I don't remember. 'Hobbs Choice', as the film would be called, went out as a short on the cinema circuit, in the days when there were short films. A short was any film under twenty-five minutes. Its *raison d'être* was to promote young film talent. Surprisingly a lot of punters seemed to enjoy our little film.

Sitting in my office after its 'premiere' I was reading the trade paper Broadcast and noticed that there were various award festivals for short films. It was my bizarre sense of humour that made me enter it in both the New York and Chicago film festivals. We had a young motorcycle messenger working for us at the time and I promised him that if we won, I'd send him over, on his bike, to collect the statue or whatever they handed out.

We won. We actually won in the category of best short film in both festivals. To this day, I never mentioned it to the boy on the motorbike. Many years later I got a call from Lyndall. She was then living with Al Pacino, but I guessed the reason for the call was that the relationship was coming to an end. She wanted me to explore some avenues for her in the UK. I told her it would be difficult as she had been away so long but if we could use Pacino as a calling card anything might be possible. Not surprisingly she passed.

CHAPTER TWENTY
MAKING IT IN AMERICA
AND CHAKA KHAN

I heard from Lisa that all the legal and accounting procedures for the LA Company were now in place and took off for LA to try to sell music videos to the Americans. I rented a house for a month in the area known as Beachwood in north LA. Not flash, but not hobo land either. I was ready to kick ass as Jon Roseman Productions Inc.

I made a showreel of all our best work and started to hawk it around the record companies. I made dozens of calls, but as there was no pop video industry as such, I was passed through every department with the refrain, 'not us'. I soon discovered that record companies had one hell of a lot of departments. Perseverance finally got me a meeting with Todd Rubenstein, one of the vice presidents of RCA. How important he was I had no idea. American companies were swamped with vice presidents.

I left the house and drove down the Strip to their offices clutching my showreel, no doubt in the same way Jack hung on to his beanstalk seeds. It was a very hot day and the air con in my car had decided to commit *hari kari*. By the time I'd parked and made it to the thirty first floor I looked like I'd just taken a shower fully clothed.

Todd was friendly enough. Tall, slim, thinning blond hair, jeans and a David Bowie T- shirt. We chatted like old friends, a speciality of the LA executive, and after ten minutes I produced my showreel. His face blanked. I looked around his office and saw no TV and no playback facility.

'Is there a conference room we could view it in?' I suggested gamely.

'I'm sorry Jon, we don't have anything here.'

RCA had been at the forefront of television and video technology for nearly half a century but they didn't even have a television in their vast LA offices. If someone popped out of a cupboard and declared I was on *Candid Camera* it wouldn't have surprised me, though I guess it wouldn't have been an RCA camera.

'Todd I could go back to my house and pick up a TV and video and bring it back here. It's no problem.' No problem! The TV had a thirty inch screen and weighed a good one hundred and ten pounds. The u-matic playback machine weighed nearly the same again. We arranged to meet again in an hour. I gunned the car back to the house, manoeuvred both sets of equipment on to the back seat and hurtled back to RCA. Up and down the lift twice, struggling not to drop either piece. I was drenched in perspiration and exhausted.

I set up the gear, shoved in the showreel and collapsed on Todd's sofa. He loved the tape. Eulogised about its inventiveness and I began to think my Herculean exertions were not entirely in vain.

'You know Jon that is remarkable work. Fantastic! If we were ever to make videos I know you'd be the first person I'd call. But I doubt if we'll be doing any. Thanks for coming by.' This was the reaction of every record company I met over the next month. I visited nearly all of them and assorted independent labels, as well as a few high profile managers and was rebuffed each time. It would all radically change in the coming months.

While videos like *Bohemian Rhapsody* should have persuaded any sane person that they had true merit in aiding sales, your average LA record executive was not necessarily sane. With no network exposure readily available for a pop video, thinking outside the box was required. Europe was a big market place and Japan was catching up fast. They all had programmes that showed pop videos and could be exploited - if there was any product to exploit. This slowly became apparent to a few execs who had travelled further than Ohio.

We did get some work while we loitered with intent in LA. We were asked to film Chaka Khan performing '*I'm Every Woman*'. Bruce came over from New York having been given a two day pass by Frost's producers. He was loving the work on the show and was infatuated with the city. He listened to my stories about trying to find work in LA with a shrug. It was my job not his, so why should he give a damn?

We used the studio on Fountain again. Chaka was a deeply troubled woman and when she disappeared off set we became very concerned. We finally found her, out in the alley at the back of the studio, among the dustbins, shooting up heroin with a couple of guys. Whether they were friends or a couple of dealers just passing by we didn't know. She managed to finish the shoot, (the video that is), but I read later that she was a constant visitor to rehab.

Lisa, who had now split up with Arnie, called me and suggested I have dinner with her father who'd been so helpful in introducing me to lawyers and accountants. Her parent's house, situated in Laurel Canyon, was a homage to Zen. It stood on one level and seemed to go on for a mile or two! The gardens were tastefully laid out with bonsais and orchids and a discreet swimming pool. There was lots of money here, but unlike most of California's *nouveau riche* it wasn't ostentatious.

Her parents were very warm and wonderful hosts though I still had this vague uneasiness about her father. He had invited an old friend to join us for dinner, Hal Brown, who was the president of a huge independent production company, American International Television (AIT). AIT was a subsidiary of American International Pictures which was owned by the legendary Samuel Z Arkoff. Arkoff's company made iconic horror B movies. Hal seemed an ok guy and over a few drinks asked if I thought it was possible to make a twenty six half hour series using music videos. The idea became *Jukebox,* the first music video show to air on American TV. It had the potential to make Gowers and I dollar millionaires. What it ended up doing was wiping me out. Before I headed back to London, Hal and I met a few times and I went away to work out how we could put the series together. Twenty six programmes with six videos a show meant one hundred and fifty six clips. That was a lot of material which, I hoped with a large grin, we'd be making most of.

I spent a couple of weeks meeting record companies to sell them the concept and they appeared very excited at the possibilities, though they remained far from convinced that spending large sums out of their marketing budgets to invest in music videos was a viable consideration. However they were all prepared to give away any clips we wanted for free and to cover any payment for residual rights. I met a couple of studios and began preparing the budget. I then flew back to London believing we were about to crack the big one.

CHAPTER TWENTY ONE
A TOUCH OF BRANSON AND MONEY

Pearl brought Gideon to meet me at Gatwick which was about a forty minute drive from our home in Sussex. I'd been away a month and lost a stone. I would spend my life worrying about my weight and would later be a regular visitor to the gym. My weight would go up and down like Sterling.

I spent a long weekend at home trying again to figure out what was wrong with America and their antipathy to music videos. I decided, that unlike Britain, there was no Top Of The Pops or morning kid shows that would churn them out. The record companies in the UK saw them as an integral part of promotion and supplied them for free to any TV station who wanted them. This was good for the station's programme cost base, though that would all change in a few years.

The States had nothing comparable on their networks. In syndication there was *Midnight Special* and Don Kirshner's *Rock Concert*. America had around nine thousand independently owned TV stations, many of them affiliated with one of the three major networks. ABC, CBS and NBC (back then there was no Fox TV). When a programme is syndicated, it can be aired at any time the station wants to schedule it. The programme's distributors, which can be one of the major networks, or an independent producer, gets paid per station. Before rock and roll became big business in television terms, we'd have to wait for MTV. That was over two years away. But *Jukebox* could start the ball rolling.

Having been away from the office for a little over a month, I feared what I'd find when I returned. The agency under Willcocks's stewardship, was doing fine.

He had settled in and seemed happy. He reminded me of a bank teller, indeed a man born to bank telling. The production company was seriously busy with bands like XTC, Thin Lizzy, Elvis Costello and the Boomtown Rats. Mulcahy and Mallet were at the top of their game. I began to expand my roster of directors by introducing people who had no track record as directors but had great ideas. Provided I surrounded them with a great crew and talented editors, it really was difficult for them to fail. My mother could have made music videos with the right team.

By now film was replacing tape. Film had a totally different feel from the rather flat two dimensional picture that video produced. Time was always of the essence in pop videos; 'We need it tomorrow!' was the constant demand. There was no time to edit on film, which was often a long and laborious process, so we just transferred the film to tape and cut it via the video editing process. This way we enjoyed the best of both possible worlds.

The editing culture in America was so different to Britain's. Their technology was always a year ahead. In order to cut the costs of editing on expensive state-of-the-art equipment, they developed a system of cutting tape on cheap u-matic machines (these were like sophisticated VHS's). This process is called offline editing. Having made all your decisions offline, it was a relatively simple task doing the final edit online, using all the expensive gear and make huge savings.

On one of my many transatlantic flights I considered how unsophisticated our edit facilities were in London. A plan took shape. I would raise the money for the first one frame, accurate offline edit suite in Europe. I discussed this with an editor I worked with a lot, and persuaded him to come on board if I managed to raise the cash. I would need to employ a quality editor to help get interest from investors as well as being an enticement for potential clients. My accountant prepared a business plan which was pure fiction, After all, I was going to introduce a unique facility whose only track record existed in America. There was no way we could predict a possible income stream. It was all one huge guess.

I needed to find a backer who wanted to get into the periphery of the glamorous world of television. Someone whose ego would make him believe that his investment would put him on the first rung of that ladder. In short, a patsy. Enter Richard Branson.

It took months of negotiating to put the deal in place, but finally the green light was given. The only way this was going to work was if the big spenders in the world of editing, the producers of commercials, would come to us to save money on their huge editing bills.

They didn't want to know.

However frantic we were in the land of music videos, I always had a nagging suspicion that we weren't actually making any money. Had I hired a proper accountant rather than a young book keeper, I might have avoided the oncoming speeding express.

We were now turning out some fine videos. Mallet's *I Don't Like Mondays* had gone down a storm. I think the freedom that directors had in those days was an integral part of this. Unlike movies and commercials, with executives constantly looking over your shoulder, record company executives, at that time, stayed away from what they didn't understand. That would all change big time in the not so distant future. Everyone loved *Mondays*, including Geldoff, a man who never seemed to love anything very much (that is if you don't count Paula Yates).

Around this time, I bumped in to an old friend, Jackie Adams, who was working with Michael Grade, then Director of Programmes at LWT. I'd known Michael for a while though it was on an occasional basis. When Jackie mentioned to him that we were having lunch, he uttered the immortal line, 'Roseman's either going to be a millionaire or a bankrupt.' Well, at least I didn't bankrupt an entire television company!

CHAPTER TWENTY TWO
OFFLINE EDITING, PAULA YATES AND THE NOLAN SISTERS

I moved my office to Poland Street, in the heart of London's Soho, courtesy of the deal I'd just made with Richard Branson. It was 1979. The building had three floors. The offline edit facility was in the basement, a crude reception area on the ground floor, my production company inhabited the second floor with an ad hoc staff of seven or eight and I took the top floor. The agency stayed at the basement in Langham Street.

The deal that had taken months off my life was so Bransonesque. He had borrowed the money from his bank and lent it to the new company at an absurd rate of interest *and* took a fifty per cent stake in the company. If the company couldn't make the loan repayments or made a loss after two years he had the right to decimate my shareholding. He was less an investor more a loan shark. I'd mugged myself. My editor found some great technicians and the company was soon to be launched. The first of its kind in Europe. The basement of Poland Street became a hive of activity, wires miles long attached to a myriad of machines and within six months we're up and running.

To an outsider, I was looking pretty good. Successful agency, very busy production company and now an offline editing business. Even I thought things appeared to be going well. I never examined my motives for anything I did. I just went with the flow. I had no plan, no ambition. Everything that was happening was just that, happening. I had no interest in expensive cars. In fact ever since my mini cabbing "career", I hated driving. I had a nice house, but it was a house not a mansion. We didn't take expensive holidays and I only ever wore jeans and T-shirts.

What I needed though was a business partner. Someone who'd look after the pennies and tell me when to slow down. I eventually found one. He ended up ripping me off for a quarter of a million pounds. But I was to experience a lot more shit before that happened.

The offline editing company struggled from the very beginning. While the intention was to use the new technology to save money, producers of commercials saw it as a knife through their greedy little hearts. Their mark up was based on the total budget on the commercials they made. So if the budget is seventy thousand pounds, their mark up, usually twenty per cent, would be fourteen thousand pounds. If the budget for the edit could be reduced by ten thousand pounds their mark up went down accordingly.

Business from these people was scarce at best. Luckily the corporate market place was our salvation. When I'd come up with the concept, I was completely unaware of this market. Large multi-nationals and their smaller counterparts made mini-films for promotional purposes and their budgets were often miniscule. Offline editing was exactly what they needed. None the less it wasn't a big money spinner at that time and I felt the shadow of Branson and our agreement hovering over me like the sword of Damocles.

The Agency's client list was becoming somewhat eclectic and occasionally bands would suggest clients to me. I first met Paula Yates when Bob came to see me and asked if my agency would be interested in representing her. At the time, her only work was writing a double page spread full of gossip for the *Record Mirror* for forty pounds a week. As it was Bob, I agreed to meet her. She entered my Poland Street office like a whirling dervish. Charisma oozed out of her every pore and she looked a million dollars. But what could I do with her?

We chatted for an hour, after which I needed to take a long weekend at Champneys to recover. How Bob managed living with her was a mystery. Whenever she mentioned his name she became childlike. At that time he was everything to her. Father, lover and best friend.

I asked her about a story I'd seen in a newspaper reporting that she was going to do a book of photos of rock stars in their underwear. She laughed and told me she'd made it up as it seemed a good idea at the time.

'You know Paula, that's not such a bad idea.' I said. 'Virgin have just launched a publishing company and if I know Branson he'll love this. He's such a whore when it comes to self-publicity.' I immediately called the MD and ran the idea past him. He called me back within the hour. A fifteen thousand pound advance and we had a deal. Paula couldn't believe it and thought I must be a practitioner of the voodoo arts. Bob was ecstatic as it gave Paula a focus which she sorely needed.

One month later, Paula had moved in to my secretary's office to work on the book. Fortunately for me I was away a lot. My secretary, on the other hand, became borderline suicidal. Who wouldn't, with Paula rushing around being Paula? Many of the pictures of what became 'Rock Stars In Their Underpants' were taken in my office. The one of Rod Stewart is particularly gross. Paula and I parted company a couple of years later and our paths never did cross again. Only good memories.

A strange phenomenon about the record industry was that some British artists who were almost completely unknown here were huge stars somewhere else in the world. Others who enjoyed some fame in the UK were massive abroad. The Nolan Sisters were a prime example. They had recently had a UK hit with I'm In The Mood For Dancing when I got a call from Epic/Sony Japan in late December 1981. In those days foreign companies were not permitted to own or set up companies in Japan without having a Japanese partner. Epic was a label owned by CBS and in Japan co-owned by Sony.

I was asked to meet three of their executives at the Savoy hotel in the Strand. I'm introduced to Joe Morita, son of the Sony founder Akio Morita. His English was better than mine having been educated both in the UK and America. We settled down in Joe's suite and I found out later that the other two execs, one female and quite cute, didn't speak any English.

'What we want to do Jon is shoot the Nolan Sisters (I'd heard that many times before but in a different context) on New Year's Eve and broadcast it live to Japan.' I nodded sagely but wondered why anyone would go to so much trouble for the Nolan's. As if reading my mind he went on, 'The Nolan's are very big in Japan and their record is at number one at the moment. Can you help us? Our mutual friend Mike Smith says you are the man to do it.'

Mike Smith was one of the first guys I met when I joined LWT a million years ago. In fact he was my immediate boss. He was now forging a successful career as a manager and promoter and is married to the delightful Sally James. We have remained friends to this day.

'It's no problem Joe. Have you a location in mind?' I was thinking of maybe hiring a large Thames/LWT studio.

'St Paul's Cathedral' he said. I think my face may have conveyed a glimmer of surprise! 'Will that be a problem Jon?' I thought it over for a second or two. No, no problem at all! 'Might raise a few issues.' I said with a straight face. 'Why St Paul's?'

'We were all captivated by the royal wedding and we think the Japanese people would love to see such big stars performing there.' The wedding had taken place earlier that year in late July.

'I'll make some calls and get back to you. Budget?'

'Whatever it takes.' It would take a lot. 'Now would you please excuse me I have another meeting, but perhaps you would care to have lunch with my two associates.'

It was only when we were seated in the hotel's restaurant that I found out that neither spoke a word of English and my Japanese wasn't really up to scratch. Somehow I managed to make them laugh and we enjoyed a lunch interspersed with mime and sign language. I would have been a wow on Lionel Blair's *Give Us A Clue.*

Getting the pictures to Japan via satellite wasn't going to be a problem but St Paul's.....

I wrote to the Dean's office and was amazed when they agreed. They would allow us to film in the courtyard adjacent to the Cathedral. We were in business. Because of the time difference Japan's midnight was four o'clock in the afternoon in the UK.

We set up at seven in the morning with the Nolans due to arrive at eleven. I used a facility company to put the technical side together. They booked the satellite and supplied all the crew, cameras and lights. It was a cloudy day so the lights became an important factor. My first hint that we were going to have problems was around ten o'clock. Hundreds of school children began to arrive to visit the Cathedral. Apparently this happens every year. Kids from all over the world come to St Paul's on New Year's Eve. By midday there must have been two thousand of them. I instructed our runners to cordon off our area with ropes.

The Nolans arrived and their roadies set up their equipment. We rehearsed with the girls miming to playback and everything seemed to be on schedule. They were totally professional and did whatever we asked. At half one, I sent everyone off for a lunch break and then the heavens opened and it poured down. This was not good as we hadn't planned for them to perform under cover. I found the runners and told them to get something, anything, to provide some protection from the elements.

Out of nowhere the Dean, accompanied by what turned out to be a French monk wearing a brown cowl, suddenly emerged from a side door of the cathedral and came marching over towards me.

'Who's in charge here?' The Dean demanded.

'I am.' There was nowhere to hide.

'Well you cannot do this here,' he waved his hand around at the cameras, 'I can hear the noise in the Cathedral.' I guess what he meant by 'noise' was the Nolan's rendition of *I'm In The Mood For Dancing*. He wasn't too happy that I'd cordoned off the adjacent courtyard either.

'But we have permission from your office,' I said. Hoping I'd brought the letter with me. Then the mad monk, who could have been the inspiration for the

111

forerunner of Dan Brown's *The Da Vinci Code* launched in.

'You hear what he say. You go away. You go away now!' There was something about his accent that made we want to thump him. It's pissing down and we're all drowning. I found the letter in my pocket and showed it to the venerable Dean. He glanced at it but he wasn't in the mood to change his mind.

'You cannot do this here today. Perhaps another time?' Being that New Year's Eve only happens once a year, there wasn't really any other reasonable alternative. By now a half a dozen Japanese record executives have joined the party. The only one who had a smattering of English is asking me what's happening. Meanwhile I'm drenched down to my underwear and the monk decides to have another swipe.

'You go, you go. Leave now.'

'I'm sorry sir,' I said to the Dean, 'but we can only do this today as it is meant as a New Year's Eve television programme for Japan.'

'Can't you do it somewhere else?' He gesticulated to some unspecified location down the Strand. Some of the crew having returned from lunch were staring rather bemusedly at our small gathering. I noticed they'd obtained umbrellas from somewhere.

'The problem is, sir, that we have to use a satellite and we just can't up and move it as it needs to be aligned in a very special way.' I might as well have been speaking in tongues.

'You hear what he say, go away.' That French monk's mantra was now seriously getting to me. I felt a tug on my arm. I looked down and saw a little old lady with a shopping basket wearing a worn, sodden coat. 'Excuse me,' she asked, 'could you tell me the way to Trafalgar Square?' I had become part of a Monty Python sketch.

The Japanese sensing a problem but not understanding what was actually going on were chattering loudly amongst themselves. The monk continued his diatribe and the Dean and I just stood looking at each other. The old lady had now left and was on her way to visit Nelson.

Finally, I suggested a compromise, no doubt much to the chagrin of the cowl headed monk. We'd move the Nolan's back a hundred metres and lower the play back volume. The Dean was happy as he wouldn't hear the 'noise', as he'd put it, and the men from Sony were happy as we could still get the Cathedral in shot.

Shooting live is one of the greatest adrenalin rushes a director can experience. There are some who can't handle the process and will lie, cheat and kill to avoid it. Unfortunately a producer doesn't know how a director will deal with it till it's too late. Years back when I'd first started out at LWT, some idiot had hired a director from ITN in the bizarre belief that as the news went out live he'd be able to direct live programmes. The shows were a live Saturday night variety series from The London Palladium.

All this poor sod had ever done was point two cameras at a couple of stationary presenters and cue in some film or tape to illustrate the stories. It would take a substantial leap of faith to believe he had the talent to direct a dozen dancers racing round the vast stage at the Palladium while ten cameras were available to him to pick out the right shots. The presenter of the show would suddenly appear and sing a song, while performing with the dancers. So now he had to cover the presenter and the dancers. It ain't easy.

After he's attended rehearsals, the director needs to 'write' a camera script. This is a script that, apart from containing who does and says what, indicates which of the many cameras available will cover which piece of action. ITN News wasn't a great training ground for such an adventure. I passed by this poor bastard's office the day before his first show and I found him sobbing hysterically. He never directed a single programme and went quietly back to the safety of ITN.

CHAPTER TWENTY THREE
JANET STREET PORTER SAYS GOODBYE

The Agency was continuing to grow and we'd started taking on directors as well as presenters. Our presenter's roster was forever growing. We recently signed Nick Ross and Frank Bough. We also represented Janet Street Porter. In fact this was the second occasion I'd acted for her. The first time was for a couple of years in the mid-seventies. She rejoined us because she'd taken up with, and married, a long time director client Frank Cvitanovich. Frank thought it would be good for her to be in the same 'family' as he called us. He was a wonderful, caring, brilliant director and I was very fond of him. He made an award winning documentary about his son Bunny. The heart breaking film was called just that, *Bunny*. It told the story of the treatment his brain-damaged son had in a clinic in Philadelphia. Bunny died shortly after.

We were having dinner one evening, Frank, Janet and a couple of my producers at a restaurant in Dean Street in Soho. The chat got a little fruity and we all got a little pissed. Suddenly Frank, who was a big ex-Canadian ice hockey player, shouts across the table at me,

'How dare you say that to Janet!' The conversation stopped. There was, suddenly, total silence. I stare at Frank not understanding.

'What?' is all I can come up with.

'That's fucking over the top. It was fucking insulting!' He's still shouting. I look at the faces of everyone else at the table. They have as much idea about what's going on as I have.

'You apologise. You apologise right now.' His left hand is curling into a fist, his right hand is clutching Janet's arm. What had I said that had kicked this off? And anyway how does anyone 'insult' Janet? I was heading for an entrée into the Guinness Book Of Records.

'Whatever I said Frank, I'm truly sorry.' I was totally bewildered. He stood up grabbing Janet and uttered the immortal line no agent wants to hear,' We're leaving and we're leaving your agency,' and he left.

'What did I say?' I ask, looking round the table. I'm greeted with shrugs. No-one could tell me. A decade later I bump into Janet at The Groucho Club, a loser's home for the media crowd. We have a drink.

'Janet,' I ask, 'I've always wanted to know what was it I said to upset you and Frank all those years ago?'

'You know.' She said knowingly.

'Actually I don't.' I replied. I looked into her eyes and could see that she had absolutely no idea either.

CHAPTER TWENTY FOUR
PAUL McCARTNEY, NEIL DIAMOND AND TED NUGENT

I had always been a huge fan of the Beatles and when we got a call from Paul McCartney to film his Xmas single, 'Wonderful Xmas Time', it was excitement all round. I'd worked with some famous bands, but McCartney was something else. As far as I was concerned, he and Linda were lovely people. They were as normal a couple as any couple could be bearing in mind they were vastly wealthy and instantly recognisable all over the world. On the shoot he was a great professional and had no problem dispensing autographs and making time to have his picture taken with both the crew and the public. I very rarely had a picture taken with an artist as I always felt awkward about participating in photo opportunities. During breaks in filming, Paul would talk happily about his time as a Beatle which surprised me. I would have thought it was a period of his life that had passed and he'd rather it stayed as a part of history.

We didn't shoot a lot of live concerts which was very disappointing for Gowers as he was such a supremely gifted director of live events. On two occasions we were asked to cover concerts but without editing them. The company or artist merely wanted a record of it. Though with Neil Diamond, it was a little more complicated. Either way we were nearly ripped off each time. Diamond's record company commissioned a live promo to be extracted from a concert he was performing in LA. We were contracted only to deliver one song. As we had eight cameras and the song was number seven in the set we shot everything up to that point. A record company executive who was watching the monitors in the OB truck was so impressed with Gowers' work that he asked us to video the entire concert. We edited the song we were contracted for and delivered it.

Two weeks later I was back home in England when Pearl woke me to take a call from my LA office. They just wanted to check that I'd authorised the release of the master tape of the Diamond concert. I hadn't. I was told his management company claimed we'd spoken and that I had agreed for its release. I called his manager and we had a 'little' row where I demanded another ten thousand dollars for the tape. I explained they hadn't paid for it and while not my property per se I did have the power to erase it. After interminable conversations they handed over the money.

Ted Nugent's performance was a similar story. His band was credited with playing louder than any other band back then. Though having worked with Rush I'd say it was a close call. CBS in London wanted us to shoot their concert at the Hammersmith Odeon. They wanted nothing else, no editing, only a rough mix which would be done, live, via the mixing desk in the OB truck. The whole thing cost around ten thousand pounds. We used seven cameras with four slaved to their own VT machine. We were not required to augment their lighting. Meaning if some of the concert was too dark to be seen clearly, it wasn't down to us. Nugent's reputation was such that between songs he came out with every curse known to man and some that weren't. So you'd hear, 'Are you having a great time you fucking cunts?' and so on.

The following day, his manager called to ask if his artist could see what we'd shot. I found a viewing room and Nugent, a couple of band members and assorted hangers on made themselves comfortable and settled down to watch the show. Ted Nugent, despite his obscenity fuelled act was, I found out, surprisingly, quite a shy man. As he watched himself cursing a multitude of four letter words at his audience he buried his head in his hands muttering, 'God this so embarrassing.' He almost appeared to be apologising to the assembled gathering though most of them had known him for years.

Then began the musical chairs. I invoiced CBS and they sent back the bill saying, it's not us you should be billing but CBS in New York. New York were quick in their response, it's not us but our label Epic. Epic were no less slower in telling me it was Nugent's management company who would be picking up the tab. The management company denied all responsibility. After a few months there were no more chairs left standing so I gave up. Twelve months passed when I got a frantic call from a CBS executive in London.

'Jon, have you got the tapes for the Ted Nugent concert? I've desperately been trying to locate them.'

'I have.' I said.

'Fantastic! Can you get them over to me immediately?'

'I'm glad you called. You're probably not aware but we haven't been paid for the work.'

'I'm sorry?' It wasn't a vote of sympathy but more of a 'what's that got to do with me?'

'I'll try and make myself clearer. I chased your record company in London and New York, your label Epic and Nugent's manager and no-one has slipped me a cheque. Is that clear enough?'

'Are you saying that if we don't pay you, you won't release the tapes?' Incredulous doesn't come close to the tone in his voice.

'Absolutely not. I'm saying that unless you pay me the ten thousand pounds plus interest, plus the costs of all my calls to New York, in three days time I'll *erase* the tapes.' A long pause.

'I'll get back to you.'

Six hours later, he got back to me.

'Ok we'll pay.'

'So kind!' I said.

'Send me an invoice and we'll cut you a cheque.'

'I don't think so.' I said. 'Certainly I'll send the invoice but either I want a certified cheque or cash.'

'What!'

'I'm not going to repeat myself.'

'You won't take our cheque?'

'I said I wasn't going to repeat myself.'

'You'll never work for CBS again.'

'I can't afford to work for you people.' They biked me round a certified cheque which included all the add-ons, and, true to their word, I didn't get any work from them - for nearly a year.

CHAPTER TWENTY FIVE
JUKEBOX, BRITT AGAIN AND SHARON OSBOURNE

It's 1980. Bruce is now living full time in LA and I'm bouncing back and forth like David Frost on speed.

He only had to commute between New York and London. I had to do an extra three thousand miles each way. I occasionally sneaked in a few first class flights.

For some time I'd been worried that Pearl was still breast feeding Gideon though he was two. I don't know why I had such a big issue with it, but fortune smiled at me. Sitting next to me on a flight to LA was a paediatrician from Orange County. We got talking and soon found out what we both did to earn a crust. I immediately launched into Gideon and the breast. He dismissed it, saying one or the other will soon get bored and it will stop naturally. He was a huge Rod Stewart fan so he grilled me for hours about the old rocker.

As we are chatting away the tannoy comes to life asking if there's a doctor on board. He didn't miss a beat and continued talking as though the announcement had never been made. Finally a stewardess came by and tapped him on the shoulder and whispered in his ear. He stood up, turned to me with a resigned expression, and vanished for twenty minutes.

On his return I asked him why he was so reluctant to respond to the call. He looked at me and said, 'Do you realise what I pay in insurance?' I shook my head. 'forty thousand bucks a year. All I need is to attend to someone on this flight and there's a problem, I get sued and my premium shoots up twenty per cent.' I was amazed. I'd never heard of doctors getting sued before. How times have changed!

I check in to the Château Marmont and get busy tying up the loose ends on *Jukebox*. A week before I have the final meeting to close the deal which had taken nearly a year to negotiate I find myself in Hal Brown's office. We're going over a few petty details when he takes a call from a guy called Frank Maloney who runs AIT's New York outfit. I'd met him a couple of times, "slime" and "ball" come to mind. Bizarrely Hal puts the call on speaker.

'Hi Frank, thanks for calling back.'

'How's the folks?'

'Fine. Look I've had a call from the Magenta people (a big New York advertising agency). They said they sent you the cheque for two hundred and fifty big ones.'

'Oh!'

'They say it's been cashed. Only our accounts people can't find it anywhere.'

'Oh!'

'Can you help me out here?'

'I'll check it out and get back to you.' I was listening to corporate fraud. This was confirmed some months later. Hal was right up to his neck in it. How did I know?

'Well Jon, I think we're in a position to close the deal. Let's meet in the boardroom here next Wednesday and sign off on it.' We shook hands. By the time I got back to my rented house, I had a message to call Lisa's father.

'Great news about *Jukebox* Jon,' he says. I could hear the delight in his voice. Only his happiness wasn't reserved for me or his daughter who would be working on the series. 'There's one thing you need to do before the deal can be closed.' I'm listening and wondering what any of it has to do with him. Sure he made the introduction but.....'I'm going to give you details of a bank account in Las Vegas. You need to pay in one hundred thousand dollars for Hal and me and that's it!' Just like that. Over the phone. Welcome to their world. I explained I didn't have a spare hundred grand and that I'd pay the money from the first tranche when AIT paid us. It was agreed. We made the deal.

I rented an office in Merv Griffin's building on Sunset and Vine and start to put together a production team for *Jukebox*. I ask several people from London to come on board. One of them, Simon Fields, turns out to be the only producer of merit. Much later his skills lead him to be a successful film producer, making movies such as *'Teenage Mutant Ninja Turtles'* and *'Maid in Manhattan'*. He currently manages Jennifer Lopez.

Our biggest problem was to find a host for the show. Simon and I were having dinner one night at some fashionable eatery when I spied Britt dining with friends. She waved at me and we joined her party. By now she was referring to me as the Methuselah of the music video. As Rod might have said, to paraphrase, 'I wore it well.'

I asked her if she was busy, because I'd suddenly realised she'd be perfect to host the series. All she'd have to do was stand by a juke box for three days reading links to camera. Good money for little work. She loved the idea but said I'd need to speak to her manager, Sharon Arden or, as we all know her today, Sharon Osbourne.

Sharon and I met and we nearly got on well. Sharon worked for her father, Don Arden, the late manager of The Electric Light Orchestra (ELO) and was one of the music business's most notorious villains. He was one man you didn't mess with. In 1977 we had made *Rockaria* for ELO where I'd met him briefly. I was invited to the Arden home, a vast monolithic place, high in the Hollywood Hills. The deal with Britt was sealed and we began making the series. After that Don and I often had dinner together, but a coincidence of monumental proportions snuffed out our relationship.

One of my first clients, Roger Cook, was presenting a consumer series for Radio 4 called *Checkpoint*. He had recently made a programme on Arden's business methods featuring a dispute between Lynsey de Paul and Arden's Jet Records. The programme ended with Don threatening to break Cook's neck and, for good measure, the necks of anyone who'd talk to him.

Roger was in LA and visited my office on Sunset and Vine. As we were catching up I had to briefly leave the office to sort something out. My phone rang, he answered it. It was Don Arden. Roger's voice is instantly recognisable and that was that. Cook answering my phone meant war. A week later Arden sued me. It was pretty frivolous stuff, something like *for having Roger Cook answer your phone one million dollars in damages please.*

We were still making videos amid the mayhem of producing *Jukebox*. Mayhem because of the sheer number of videos offered to us. While we wanted the latest ones that were available, it wasn't a deal breaker. The record companies, wanting to promote any new single they were about to release, wanted us to choose material from any of their current product and in those days there was a lot of it. They'd discovered the merits of making videos with a vengeance.

We were contacted by CBS to make a video for Michael Jackson's *Rock With You*. His years of meltdown were still far in the future. He was, of course, still accompanied by a large entourage, but then he was friendly, funny, intelligent and black. No Bubbles in those days. I was struck by how good looking he was. Plastic surgery, like his breakdown, would eventually take away the essence that was Michael Jackson.

It was a simple shoot. He performed in our favourite Fountain studio wearing a spangled jump suit and matching boots. It was uncluttered without the usual gaggle of accompanying dancers or backing vocalists. Looking at it now, it seems almost parochial, but it did its job.

CHAPTER TWENTY SIX
COCAINE, HEROIN AND MARK SPITZ

I didn't know it, but coke was turning me into an aggressive, 'don't give a fuck' lunatic. I only ever used it in LA, never in England. It wasn't because of health and safety: it was because I didn't know any dealers in London. I was now renting an apartment at the Marina City Club situated in Marina Del Rey. It was, as it says, right on the Marina, with multi-million dollar yachts moored as far as the eye could see. I shared the rent with Reed. Big mistake. Don't get me wrong, I loved the guy. He only ever showed me true friendship, but his lifestyle would make Hugh Heffner's Playboy mansion look like an old people's home.

Every night was party time for him. He'd come back at two in the morning with a few friends. The friends were always nubile young girls. I had to work for a living and often had to rise at the crack of dawn, just when he was going to bed. It got so I had to lock my door to stop his 'friends' from entertaining me. There would be loud knocking on my bedroom door and coked up girls giggling and shouting, 'Reed says we've got to give you a blow job. Open the door.' The knocking got louder. The door didn't always stay locked!

Hanging out with the Reedster meant beautiful girls and lots of coke. Often, of course, his life style created problems, apart from the illegal nature of the way he made his money.

The American legal system is a strange animal. The guilty seemed to get off, no matter how damming the evidence. OJ and Jackson come to mind as well as the cops who beat Rodney King to a pulp. Even video evidence isn't enough it seems. Reed's apartment was raided by LA's finest waving a search warrant for cocaine. They only found heroin. The warrant didn't include heroin and they had to leave empty handed and return with a new warrant later in the day. Surprise, surprise there wasn't a trace of the stuff on their second visit.

Sometime later, when we had both evacuated the Marina City Club, he rented a vast apartment from the manager of Earth Wind And Fire. It was decorated by someone whose appreciation of the goddamn awful could only have been surpassed by a dozen coked-up monkeys with paint brushes. As usual Reed has a couple of ladies around and the drugs are swinging back and forth. He offers me a piece of aluminium foil with some brown powder on it which I thought was some strange brand of coke. He lights a match under the foil and instructs me to inhale. The two girls are kneeling at my feet sharing my cock. After a few minutes I can't feel my legs or anything else for that matter. I try to stand up but my legs have taken a vacation. I manage to stagger to a spare bedroom and collapse on the bed. I lay there for what felt like hours feeling a terrible sickness invading my body. Finally I make it out of the apartment and grab a cab back to my hotel. It's seven in the morning. When I get to my room the maid is changing the bed. I sit in the living room while she goes on to vacuum. I just want to be sick. I could have asked her to go but that wasn't my style. I'm much too polite. I sit there waiting for death while she finishes.

I throw myself on the bed and come to twenty hours later. What the fuck had just happened to me? I called a friend who told me that I hadn't been doing coke but heroin. I wasn't best pleased that my buddy had foisted heroin on me without my knowledge or consent. In fact I was fucking mad. I stormed round to his place and when he opened the door my clenched fist met his chin. He got up looking vaguely surprised.

'What the fuck was that for?'

'Payment for the heroin.' I said. He just didn't get it. 'You fucking gave me heroin you shit. I was sick for a day.'

'It's always like that first time.' He explained. 'After you've tried it a few times it's a great buzz.' He *really* didn't get it.

'Are you fucking crazy? I don't want to try it a few times, I never wanted to try it at all.'

Hanging with Reed was always a little different.

He called me one afternoon and said he needed a favour. I didn't take up the baton quite so quickly this time around.

'I always seem to get grief when you call me lately.'

'Come on Noseman, you know you *love* it!' I was never a great fan of his personal endearment, the 'Noseman.' 'It's only dinner. I just want you to come to dinner, I promise that's it.'

'Sure,' I said, totally unsure.

'It's with my parents and my brother,' I wasn't buying it.

'Who else?'

'A couple of friends of the family.'

'Reed either tell me what's going on or fuck off.'

'It's Mark Spitz and his wife.'

It turns out that Reed's brother put together the training programme that enabled Spitz to win his seven gold medals in 1972 at the Munich Olympics.

'Why me?'

'You're the only person I know who would be acceptable to my parents.' In a strange way I took that as a compliment. Reed's family were very wealthy owning a steel manufacturing business on the East coast. They were normal family folk which begged a lot of questions as to how Reed turned into the man he was.

At the dinner I was sandwiched between Mark and his wife. Reed's elder brother came from an altogether different planet than his sibling. He was a computer specialist and very low key. He was tall and gangly with thinning brown hair, wore a Brooks Brother's dark blue suit and said very little and smiled a lot.

Mark's wife spoke only if spoken to and the swimmer talked exclusively about real estate till blood started to ooze out of my ears. He was a man without equal in the boredom stakes. Reed could only take it for an hour, kissed his parents goodbye, pleading another engagement (yeah right!) and grabbed me by the arm and forcibly ejected me from the table.

CHAPTER TWENTY SEVEN
PETER COOK AND DUDLEY MOORE AS DEREK AND CLIVE

Back in London we were incredibly busy turning out videos. Russell did a brilliant job on The Buggles' *Video Killed The Radio Star*. Other directors I'd taken on, included Julien Temple, who later had great success with the Sex Pistols' *The Great Rock And Roll Swindle*. We were working with Bonnie Tyler, Elvis Costello, the heavy metal band Samson and Hazel O'Connor. When the record companies heard about our American series, it increased our work load and certainly my liabilities.

The agency was attracting more clients and we took on another agent. I was now having almost nothing to do with the day-to-day running of it being up to my eyes in the UK production company, the ongoing problems of offline editing and trying to oversee the LA operation.

Anyone looking over my shoulder would have thought, wow! he's only thirty two and look what he's achieved from sod all. No rich dad, no inheritance, he did it all on his own. Oh! I did it all on my own all right! And that express train was now hurtling towards me at an unstoppable speed. Collision was imminent. If only it had been a Virgin train, then it would probably not have arrived at destination Roseman.

Branson and I were still 'buddies' at this time and he rang me to see if we'd be interested in filming Peter Cook and Dudley Moore doing one of their Derek and Clive albums. I wasn't a fan but Russell Mulcahy jumped at the chance. We met them, Moore, articulate and funny, Cook, sullen and bitter. Talked through some ideas that would allow a visual representation of what was, after all, only supposed to be two guys making obscene impromptu conversation. It was a two day shoot at a recording studio near Shepherds Bush, West London.

I spent a lot of time planning it out with Russell. Two guys sitting on stools in a studio nattering away was great for a CD but not nearly enough to carry a ninety minute film. We needed to add some strong visual elements. I came up with two basic ideas. We'd have a stripper as part of the production team and give her a clip board. Cook and Moore would assume she was a secretary taking notes until we gave her the signal to suddenly stand up and strut her stuff. I remember when she arrived at the studio we gave her an office so she could try on different outfits. She insisted I stay with her while she tried out a variety of lingerie seeking my approval for black seamed stockings or a myriad of lacy bras. It was an onerous task but someone had to do it.

I also devised a police raid. Various actor friends were hired. We had five in uniform and a wonderful plain clothes man who, on the day, was so authentic that even I began to believe he was the real thing. Branson and I were in the control room when the 'raid' took place. As soon as they marched in, Cook was trying to stuff his cannabis down a gap in a chair.

The questioning of the pair went on for nearly half an hour and Peter was getting more and more paranoid. Dudley on the other hand was all smiles and cool. Branson and I were nearly sick with laughter. I soon noticed that things were getting a little out of hand. I thought Cook was going to thump our plainclothes man and took the decision to walk into the studio and end the stunt. Relief and laughter all round though 'Clive' hadn't enjoyed the experience very much.

When Dudley broke away from Peter to sit at the piano, that was the cue for the stripper. She stood up from behind one of the cameras and did her thing. Dudley, who had already started tinkling the ivories, nearly fell off his stool. She sat next to him wearing the lacy black undies and he could hardly get a word out. He managed ultimately to take it all in his stride and it became a high point of the film.

I had various meetings with Cook about the release of the film, but we didn't get on. I had to go back to LA and check on the progress of *Jukebox* and take the rough cut to Dudley who was now living in Malibu, right on the beach. I left Cook to his own black thoughts and ultimately his lawyer, Oscar Beuselinck. Oscar was right up there with Don Arden. But whereas Don would use fists, Oscar would just use words. Oscar would have taken Arden to the cleaners. He sure took me there. He's the only lawyer I've ever received a letter from that ended with 'go fuck yourself.'

I visited Dudley at his beach house and we lay on his bed to watch the film. He had one television and it was in his bedroom. He loved it. We got on well and had a few dinners together and regularly bumped into each other at various LA clubs. He was the antithesis of his partner and sometimes alluded to the jealousy that had infected Peter Cook because of his successful career in the States.

Jukebox was coming on well and after a week I flew home.

The return flight held an interesting diversion. In those heady days, some jumbos had a first class lounge on the upper level. Access was via a spiral staircase. The lounge had a bar and first class passengers had the luxury of sitting down around tables to sip their champagne. I was duly doing my sipping when a stunning girl, who I later found out was the daughter of an African ambassador to London, sat opposite me.

We exchanged glances and I went back to my book and sipping. After ten or fifteen minutes she handed me a note. It read, *My name is Inikpi Abebi Adebola and I like to meet people and I would like to meet you.* I told her I thought it was a lovely note and a very special, if wholly unpronounceable name. We started talking. After a while we were called down for dinner. Real plates, cutlery made of stainless steel, wine served in proper glasses. I miss those days.

We sat next to each other and enjoyed our dinner together. After the plates were taken away she suddenly thrust her hand on to my crutch and whispered in my ear, 'I want you to fuck me, now!' I wasn't used to this kind of extended foreplay! I think I may have mumbled something like, 'how delightful', and said I was just going to nip upstairs to have an after dinner cigarette. I tootled up the spiral staircase and took a seat at the back of the empty lounge. As I fumbled for the packet I found a joint that someone had given me, jokingly telling me it was for the flight home. Why I took it I don't know. Apart from the danger of being caught with an illegal substance I didn't smoke dope anyway.

I sat alone in the cabin and for reasons known only to him above I lit the joint and had a few puffs. I woke up three hours later. On my way back down the staircase I met Miss West Africa coming up. There was no escape. I shrugged and smiled shamed-faced and took off for my seat. We didn't speak again.

On September 14th, 1980, my daughter made her way into the world. Pearl woke me at six in the morning and we were on our way to Cuckfield hospital, a fifteen minute drive from the house. Pearl as ever was completely prepared. Her bag packed and ready under the bed. Everyone says that the second child is delivered so much more quickly than the first. I wasn't so sure. So on the way to the hospital, I stopped off at a petrol station to buy the Sunday papers. Unforgivable I know.

Now there were four of us. I was spending far too much time away and living a life that Pearl couldn't share. Or perhaps I wasn't prepared to let her share. What I do know is that if it wasn't for my family, the excesses I was putting myself through in LA would have ultimately left me a dribbling wreck in some cheap motel room. My family was, and always has been, the rock that has anchored me to some sense of sanity.

CHAPTER TWENTY EIGHT
BYE BYE AMERICA AND BRANSON

1981 was a special year for me. The birth of MTV. At last a network existed to play the videos that took so much time and effort to make. It would spit out so much material that the record companies would be screaming at us to make more product for them. *Jukebox* had been doing some good numbers in syndication so the future was looking promising. The express train had, however, arrived at its destination. Me! I was about to shoot myself in the foot, leg, heart and let's add for good measure, the head.

I'd done an interview with a newspaper while I was obviously on the marching powder and managed to diss the entire record industry as well as a few rock icons. Not bad going for sixty dollars a gram. Imagine you own an airline and let it be known your planes aren't safe. Now that would not be a good move. My production teams on both sides of the pond are pissed with me and begin to think about an exit strategy from crazy Roseman and his big mouth and even bigger coke filled nose.

Now I could have probably contained this, at a push, if it wasn't for AIT being taken over by a company called Filmways at exactly the same time. It didn't take Filmways' accountants long to uncover some seriously dodgy dealings. The AIT deal was Bruce's and my nest egg. It was about to go the way of all flesh. Within a week of the take-over, Filmways suspends all AIT's contracts. Our money is frozen and the series cancelled. The contract we had, hadn't legislated for this kind of incident. Fucking lawyers. The corrupt AIT executives all lose their jobs. I'm left alone.

I call the company's American accountants to find out how big a hole we're in. It isn't a hole so much as a canyon. An eight hundred and fifty thousand dollar canyon. That's what is still owed by Jon Roseman Productions Inc. to the facility houses, studios, crew and the lovely Britt Ekland. I'm not sure what worried me more, the vast sums owed to all the back up companies, or the wrath of Don Arden. It was a close call. I still had the music video company, just, and MTV were up and running which should still be good for business.

I began negotiations with Filmways and managed to get them to agree to pay all the outstanding liabilities and signed off on it. Bruce, apart from being paid a few bucks as the series director, never saw his million dollars and nor did I. The flight back to London was immensely depressing, the phone call from my American accountants two days later even more so.

Oops! They told me, we got the numbers wrong; it should have been one million one hundred and fifty thousand dollars. I was nearly three hundred thousand dollars in the hole. It's nine o'clock at night, I'm sitting in my Poland Street office, everyone has long since left, and staring into the abyss. I haven't got three hundred thousand dollars and Filmways as sure as hell aren't going to cough up any more though that doesn't stop me from asking them. They tell me politely to fuck off.

Word gets out and the guys who are still owed money in the States close down my American production company. Add all this to the unrest already existing in my UK production company since my coked up interview and I have a disaster of cosmic proportions. Poor Pearl had no idea what was going on and I didn't tell her. I figured something would turn up. It did.

The following day Mulcahy, Mallett and the entire production team decamp to pastures new. I'm not having a good week. At least the Agency remains completely unaffected and there was always the offline editing business, though it was still struggling.

I knew I'd have to tell Pearl and I knew she wouldn't care. For her it would mean no more trips to the States and no extended stays in London. She and the kids would see a lot more of me and for that I should be grateful. Before I could tell her, I needed to explore, within myself what it all meant to me. That's when I got the call from Branson. Lunch on the boat tomorrow.

His houseboat was moored on the Thames in Maida Vale in West London. I arrived just after one and he was the perfect host. A glass of wine, a whinge about record sales and we sat down to lunch courtesy of some cheap catering firm.

'So I hear you've had a few problems in America,' he begins. I hadn't even had time to touch the starter, though looking at it I wasn't sure I wanted to. 'Doesn't sound good,' he went on, 'Is it true Mulcahy and Mallet have left to set up on their own?' A rhetorical question at best. Where was he going with this? 'It's going to cause me some problems,' he said forking some dead thing round his plate. Cause *him* some problems. I'm not exactly dancing the fandango myself. 'I'm not sure we can still do business together. Having a partner with all this shit going down reflects badly on me.' Was he suffering from some kind of dementia? Wasn't he the guy who defrauded HM Customs and Excise out of two hundred thousand pounds not that long ago?

'I don't see why any of it should be an issue for you Richard,' I said pushing the starter plate away. 'It's hardly going to impact on our offline editing company.'

'Can't agree with you Jon. It's all based in the same building in Poland Street and potential clients won't be comfortable knowing you've just bankrupted both your production companies.'

'Hang on mate don't start fucking telling me about bankrupting my production companies. You have no fucking idea what happened in America.'

'I heard you owe a quarter of a million dollars.' He was starting to lose his cool and I was getting close to giving him a smack.

'Well that's not even close to what you ripped off from the Customs and Excise.' I retorted. This was getting nasty.

'I'm willing to buy out your shares in the edit suit.'
'Fuck you!'

'I've taken advice and I don't have to pay you anything. I can just take back the shares.' Course you can Richard.

'Fuck you!' I say again.

'I'll offer you a hundred thousand pounds if you sell them to me within the week.'

'Fuck you!' I stand up. I'm shaking with rage. 'Branson do the world a favour and fuck off.' Very articulate! I'm beyond articulate. I march off the boat via the gangplank. Very apposite. I walk about half a mile and the rage begins to dissipate. I've lost everything in America, I don't know if it's going to be possible to start from scratch again over here and I've just told Branson to stick a hundred thousand big ones up his arse. This really was becoming a very, very bad week.

I go back to the office. With the entire production team gone apart from one secretary, things are a little quiet. I ask her if she's alright and tears well up in her eyes. I put my arm round her and tell her everything was going to be ok. Then I saw the huge folder on her desk. They were outstanding invoices from shoots that went back nearly four months. I asked where Roger, our bookkeeper was. Ill, apparently. I caught him at home and told him that unless he had the fucking plague to get over to the office immediately.

It took him two days to tell me that we owed seventy thousand pounds and we only had eighteen thousand in the bank. I wanted to know how this could have happened and his explanation told me nothing I didn't already suspect. The producers let the directors roam free and spend whatever it took to make a video that would look great on their individual show reels. I could and should have acted on my deeply held suspicions a long time ago but I was out of touch. As the years rolled by my touch didn't get any better. If the truth be told, it got worse. Rats in a maze learnt quicker than me.

Finally I told Pearl the situation. She took it well, said she trusted me to turn things around. I had a couple of glasses of wine and tried to figure out my next move. I was going to need a bucket full of luck to get out of this mess. A dumper load probably. I took little comfort in the knowledge that at least the American debacle wasn't my fault. At about ten o'clock I went up to check on Gideon and Elie. They were asleep in bed and cot respectively. I gazed at them for a long while and that was what it took. Fuck 'em all. No one is going to hurt my family I'll find a way. As Macarthur said, 'I'll be back.'

CHAPTER TWENTY NINE
EURYTHMICS AND THE NOLANS AGAIN

I had to put my production company to the sword. A very painful experience. I start again. The new company consists of me and a secretary. I have no directors, only a reputation for producing quality work. My only technically creative skill at that time was in the edit. No matter what problems the directors found themselves in, I could pretty much save it in the edit.

I get a call from the Eurythmics' management. Let us not forget that I hadn't heard of eighty percent of the bands I'd worked with until I met them. The Eurythmics fell wholly into the "never heard of" category. Now there was no Bruce or Russell to meet the bands with me. When I first met Dave Stewart and Annie Lennox, I think they were under the impression that I was *both* producer and director. I just went with the flow.

Their first single was *'Never Gonna Cry Again'*. Dave had a million ideas but we were only given a five thousand pound budget. We shot it all on a beach in Southend in Essex. It was cheap and strange. The forerunner of a very successful collaboration. The video was never broadcast as some idiot in the record company hadn't obtained clearances for some of the musicians who played on the track. It was my first solo video. The express, for the time being was on a different course.

It was December 1981 and I was looking forward to the Christmas break. It had been a *very* long year. We'd planned a quiet family time together. Pearl and I had agreed, after we got married, never to invite either of our families over during the holiday period. That way we got to offend everybody equally.

It was then Joe Morita called me. He was in London and asked if we could meet. He was staying at the Westbury hotel near Park Lane. I liked Joe. For a man who was a major celebrity in his own country, he was just a lovely normal guy.

'Jon we need you to do another satellite broadcast to Japan. The first one was very successful.' I wondered where he wanted to do this one from, Buckingham Palace?

'Do you think it's possible to film from the Embankment?' This was more like it.

'I'm sure that can be arranged.'

'We'd like to be close to the Houses of Parliament. I think it would make a good backdrop. Also we love your black cabs and red double-decker buses so it would be good if we can get plenty of shots of them. Maybe we could use a helicopter.' It's never simple with these guys.

We found a jetty a few hundred yards from the Houses of Parliament and I arranged the crew and facilities much as before. Joe liked the idea of a putting a thirty foot Christmas tree on the jetty and I hired set dressers to decorate it.

The first problem I encountered was the mount for the camera in the helicopter. There were only three in the entire UK and they were all out with various film units. No mount meant no helicopter. I'm no expert on helicopter camera mounts and it was only by luck that I overheard that they were manufactured by Sony. I called Joe and told him the situation. Let's face it, his dad *was* Sony. Within twenty four hours we had the mount! It was flown down from Scotland by helicopter. Naturally.

It was a cold, but sunny New Year's Eve as we rehearsed the Nolans. The set decorators had done a great job on the tree and the helicopter was airborne sending us shots of cabs and buses. The Japanese contingent were standing behind me in the OB truck and watching the pictures coming through on the monitors. Everything was going very well, a sure sign of impending doom.

We'd made audio contact with NHK the TV station in Tokyo and were about a minute away from the live transmission. NHK told us they had the pictures and then told us they didn't. There was a problem with the satellite. No pictures. With forty five seconds to go the guys from Sony were audibly panicking behind me.

'What are you going to do?' The only English speaking one asked me. I liked the "you". I was less certain about the terror in his voice.

'Well, apart from jumping aboard a rocket and attempting to fix the fucking satellite there's nothing I can do. It'll be ok. There's no reason for panic.' I said, hiding my panic. Fifteen seconds to go we're all back on. Smiles all round. The hard bit's over and now we're on easy street. Not a chance.

The helicopter is dong a few dry runs above the Thames when I'm asked if it can go any lower. I speak over the radio to the pilot who tells me that with the current terrorist alert the rule is nothing flies below a thousand feet near the Houses of Parliament. The men from Sony get more and more insistent. Finally I beg the pilot to come in on just the one occasion at five hundred feet. He agrees.

We've been live to Tokyo for thirty seconds and the Nolans are banging out some forgettable number as the helicopter swoops low across the Thames giving us great pictures of those iconic cabs and busses crossing Westminster Bridge. Unfortunately because he's flying so low the updraft created by the rotary blades blows the Christmas tree into the Thames nearly taking a Nolan with it. We cut to a close up of the girls who amazingly were following that old rule of showbiz, 'the show must go on.' By carefully shooting around the girls, no-one realised that the Christmas tree had vanished. I think it ended up being washed ashore somewhere near Chelsea. For some time afterwards I had dreams of newspaper headlines declaring *Nolans' Career Ended By Decapitation*. But then again, who'd have complained?

CHAPTER THIRTY
THE WHITE ELEPHANT, NIK POWELL AND EDITING

Since my *tête-à-tête* with Branson, I'd heard nothing. It was 1982. What I didn't know at the time was that he and the Virgin Group were in deep trouble with their bankers Coutts. They had given him an ultimatum - get some seriously qualified person in to run the financial side of the company or it's sayonara.

Virgin Holdings, which owned all the companies in the Group, was split sixty-forty between Nik Powell and Branson, with the bearded one owning the majority. Nik had always run the money side. Supremely without qualifications, he had done his best to hold back Branson's more absurd ideas. I could have done with someone like that. Hey ho! As Nik tells me the story, Branson had the company valued and it came out broke. So a deal is done. Nik can take any three of the smaller subsidiary companies and three million in cash with a guarantee by Branson to pay the capital gains tax when it fell due in a year. Another million!

One of the companies he wanted is offline editing. Now I began to understand why Branson was so keen to buy my shares. At our little lunch he would have known Nik wanted the company but knew I could block its sale because of our shareholders' agreement, a document that lays out what can and can't be done with a company.

Nik has started to make plans for his departure from Virgin, but wants the offline business as the start of a move in to television and film. An office in Poland Street wouldn't be a bad thing either. He calls me and arranges to drive down to Sussex where we go out to lunch. As he's paying I take him to Gravetye Manor, an expensive multi-award winning hotel and restaurant near East Grinstead. He tells me his plans and is surprisingly open about his situation with his soon to be ex-partner.

Nik is not one of life's extroverts. He's tall and thin with a face that says 'what do you want, I'm busy.' He calls it as he sees it, which often comes across as loutish. We hadn't met to become friends and never were. We only ever barely tolerated one another. We cut a deal that was great for me, a big salary increase for my part time running of offline and an issue of shares that made us more or less partners, at least in the decision making process.

I persuaded him that we needed to move on from being a mere offline editing facility and get in to the online market. At that time online editing was almost the exclusive preserve of studio based facilities. The concept of a 'bijou' edit facility would be breaking new ground. After shaking hands on our new association, he asked me to put together a budget for my proposal. I set to work with our brilliant offline editor, who I'd enticed away from another facility, to work out the costings.

I spent long hours thinking about my new situation. No more trips to America. Would I miss it? I didn't think so. What was there to miss? I knew there would be occasions when I'd need to travel to LA, so at least I could still see my friends there. But the excesses would remain a thing of the past. Perhaps, most important of all, I no longer had to try and run an American production company from England. Back and forth to LA two, and sometimes three times a month, screwed with your head.

The White Elephant in Curzon Street had been a haunt of mine for a few years. It was a private dining club for the super rich and nearly every movie and TV star. American celebrities always dined there when visiting London to promote their new films or books. The only reason they allowed me in was because it was owned by Stella Richman, my old LWT boss. Cookie, her daughter and my friend, was now running the place. But I didn't get discounts.

The club had been in their family for over thirty years. What made it special was that the staff had been there for most of their working lives. They literally saw my children grow up.

One evening, I was having a drink in the bar with Nino the barman, when King Hussein of Jordan popped in, accompanied by plain clothes police officers and his own team of bodyguards. Nino was familiar with the King having looked after him on his visits to the club. After they shook hands he escorted the King into the restaurant, 'Your Majesty, you have no need for all these bodyguards,' he gestured at the men accompanying him, 'not when you have James Bond over there,' he pointed to Roger Moore who was with his wife, 'and the other James Bond over there.' He pointed again to the far end of the room where Sean Connery was also entertaining his wife. It was that kind of place. As the years rolled by, I tried introducing some music stars to the restaurant like Annie Lennox and George Michael, but the economic climate worsened in the late 80's and forced its closure. A very sad day in my life.

CHAPTER THIRTY ONE
THE VIDEO EDITING CENTRE AND THE EURYTHMICS

I finally presented the online editing budget to Nik Powell. It was around seven hundred thousand pounds. All the equipment was state of the art and had never been configured before though the suppliers guaranteed it would work. They were all very wrong.

While we were building the new edit suite, which was to occupy half of the ground floor of Poland Street, with the other half acting as a reception area, I was embarking on video number two for the Eurhythmics', *Love Is A Stranger*.

Production companies are always inundated with showreels. They could be from directors, set designers, make-up artists and directors of photography (DP's). A DP arranges all the lighting on a production and often operates the camera. A lot of cameramen don't always light, since lighting is a very special skill. To find a great DP who is also available is a rarity.

Chris Ashbrook came in to my world by sending me his showreel. He had been working in Australia for a decade or more. A love affair had brought him back to the UK. I liked his stuff a lot and asked him to come and see me. He reminded me of Worzel Gummidge. Tall, thin with a mop of unruly fair hair and an intensity in his eyes last seen, no doubt, in the occasional cardinal from the Spanish Inquisition. He was passionate about his work and never left home without it.

We were once at a New Year's Eve party together. A girl sitting in an armchair beside a table lamp caught Chris's attention. She was young, blonde and beautiful. He stood up and went over to her. I had no idea what she must have thought having Worzel Gummidge seemingly coming on to her.

'You know that light is fantastic on your face,' he said to her with great seriousness. He then started to adjust the pale shade of the lamp giving a little shadow to her long blonde hair. He stood back to admire his work and then re-joined his girlfriend on the sofa!

He told me he was desperate for work and had sent his reel to every production company in London but no-one had got back to him. I hired him immediately to work on *Love Is A Stranger*. I still needed someone to call the shots. Not a director as such, I'd had enough of them spending the budget and much more to enhance their careers. A young guy I'd known for a while, Mike Brady, had been pestering me for an opportunity to direct. He had no experience, having only worked as a boom operator at LWT. A boom operator is the guy who swings a microphone on the end of a fourteen foot pole to record the artists' voices. He impressed me with his ideas and calmness. I didn't like directors who threw tantrums. It upset the whole equilibrium of a shoot. After all, we were in the business of making pop videos, not *The Godfather*.

We shot the interiors in Dave's mother's house in Maida Vale. The rest we did on location around London. The single didn't do very well but the video received a barrage of plaudits. Many Americans were outraged by it, believing Annie was a male transvestite when she pulled off her blonde wig revealing close cropped flame red hair. It cost eleven thousand pounds and all the budget was spent on the clip. The production crew worked for nothing and so did I. It didn't matter because it meant I was back in business. I'd put myself and my family though a lot and I needed to know I hadn't lost whatever it was I had. There was still a bit more in the tank and although it would never be like it was before, that in itself was a mixed blessing.

There were four basic elements that made up the new edit suite. 1) A computer that would control all the machines. 2) A Grass Valley mixer that would allow cuts, fades, split screens and alter the colour of the pictures. 3) A Quantel digitital effects device. This allowed the editor to provide some very limited special effects. 4) Five one inch tape machines.

The moment came to switch it all on and test everything. It didn't work. The computer failed to operate the mixer and the Quantel. Whatever the engineers did, the machines objected. As the days turned in two weeks, I was becoming seriously worried. We had spent nearly three quarters of a million pounds and it didn't bloody work. Something in the configuration was preventing the machines from 'talking' to each other. Believing what it had said on the packet, as it were, I'd started to advertise the new facility, now called The Video Editing Centre (VEC), and named the date we'd be open for business. Having allowed four weeks for testing, that date was now a few days away.

I had been assured by the manufacturers that there would be no problem in configuring all the machines. The mixer and the Quantel were made by the same company for God's sake. I called them in the States. I was put through to their technical department

'Is that Roy Baker the technical supervisor?' I asked.

'Yes, Roy Baker speaking.' the voice said. Grass Valley was then based in Grass Valley California. Getting straight to the point I dove in.

'I've just spent two hundred and fifty thousand pounds on your Grass Valley 300 mixer and another two hundred thousand pounds on a two channel Quantel. When I ordered this kit your Mr Leonard Goldstein (their UK sales agent) assured me it would all work happily together. I've had your engineers nearly living with me for the last three weeks and believe me nobody's happy.'

'That's Mr Roseman isn't it?' I was now famous in the 'valleys!' I agreed it was me. 'I have been made aware of the difficulties you're experiencing and we hope to sort it out very quickly.' I wondered what quickly meant to this man. 'I've spoken to our engineers and we think that the problem lies with the Quantel machine's interface. They've spoken to your tech man at VEC and he needs to call Quantel so they can run some tests.'

145

'Let me get this straight,' I said pushing the sarcasm button,' you are Grass Valley and you guys developed and made my mixer. Right?'

'Yes sir.'

'You also make the Quantel machines. Right?'

'Yes sir.'

'So Roy, tell me this: why the flying fuck do we need to call you guys again, if you're all owned by the same bloody company?'

'Mr Roseman, I'm sure you can appreciate that the technology involved in both sets of machines is secret. We run Quantel and Grass Valley as totally separate divisions. So neither company will reveal to the other any direct technical data.' They lived in another world.

'Ok,' I said, 'what I've just heard is a lot of bullshit. Who's your Company's President and where do I reach him.' I think our laid back Californian was rather taken aback by my forthrightness.

'He's away at an international exhibition. He won't be back for ten days.'

'Where is this bloody exhibition?'

'A place called Brighton, somewhere in Britain.' Serendipity paid a visit. A cloud lifted from somewhere in the right hemisphere of my brain. I'd read in some trade paper that once a year the great and the good suppliers of new video technology had a jamboree in my old home town. After getting him to give me the name of the President I hung up and dialled The Corn Exchange in Brighton where the exhibition took place. Nik was giving me grief, rightly so, as he was guaranteeing all the money. 'It's not my fault' wouldn't have washed with him, or with me if it had been my cash.

Luck got me put straight through to Grass Valley's stand and Ryan Connell the President.

'Ryan, you don't know me but I've just been speaking to your Mr Roy Baker.'

'I'm sorry, I really can't talk to you now Mr...er..'

'Roseman,' I said helpfully.

'Mr Roseman. I'm in the middle of...' I cut him short.

'I don't care if you're in the middle of life saving surgery.' I said. Let's face it. Enough was truly enough. 'Listen to me very carefully. I've just spent four hundred and fifty thousand pounds on your fucking mixer and Quantel. I've suffered your incompetent engineers for three weeks and nothing works. Did you get that? Nothing fucking works. Now unless you get it working in twenty four hours, I'm coming down to Brighton and I'll stand outside The Corn Exchange with a banner telling the world what I think of your fucking company.' I took a deep breath and went on, 'Ask anyone who knows me and they'll tell you I'm mad enough to do it.'

At four the following afternoon a rather haggard looking engineer turned up. He'd just flown in from Germany and had been roaming Europe sorting out various technical disasters. He was one of their senior R&D people. He sat in front of the editing desk played around with it for ten minutes, opened up the mixer's panel, removed a board and replaced it with one from his huge metal case. Everything came to life. Someone from Grass Valley had installed the wrong board. Maybe they'd been smoking the stuff they'd named the Valley after. I got them to knock off thirty thousand pounds from the bill.

Two days later we're open for business. I greet our first client with an early morning glass of champagne and watch as my editor whirrs into action. I hang around for a couple of minutes and am about to shoot off when I smell smoke. The one inch tape machines and ancillary equipment are separated from the edit suite by two large glass sliding doors. I turn towards the glass doors and see smoke pouring out of one of the machines. You couldn't make it up.

CHAPTER THIRTY TWO
CHANNEL 4, A YIDDISH DOCUMENTARY AND A HIGH COURT INJUNCTION

It was around this time that the Gods gave birth to Channel 4. Ian Bloom, a lawyer I'd recently met, called me. We'd met a year before, after a client introduced us. I had gone to see him when I thought Private Eye had published a libellous article about me. They had cobbled together a story about my defunct production company's fall from grace. He persuaded me that given the company's losses and failure to pay some creditors, suing might be a problem. Some years later he was able to use his talents when I became involved in a big libel action with Haymarket Publishing. At this time he had the good fortune of not actually representing me. That was left to a firm called Denton Hall and Burgin, a substantial law firm in Grays Inn. Like many other firms, they've since changed their name.

He wanted me to meet a director client of his, Russ Karel. Karel was probably the only fluent Yiddish speaking Australian on planet Earth. He wanted to make a documentary history of the Yiddish cinema. I loved the idea and thought it perfect for the new Channel 4. We put together the concept and a preliminary budget took it to them and they commissioned us to make it. It was to become *Almonds And Raisins*. "Raisins and Almonds" was a lullaby written by Abraham Goldfaden and is now firmly established as a folk song. There's an old film expression, 'never work with animals and children'. They should have added "and Jews who 'claim' ownership of film rights".

Karel was a strange man. Very small, very thin, almost emaciated, all of this hanging off a tiny frame. He came across as more Jewish than my old Rabbi. He flew to New York to meet with the so-called owners of many of the classic old movies. He also headed to the National Centre for Jewish Film at Brandeis University in Waltham, Massachusetts. Their archives would provide much of the material for the documentary. As executive producer i.e. the plonker who looks after the budget, I became seriously worried by these old New York Jews who claimed copyright ownership of much of the material. They wanted fortunes for the use of a thirty second clip but could never find any documentation that proved they actually owned any of it.

Karel was now editing the film in a Soho edit suite. Great care had to be taken with copying most of the footage as it was shot on nitrate film. This was highly flammable and, not to put too fine a point on it, downright fucking dangerous. Karel kept insisting that the releases we obtained from the New York Jewish fraternity were legitimate. I couldn't agree. It became a huge problem between us to the extent that he went to Channel 4 to get me removed from the film. I, in turn, sent along a couple of rather large framed production runners to bar Karel from the edit suite. Stand-off.

The following evening I was going to dinner with Pearl at the White Elephant. As I walked up the steps to the restaurant I was tapped on the shoulder by some anonymous looking man. 'Jon Roseman?' he asked. I nodded. He then slapped an envelope in my hand. It was a High Court Injunction courtesy of Channel 4.

It told me that I had no rights in the film and that it was their property. By this time in my life I'd been through so much that a High Court Injunction was merely par for the course. I called the Head of Acquisitions at Channel 4, David Harris, the following morning.

'Got your letter last night,' I said. 'What's it all about?'

'Karel says you're screwing up his film.'

'David, the guy's putting a bunch of clips in the documentary that will never survive any legal scrutiny. I wasn't prepared to let that happen.' A pause while he digested this.

'Will you agree not to tamper with the film in any way?'

'Fuck off.'

Will you agree not to remove the film from the edit suite?'

'Fuck you.'

'Will you agree not to damage the film?'

'Fuck you and fuck your injunction.' I hang up. It's all show biz. He knew I wasn't going to mess with the film. I was just creating the environment for a negotiation. None the less I hand it over to my lawyer, Charles Harding. At my instigation we seek a barrister's advice. Harding calls me from the conference. I couldn't go as our third child was imminent.

'I'm here with Nigel Thompson,' he tells me. 'Nigel says you haven't got any leverage, Channel 4 have you over a barrel.'

'Charles I'm not paying you and Nigel whatever to tell me I'm screwed. I want *something* that will help. Anything.' Harding calls me later and apologises for the complete negativity of the meeting and, surprisingly, tells me there will be no charge. I decide to deal with Channel 4 myself and do without lawyers. As time is of the essence for Channel 4, I know I'll get a call.

Later that afternoon I got the call.

'Ok Jon can we work something out where you hand back the project to us for an agreed fee?' I had no problem with that. The budget was out of control and this was the only way I was going to see a penny. I was in the budget for five thousand pounds with no back end. The back end refers to repeats and overseas sales.

A few days later I sit in Channel 4's offices across a desk from David Harris. He shoves a ten page document across to me. The bit that's blank provides for the financial settlement. The pages are all gobbledygook to me. In essence it states that I'm to hand over all rights that I may have until the universe bends back on itself and reverts back to the primeval atom etc, etc. After a lot of hardball we agree a figure of twenty thousand pounds. It's absurd. More than double I'd have paid if I were him. He leaves the office and ten minutes later he comes back with the cheque. I sign the paperwork and offer it to him but don't release it till I have the cheque clasped in my other hand! *Almonds and Raisins* was a great documentary, but it was broadcast only once. Immediately after transmission the real owners of the clips began to bombard the station with claims. I missed its transmission as I was on holiday in Spain. I was told it was good. But to this day I've never seen it. Not surprisingly, Channel 4 could never re-show it, since the cost of getting real clearances was prohibitive. Karel, despite his cavalier attitude towards the legalities (and who am I to talk?), was a fine filmmaker who died young in Italy of a sudden heart attack. I found out later that he wasn't even Jewish!

CHAPTER THIRTY THREE
SWEET DREAMS

Dave and Annie were very disappointed with the chart position of *Love Is A Stranger*. It reached only 81 in the UK charts. *Sweet Dreams* however was a winner. The budget was a meagre fifteen thousand pounds. Again no profit materialised but the quality of the work was so much more important. We shot on location in a Sussex field with a herd of cows as extras and a studio in London. We actually bought in a cow for the studio shoot. Months later I got a call from a friend in LA saying that *Sweet Dreams* was up for a video award for 'best use of symbolism in a pop promo.' It wasn't that long ago when our American friends couldn't even envisage making videos, now they were having lavish award ceremonies for them. As for 'best use of symbolism' I couldn't buy into that. I'm not sure whose idea the cows were, probably Dave's, but was it some kind of esoteric metaphor? Give me a break. The success of *Sweet Dreams* was such that the record company decided to re-release *Love Is A Stranger* which went to number 4 in the charts.

I have always maintained that clients, which included the bands I worked for, as well as presenters are not your friends and never will be. They view you only as a means to an end. It doesn't matter how long you've known them, the relationship that exists lies somewhere between a lawyer and a priest.

I began spending a lot of time with Dave and Annie, perhaps more with Annie. We'd often have dinner together and when she was going out with someone I'd still be asked along. We'd see each other four or five times a month. She was great company and very left wing. We'd discuss/row/laugh/shout at each other. I enjoyed the time we spent together. They were looking for a manager around this time and Dave mentioned in passing to me that I was on their list. I told him I wouldn't have done it. I preferred not to alter the dynamics of our existing relationship.

CHAPTER THIRTY FOUR
WHAM AND DAVE AND ANNIE

The world of music videos had marched on a pace. On both sides of the Atlantic there were now scores of production companies churning them out. It was 1983. Record companies in the States had East and West Coast video vice presidents responsible for commissioning pop promos. Things had come a long way since my first meeting with RCA when there wasn't even a television to be found in the entire building.

The American president of RCA's video disc division was in London and asked me to lunch. Tom Kuhn was a little older than me, medium height and neat fair hair. He wore expensive suits and emitted an air of casual calm. He looked fit, courtesy, as I found out later, of his passion for tennis. I was jealous of the immense calm that clung to him like a second skin. I only ever exuded manic disassociated excitement. He was a very experienced TV network executive and had been Vice President of Warner Brothers TV Division.

We lunched at the White Elephant and our common interests made us life-long friends. Over the years we enjoyed each others' company in some of the great restaurants in London, Los Angeles and New York. We also shared some rather bizarre adventures which usually involved beautiful girls and copious amounts of the marching powder. He was one of the senior executives behind the late David Carradine's popular TV series *Kung Fu.* Though, to begin with, it wasn't necessarily going to star David. Bruce Lee, who was desperately trying to break in to American TV, met Tom and performed all his legendary kicks in his office, scaring the living shit out of him, but sadly Bruce's voice let him down.

He told me that his division had made a long form video (a DVD in today's parlance) with the Eurythmics. Not with me?!! Tom was very complimentary about my work but didn't mention why I hadn't been invited on board. When I next saw Dave I asked him why he hadn't wanted me to produce it. I wasn't so naïve to assume that however good my relationship was with him that I would always be involved with their videos, but it would have been nice not to have heard about it second-hand. All artists want the creative freedom to change their working relationships. He explained that he hadn't really been given any choice in the matter. Later I found out that he'd been rather overwhelmed by the Americans and hadn't pressed them on the producer/director. It was the only time he'd ever let creative control slip out of his hands.

'We've got a major problem with the long form video,' Tom was saying.

'What sort of problem?' I asked sipping a very expensive Burgundy courtesy of RCA.

'Dave hates it.' Tom said simply.

'I see,' I said, seeing.

'Can you talk to him? I know you're close.' He told me who had done the original shoot.

'I know the director and he's bloody good and Dave's got great vision. What happened?'

'It was put together a while back and Dave feels the band have moved on and wants us to take it off the market. He's just doesn't like it. He's really pissed.'

'How pissed?'

'He won't talk to us.'

'What can I do?'

'If you could persuade him to make another one, with you at the helm, then we'd take it off the shelves.'

'A big ask.' I said.

'Between you and me Jon, if he doesn't go for it we'd take it off the market anyway. They're going to be big in the States and the record division won't be happy if we make them unhappy.'

I told him Dave was on holiday in Barbados with his then girlfriend the TV actress Leslie Ash.

'Would you fly over there and speak to him?' A trip to Barbados paid for by RCA. How could I refuse my new friend?!

'Look I can only go so far with this, but you'll need to come over for a couple of days as well. I need to show him you're one of the good guys.' It was agreed.

Two days later I'm first class on the plane to Bridgetown. I get to Dave's hotel and he greets me like a long lost friend. I'm suspicious. It turns out he and Leslie aren't getting on too well. The hotel is a paradise. He has an exclusive bungalow right on the beach. I have some telephone booth right at the back of the hotel. I don't mind. After all, I'm not paying!

We all had dinner on my first night. Cutting air and knives comes to mind. He completely excluded Leslie from our conversation which made me very uncomfortable. I am a very 'correct' kind of guy and this overt rudeness did not sit well with me.

The next day we took a boat out and the situation didn't get any better. I managed to get a nasty case of sunburn. The atmosphere at dinner that night was just as bad. It was half an hour before a waiter stopped by to take our order. The conversation was desultory at best. After we ordered, Dave just stood up and left the table not to return. Leslie burst into tears and I'm pissed with Dave for leaving me with a very distressed young lady. She pleads with me to intervene on her behalf and tell him how much she loves and cares for him. My heart goes out to her, but it's not something I'm prepared to get involved in.

Tom arrives the next day and walks in to a pretty unresponsive artist. I warned my friend what he would have to contend with but he'd flown too far not to make his pitch. The following day, he flew back to New York with Dave's complete non co-operation ringing in his ears, leaving me to try and talk to Dave. We hung out together but there never was the right opportunity to raise the topic. I figured I'd just enjoy myself. I suggested to Dave we get some coke. He went along for the ride but his sniffing days were long over.

He told me that when he'd signed a deal with Elton John's record company, Rocket Records, he'd been given a thirty thousand pound advance from John Reid, Elton's manager. He took the money and spent a lot of it on copious amounts of cocaine to fuel his then large coke habit. When he got back to his top floor flat, part of a large converted house in Crouch End, he tipped one particular purchase onto the kitchen table intending to crush it up ready to use. Dave tells me in the middle of this the door bell rings. No intercoms in those days. He opens the window to check out who it is and chucks his keys out the window then gets back to his crushing. His friend opens the door of the flat, and then physics intervenes. Open window plus open door creates strong current of air. Coke blown all over the place and so is much of his advance.

Some weeks later he had to present the demos that Rocket Records had paid for to Elton and his manager. Hands shaking from weeks of over over-indulgence and barely able to put the tape in the cassette deck, they were treated to an endless bass guitar riff droning out of the speakers. They weren't particularly pleased with the results of their investment but they'd been round the block quite a few times themselves and handed over some more cash to the trembling Stewart. They told him to come back with a demo that would include more than just a bass guitar.

Meantime back in Barbados I talk to some local dude on the beach who was trying to sell me some ganja. I tell him I want some coke. He says he'll make a call. An hour later the dude, Dave and I are motoring in a Mini Moke to some isolated place in the island. We park up and our new found buddy walks a couple of hundred yards to a derelict hut with my hundred dollar bill. He's gone for about half an hour and Dave and I are getting pretty nervous. Finally he ambles back to the car and gives me a packet. Normally, I use the word loosely, you buy a gram. What he'd handed over was at best half a gram. I tell him I'm not happy and to go back and get the other half. What was I thinking! We're alone, in the middle of nowhere and I'm complaining about some insignificant drug purchase.

He returns back to the ramshackled abode and after a few minutes I see him running back to the car followed by a big muscular local brandishing an Uzi. We fired up the engine and sped back to the hotel. I'll settle for the half I told our man. No I wouldn't. He'd left it at the hut when he'd fled in panic!

We all flew back to London the following day. Wearing only shorts and a tee shirt at the British Airway's check-in desk, I was told that my clothes were inappropriate for first class travel! We had words. Mine perhaps were more explicit. We arrived at Heathrow after a very long and tedious flight. I felt that Dave and Leslie were getting on a little better and the flight, for them at least, had applied some balm to their fraught relationship, that is until we passed through passport control. As we walked through those endless corridors to the baggage claim, Dave suddenly about turned, said he was going to Paris and left me with an hysterical Leslie. Thanks mate, that's all I needed!

My new production company wasn't on a par with the old days, but that was never an issue with me. I had never intended to build some vast global organisation. What happened, just happened. I had no long term Murdochian plan to rule the world. I didn't want to make millions and have three homes. I always just went with the flow. Looking back, I really could have done with a professional looking after the financial side and then perhaps I might even have ended up with something to show for all the effort I'd put in. But hiring staff in the pop promo business was always going to be a problem. You never knew from one week to next if you were going to get a commission, and it was impossible to forecast turnover, far less profit. Financial planning was a complete lottery. My biggest regret has always been that my mistakes cost other people as well as myself our own hard-earned money. I've been stuffed financially on so many occasions that I just got used to it. If a company owed us money I tried to work something out. If they were insolvent, I let it go, no matter how much it was. If the only recourse is to bankrupt them, I took the view it wasn't worth it and walked away. I guess I always assumed other people would see things the same way. They didn't.

Simon Napier-Bell, the manager of Wham! called me about making a video with the formidable twosome. The song was *Bad Boys*. I first met George Michael with Mike Brady who'd worked with me on *Love Is A Stranger* at a recording studio in Notting Hill Gate. He was about twenty one at the time, a shy young man who nonetheless appeared in total control. God alone knows how he got along with Napier-Bell who considered himself both the belle of the ball and a leader of men!

We listened to the track which was hot off the press and talked ideas. The budget was around twenty thousand pounds and we'd spend every penny of it and more. In retrospect it was a step too far for Mike. A more experienced hand on the tiller would have been safer. It was a two day shoot involving actors and ten dancers. One of the days ran for twenty three hours. The dance sequence in the street at the end of the clip took eight hours to shoot and we didn't start filming it till ten at night. By three in the morning the dancers (all male) went on strike. They wanted more money or they were going to walk. Who could blame them? The choreography was all over the place and they were exhausted. Michael and Ridgeley did not find dancing in the street in the middle of the night particularly appealing and to cover up their dreadful performance we had to resort to slowing the images down. Always the last resort for a director in trouble. It obviously didn't put the boys off from working with us again as *Club Tropicana* was next up. Apparently, in order to exert total control over all things, Napier-Bell had agreed with the record company that, with a fixed contribution from them, the band would pay for, and have the final decision, over all their videos.

Club Tropicana was shot in Pikes Hotel Ibiza. It nearly didn't happen at all. I had some urgent VEC business and was due to follow the crew out the following day when filming would begin. Samuelsons' were the most experienced provider of film equipment at the time and had their own shipping company. They supplied major movie companies with kit which often required shipping anywhere in the world. The band, accompanied by their two girl backing singers, Helen

'Pepsi' DeMacque and Shirlie Holliman, flew out with my crew in the morning.

It was around two o'clock; I was sitting with Nik Powell and some of VEC's technical people when I got an urgent call from Samuelsons shipping company. When do you want us to fly out the equipment they wanted to know? I was a little surprised as it should have gone on the same flight as the crew. In real time I wasn't actually a 'little surprised' I was seriously pissed off. How the hell could they have done this? I called their MD and explained that the next available flight wouldn't arrive till the middle of the following day. And by the time customs had cleared the equipment we'd have lost a days filming. The kit needed to be sent today. So there was only one solution, a private plane. He called me back within ten minutes and agreed. I guess it must have cost them a few thousand.

Michael was a reasonable man in those days, so everything went fine. *Careless Whisper* on the other hand was a shoot from the planet of the damned.

It was always a pleasure to work with Dave and Annie. *Who's That Girl* was our next collaboration. That's the way we worked. I've read so much drivel on Google about who directed what, but the truth is simple: the only consistent people on all the videos we made together were, apart from Dave and Annie, Chris Ashbrook, the DP, me and Bill Saint my video editor at VEC.

Dave dropped by my office late one afternoon. He was bored and wanted to play. We took off for The Carlton Tower hotel. I often used to stay overnight in London and had struck a deal with the Carlton Tower in Knightsbridge. They waived the room fee and would just charge for room service. As I liked a drink and entertained a lot, their shareholders need have no fear of the arrangement affecting their profit margins. I finally ended the arrangement after a year and rented a tiny flat in Conway Street just off Marylebone Road near the underpass. The rumble of tube trains was a constant reminder of my central location. A long term relationship with a hotel affords you no privacy. They know all your business!

Dave loved hotels. We settled down with a drink and chatted. Suddenly he stood up and took a little black book from the inside pocket of his jacket.

'Let's call some girls!' he said. He started manically flicking through the pages stopping every now and then to dial a number. Thirty minutes and nine girls later he gave up. We ended up at his mum's flat where she cooked us spaghetti bolognese. You just can't beat a rock star's lifestyle.

Dave was always on the look out for new experiences. We'd been out for an Italian meal one evening in Soho and were walking down Brewer Street when we passed an 'encounter parlour'. At least that's what the grimy sign outside said it was. Dave wanted to try it out. We walked down a narrow hallway where a man and two women were seated behind a small table. He looked like Don Vito Corleone's son, Fredo (the emaciated one) and the women both resembled page three girls via abusive husbands plus twenty years. One was tall and thin, the other obviously enjoyed a Big Mac or three, probably intravenously. A handwritten sign on the table gave the prices. Fifteen pounds for twenty minutes and twenty five pounds for half an hour. A half hour for what I wondered? Dave handed over his money and followed the tall girl down some stairs. I was left with Fredo and Ms Tubby standing by the table. Anyone looking down the corridor from the street would have thought I was part of the set up.

Ten minutes passed and the woman returns adjusting her dress and tells Ms Tubby to go down the stairs. What the fuck was going on? I was a little concerned that Dave was tied to some bed after being thrashed with a whip with washing pegs attached to his nipples. Finally he emerged and we wandered down the street towards the Hippodrome night club.

'So what happened?' I wanted to know.

'What you get is to sit behind a glass screen and the girl lies on a bed and asks what you want her to do.'

'Sounds fantastic!' I lied. 'So what was all that business with the other girl?'

'The first girl had a huge caesarean scar. It was a bit off putting so I asked for the other girl.' He said this as if he was merely returning goods to M&S.

'Oh!' was all I could come up with. I had no intention of asking him what he wanted them to do.

We walked up the steps to the entrance of the Hippodrome and past the queues of revellers. The bouncers recognised Dave immediately and we were guided to some private bit of the club. I'm no clubber, and have never enjoyed anything they had to offer, which seemed to me only to be a noise so loud that human conversation was made impossible. We hung out for an hour trying to look cool, easy for him, impossible for me, before we both decided enough was enough and left for our respective beds.

By coincidence I had dinner with Annie the following night. Our dinners were lively affairs. Always politics, the environment and whatever social issues were headlining in the press at that moment. After we'd eaten, I'd normally put her in a cab and go back to the Carlton Tower. That night she felt like doing something. I told her that Dave and I had done the Hippodrome the night before. She'd never been so she decided to give it a try.

My relationship with Annie was as 'friend' and walker. The inverted commas represent the fact that it could never be a true friendship as it was based on a professional relationship. The 'walker' bit is because she found it difficult to meet guys since they were all a little in awe of her. As we strolled up the steps of the Hippodrome one of the bouncers said with a grin, 'That's all of them then!'

We were shown to a VIP table and given complimentary champagne. Annie told me she wanted to dance. The floor was packed with people gyrating, spinning, hands akimbo. It looked pretty scary to me. I have never been able to dance and am totally rhythmless. I gave it a shot. The fact I was wearing a sweater didn't help. My body temperature went from nought to a hundred in thirty seconds. We stayed on the dance floor for twenty minutes, she moving at one with the music. I moved like a Duck Billed Platypus on steroids.

When we went back to our table I was so hot I took my sweater off leaving me bare chested. Suddenly over the tannoy a voice announces, 'We'd like to welcome tonight to the Hippodrome from the Eurythmics, Annie Lennox.' A spotlight swung round to where we were sitting. Annie is caught sliding under the table desperately trying to avoid it. For someone trying to preserve their anonymity slipping beneath a table next to a half naked man wasn't her best move perhaps.

CHAPTER THIRTY FIVE
KOO'S DAD, PORN, MORE EURYTHMICS AND RCA

I was used to receiving some odd requests throughout my time in the music video business. I took a call one day from Wilbur Stark, Koo Stark's father. She had just ended a much publicised romance with Prince Andrew.

He invited me to lunch at the White Elephant. Stark was an American film producer and director. He'd been responsible for giving us Joan Collins in *The Stud*. He was a large man with a ruddy complexion and a huge appetite for food and wine. We shot the breeze for a while and as the main course arrived he got down to business.

'As I said Jon, I love your videos. What really appeals to me is the editing technique. Fast, furious but right on the beat. And your lighting is fantastic.' I nodded my thankful appreciation and swallowed a mouthful of sole meunière. 'What do you know about the porn market Jon?' Thank God I'd just swallowed.

'I'm no expert.' I said. Though I've had my moments!

'Well, I've been thinking about how your techniques could be utilised in making some classy porn films.' He cut through his steak, so rare a blood transfusion would have it up and walking. I offered what I hoped wasn't an encouraging smile. 'So what do you think?'

'Well I don't have any copyright on the way we make them, but I would have thought that porn..er..aficionados might want to go for the long lingering shot.' That's what I would want anyway.

'Sure, sure. I'm not suggesting you'd use fast cutting in the whole picture just enough to give it a touch of class.' It was the *you'd* bit that felled me.

'So what do you think?'

'About what?'

'Making a porn film.' I had to admit it had its appeal though it had never been very high on my Christmas wish list.

'Wilbur, I couldn't possibly do it. In my other life I'm also an agent for some serious journalists and having a director of porn films as their representative might make them baulk a little.' We'd recently signed Jonathan Dimbleby and I could already see the headlines in the trade paper. *Dimbleby's Agent Makes Fuck Film.* We parted amicably and never met again.

March 1983 ushered in the birth of my son Alex. In the children stakes I didn't have a vote. Pearl decided everything. At the time I wasn't sure how many children I wanted. Now I wouldn't want to have had it any other way. Pearl was a true Earth mother. I'd often watch the way she played with them, held them, talked to them. I think I did too much watching and not nearly enough holding. My head was always full of other things. The next video, ongoing problems with the edit suite and client issues. When I did cuddle I cuddled with a vengeance!

The most difficult shoot with the Eurythmics had to be *Here Comes The Rain Again*. Dave and his mad ideas. He wanted to film in the Orkney's in mid-December and shoot atop of the Old Man Of Hoy. This is a four hundred and forty nine foot sea stack of red sandstone that took Chris Bonnington three days to climb! It was an expensive operation. Helicopters aren't cheap and I couldn't see Dave hoisting himself up a gigantic pillar playing his guitar.

The island of Hoy is not a busy place. A few crofters' cottages, a hotel or two and a couple of bars and a few shops that specialise in arts and crafts. I had to fly a large crew up there and we stayed in a hotel that could have been twinned with Potosi, Bolivia (you look it up). We enlisted the help of a lovely woman, Sarah, who ran one of the arts and crafts shops. She helped us with all the locations. The only way we were going to get to the top of the Old Man Of Hoy was by helicopter. Dave and a cameraman took off for the towering sandstone pillar and I stayed safely on terra firma. There wasn't a hope in hell that I was going to get involved with that sequence. I don't do heights.

The weather was colder than a penguin's foot. We were there for two nights. The hotel staff would hang our damp bath towels over the radiator to dry. This would have been OK if the radiators worked. Apart from the hotel I nicknamed, 'Fuck You, We Don't Give A Shit', there was the problem with the light. There was barely any. We had perhaps five hours of daylight.

We were filming one scene by a beautiful old crofter's cottage when Annie asked if I'd speak to the owner about selling it to her. The owner was an elderly woman who had probably lived there all her life. They were canny people these Orcadian's. At first she didn't take the enquiry seriously (knowing Annie nor did I) but after some gentle prodding she came back with, 'If you're serious you must speak to my lawyer!' Needless to say no purchase was made.

On our last night, the entire crew and Dave and Annie were having a farewell drink or three in the hotel's little bar. I left them to it and went in search of the owner to discuss the bill.

I found him in his normal position behind the reception desk gazing at his tiny black and white television. I was determined to get some kind of discount on the hotel's appalling service.

'I'm sure you'll appreciate we haven't had a great stay here,' I began,' the breakfasts were suppose to be hot, they weren't. The food generally was, how can I put it, tepid and tasteless. The radiators didn't work and we were freezing cold and the hot water was almost non-existent. I'd like to see if we can come to some arrangement over the bill.' I looked at him. Nothing. After we stared at each other for a couple of minutes he finally spoke. 'Pay the bill or I'll call the police.' You had to hand it to him he was a tough negotiator. I decided that there wasn't much future in diplomacy and handed over my Diner's Club card.

'We don't take Diner's Club.' I looked around the reception desk at the numerous signs that screamed, *We Accept Diners Club*. I pointed them out to him.

'I said we don't accept them.'

'Forgive me for being a tad churlish but what exactly do all those signs say?'

'That's it! You bloody English think you're so fucking important.' Next up the police!

I went back to the little bar and told Dave what had happened. He shrugged. It was his way of saying, *'You the man.'* Roseman can sort it. Roseman couldn't. Two policemen arrived. I returned to reception and the farce continued. Owner shouts a lot. I point out all the places where it says the card is accepted. The police try to calm down the owner who is fighting some war that I'm not party to and do not understand. Finally the police get through to him and tell him that he has to accept my card. Phew! It's all over. It wasn't. It's now twelve thirty am and all I want to do is sleep in my freezing room and catch the first plane out in the morning.

Mr Owner, after getting the card approved, shoves the receipt across the reception desk for me to sign and after I gave him my signature he says,

'Now you (i.e. me) get out.' I understood the words he used but couldn't comprehend exactly what he was getting at.

'What?' I said.

'Get out of my hotel.' He repeats. I turn to one of the policeman.

'He can't do that can he?'

'I'm afraid he can.' I'm told.

'But it's the middle of the night. Where am I supposed to stay?' Blank looks from the Orkney police academy.

'What if I refuse?'

'Then we'd have to arrest you.'

'Would I have to spend the night in a cell?'

'Yes sir.'

'Is it heated?' I want to know. He nods. 'What time do I get out?'

'The procurator sits at ten.' Damn, the plane leaves at nine thirty. I pack my bag and leave the hotel. It's now minus ten and the streets are deserted and dark apart from the occasional street lamp. I'm screwed. I can't sleep outside, I'd freeze to death. I bump in to

Sarah our recently appointed locations manager. She'd been drinking with the crew in the hotel bar. I tell her what's happened and she lets me sleep on the floor of her shop. There's no heating and only my coat for warmth. It was still more comfortable than the hotel.

If only the hell of making the video ended there. It was only the beginning.

Bill Saint, my video editor, and I are looking at the pictures from the shoot. It's a disaster. The light, what there was of it, changed in every shot. We couldn't match any of the pictures. It cost RCA a fortune and I wasn't even able cut a ten second sequence together. Bill looks at me ruefully and says, 'You always say you can save it in the edit. I know you're good but...' his voice trailed off.

I stare at him with eyes that pleaded, 'Help me!' He shakes his head and looks at the ceiling as though in supplication. We gaze at a freeze frame picture of Annie holding a lantern for ten minutes. A bleak dark picture. Tea arrives. The trainee engineer puts my cup down next to the mixer and inadvertently touches the lever on the mixing desk. It alters the colour of the background, the sky turns from grey to black.

'Bill look at that. If we key in a black sky, we eliminate all our problems.' He looked doubtful but tried a few edits. It worked!

Sometimes strange things happen in the edit. Odd pieces of luck materialise. As Annie mimed to the line, *I want to walk in the open wind*, in the third verse a gust of wind ruffled her clothes as if on cue. What with the break of the mixer accident and the wind I thought of it as a lucky omen.

Everyone seemed pleased with the result, everyone that is apart from Jose Menendez. It just so happens he was the head honcho at RCA, and he hated me. I had never met the man and never had any direct dealings with him and had no idea why he felt that way.

After finishing editing I had to take a trip to New York to see Tom Kuhn. I went to his offices on 6th Avenue for a meeting with some of his key execs to discuss some new projects. We were chatting away when he took a call from Jose Menendez. Somehow

Menendez found out I was in the building and summoned Tom for an urgent meeting. The lucky omen began leaking away.

Twenty minutes later he returned wearing a large grin. 'Well that was interesting,' he said breaking open the scotch. 'Jose is a not happy man.'

Knowing his feelings toward me I wasn't surprised. 'How so?' I asked gulping down my scotch.

'He's just seen *Here Comes the Rain Again.*' Here we go.

'And?'

'His exact words were, 'We've got him this time. It's a piece of shit!' It was my duty to have to point out to him that it is currently the most requested video on MTV.' A wry smile from Tom. 'He didn't like that at all. What he said was, 'we'll get him next time.'

'Wonderful.' I said.

'Lunch?' Tom offered. We went to the Four Seasons, the most expensive place that New York City had to offer and forgot about the Cuban born egomaniac. In 1989 both Menendez and his wife were blown away with shotguns by their two sons. Nice family.

CHAPTER THIRTY SIX
A WRIT, BRITT AGAIN, AL PACINO AND HERBIE HANCOCK

I had always been aware that I needed help with the running of my company's finances but could never find the right person. I was introduced to Howard Kruger by Steve Foster then the Brighton football skipper. Here was a man, ostensibly independently wealthy, steeped in the music business who sent out all the right signals. I didn't know it then but I might as well have got in to bed with Bernie Madoff. He became involved in my production company.

Kruger's father used to be a big time promoter. His .clients included the likes of Glen Campbell and Vic Damone. The family lived in Brighton in a substantial bungalow. It was no ordinary bungalow. Deep below the earth beneath their living area lay a myriad of offices all of it strangely redolent of Hitler's bunker.

His father's office belonged to the early sixties. A huge grand piano at one end of the room, a vast desk at the other. Photographs of everyone he'd worked with cluttered the room. Pictures of the aforesaid Vic Damone and Glen Campbell had pride of place. He reminded me of the old time wrestler Big Daddy! and thought of himself as a latter-day Don Arden.

Howard went on to divest me of two hundred and fifty thousand pounds. I remember his father's words when I confronted the pair of them in the Fuhrer's bunker.

'I told you Howard, didn't I warn you for fuck's sake!' He raged at his son. 'I told you: *don't get caught.*'

Howard, round faced, with a permanent six o'clock shadow and stocky with a leaning towards tubby, had this penchant for wandering up Tottenham Court Road with the company credit card and buying anything that took his fancy. This plethora of spending soon expanded itself to clothes, the best restaurants and a second hand Bentley turbo. The company sued him. It would go on for a year and a half.

It was a painful time. The Krugers used every device they could to bleed the company's limited finances. Often we'd be dragged into court for some interlocutory hearing, where irrelevant documents were asked for or unnecessary extensions sought. While the judge always ruled against them it would cost the company five thousand pounds every time this happened. The company's barrister and solicitors had to be paid to deal with these absurd applications. The judge's ruling always stated, 'costs in any event.' This was translated as, if or when we go to court, they would have to pay the costs of the hearing. Even then you never received the entire amount as it would be argued that only a proportion of the costs were applicable. However unfair the system and whatever methods the Kruger's tried, I was not about to cave in to their use of legal thuggery.

I was surprised to meet with Britt Ekland again. I was in LA having been asked to direct a couple of videos for The Stray Cats. The band were all well-known rockers in their own right before they became The Stray Cats. Brian Setzer, Lee Rocker and Slim Jim Phantom the drummer. Phantom was now married to Britt. He invited me to his home for some drinking sessions and an ounce or two of marching powder. We became best buddies for a week. As I rip through my life it often occurs to me that my involvement with some of the bands, while being memorable to me, would mean absolutely nothing to them. I was merely some inconsequential director/producer who unfortunately they were called on to work with. Hence instantly forgettable. This guy appears for a week or two in their busy drug fuelled lives, then vanishes hardly likely to appear again. I am a mere shadow to them.

Some years later I get a call from Lyndall Hobbs inviting me to the premiere of her then partner Al Pacino's film *Looking For Richard.* An in-depth dramatic analysis of Richard III and his relevance to the modern world or so the blurb said. I loved it. Lyndall had long since broken up with Michael White and had gone to LA looking for fame and fortune and was now living with Al Pacino.

I went to the party afterwards and Lyndall introduced me to the great man himself. We spoke for thirty seconds and nearly fifteen years later I remember it as if it was yesterday. There's probably upward of a thousand air stewardesses who dine out on the famous people they've served. What is it about these encounters? A fleeting meeting and we pretend to 'know' the star. We embroider the encounter to such an extent that we've become their best buddies.

I also met Glynis Barber and Michael Brandon (Dempsey and Makepeace) at the party. Several years later, at the Daily Mirror's Pride Of Britain Awards, I found myself sitting next to Barber and Brandon. We were introduced. 'Actually we've met before,' I told them, 'at Al Pacino's party.' I turned round to the other people on the table with a big grin, 'I've always wanted to say that!' having now said it. Ms Barber peered at me and uttered the immortal put down, 'which one?'

While Slim Jim and I were putting away the nth bottle of beer and the endless lines of coke in his living room at two in the morning Britt appeared. She told him to get his arse up to bed and for me to leave. Only she was more forthright. That said we always did get on.

The video I shot was memorable only for the fact that Slim Jim was so pissed that his sticks would fly off in all directions as he did his best to keep up with the playback. Normally I leave all the tight shots on the drummer till the end. By this time they're hot, sweaty and the pictures are much stronger. With Slim I couldn't risk it. I did all his stuff within the first hour. If I waited any longer he wouldn't have been able to hold the sticks at all.

It was after the Stray Cats that I had dinner with Herbie Hancock. He'd just had a huge hit with *Rockit,* illustrated by a brilliant video by Godley and Creme, ex band members of 10cc and now pop video directors.

Mutual friends had invited me to a new restaurant opening in LA. Herbie and I became instant soul mates. After dinner everyone wanted to go on to a jazz club where Herbie would always do an impromptu performance. I was more than happy to go along for the ride but I wanted to go back to my hotel to get some reinforcements (coke). I told the party I'd join them later as I wanted to drop by my hotel first. Herbie immediately said he'd be going with me. In the car I asked him why he'd decided to come back with me. He laughed, 'For the coke man,' he said. How did he know!? We got to know each other well over the next two years. He would even drop by my little flat in Conway Street in central London unannounced, ready to party.

Herbie and I shared a few lines and then drove on to the club. It was a large room with about eighty tables and a long bar facing the stage at the back of the club. The décor was white and unobtrusive. The lighting was just bright enough to allow you to read the menu without taking away the ambience from the small stage. Herbie was greeted by the owner and we were whisked away to his little cluttered office behind the stage, where the three of us drank beer and did copious amounts of the powder.

Herbie took to the stage, unannounced an hour later. The packed club rose as he entered to applaud the maestro. I stayed for a while but needed to leave about one o'clock as I had early morning meetings and needed time to recover from the evening's excesses. I tried to attract his attention as his fingers tore across the piano's keyboard to say goodbye but he seemed entirely involved in the moment. I stood up and began to make my way toward the exit, he looked up, saw me leaving, did a quick twiddle on the keys to end the piece and shot straight after me. I realised I was going to be in for a long night.

We ended up at his house in the Hollywood Hills shooting the breeze. It wasn't one of those vast rock and roll mansions. It was large but understated. His living room was filled with keyboards of every description. I thought I'd walked in to Chappells of Bond Street. A drink, more coke and speed chat ensued.

'Herbie someone told me you're a Buddhist,' I said handing him over a rolled up hundred dollar bill.

'Yeah, for fifteen years. You?'

'Jewish.'

'You should look into it. It's helped me a lot.'

'How so?'

'Well I used to spend quite a bit on coke, so I chanted to stop buying it. Now I don't spend a dime on it anymore, people just give it to me!' He was absolutely serious. I didn't think Siddhartha Gautama necessarily had this rather bizarre attempt at spiritual enlightenment in mind when he came up with the concept of Buddhism a couple of thousand years ago. I didn't get away till four. My early morning meetings became perfunctory affairs!

Me aged 1 – part of the
Balham Possee.

My mother Edna
& I, the bamitzvah
boy, January 1961.
How I long for the
comfort of those
days!

My father Norman. D-Day landings. Shortly after, dishonourably discharged for excessive casual wear.

Wedding Day, 1974. I'm the one in white.

Me, 1981. When hair was in.

Paula Yates and I, 1980 having just completed Rock Stars in their Underpants. The weight of my wallet forcing me to lean to the left.

Chris Rea, Bill Wyman, John Entwistle and Paul Rodgers at launch of Willie and the Poor Boys video. Who are those other two guys?

Dave Stewart and I on the Bob Dylan shoot. The last time my hair blew in the wind.

Annie Lennox, Billy Poveda and me circa 1875.

Dave Stewart and Leslie Ash in Barbados. A day in the life. His life.

Bob Geldof grabbing a photo opportunity with me, 1980.

Aretha Franklin and Annie Lennox I can recognise - on the set of the *Sisters are Doing it for Themselves* video. But who the hell are the bookends?

Tom Kuhn, President of RCA's video disc division - at a vital business meeting in Barbados.

1. Jack Steven, A&R guru, 1987 and I. Fact or fiction?

Pearl and Danielle in 1991. It's a lucky man who can have two such beautiful women in his life.

Tommy Vance, Danielle and I at VH1 launch party 1994
shortly before Danielle broke us up!

My friend Ian Bloom just after I'd said
I'm leaving the country.

CHAPTER THIRTY SEVEN
BRANSON AGAIN, EURYTHMICS,
BARBADOS AND DAVE'S ACID TRIP

I'd hoped that my involvement with Branson had ended back on his houseboat but it was not to be.

Dave and Annie's recording contract with RCA did not include movie soundtracks. Branson had been involved in the remake of the movie *1984* and, being the clever operator he was, asked them to do the soundtrack. Dave told me they were paid a million pounds for it. Branson, of course, didn't care whether their music would add anything to the film. It was a shot across RCA's bows to seduce them away when their contract was up for renewal.

Michael Radford, the movie's director, actually said they were 'foisted' on him by Virgin. When Dave told Branson that he wanted me to do the videos, Branson had a minor fit. I, for my part, was unaware of all the politics going on and merely expressed surprise that Branson had agreed that I could make the videos.

Dave had been fighting a rearguard action with the bearded one who finally caved in. I flew to Barbados where they were recording the album to discuss what we were going to do. Branson, apparently, required the videos urgently and as they couldn't fly to Britain because of tax issues, I had to go to them. It was a bizarre situation. Annie had recently married Radha Raman, a Hare Krishna monk, and they and some of his acolytes were holed up in a house near the beach. Dave had his own place a few hundred yards away where I stayed. One of the big problems on the island was power cuts which happened a few times a day. As Dave and I left the studios one evening after yet another power cut we passed by Annie's house. The place was lit up by vast numbers of candles. I mentioned it to Dave. 'It's not the power cut,' he observed somewhat curtly, 'it's always like that.'

Dave wasn't a fan of Raman. That was easy to see but he never talked about it. Annie and I spent a lot of time together and she would speak to me about what was going on with her marriage. It wasn't rocket science to see it had all been a big mistake. But life is for making mistakes. As someone once said, 'if you don't make mistakes you don't make anything.' According to that aphorism I should have been a millionaire several times over. In all the time I knew Annie, this was her lowest point.

After a week we set off for Dublin to film the first of three videos. They still couldn't come back to the UK for another week. Dave had bought over from Barbados a couple of musicians who'd played on the album. One evening in a Dublin bar the talk turns to LSD. I mention I've never done it. Dave thinks I should give it a try. The musicians from Barbados nod in agreement. He tells me in one particular year he'd done acid every day bar one. How he could remember his day off is probably beyond the reach of medical science. He then tried to persuade me it was a great idea even offering to be my guide/nurse. When I declined for the fifth time, he told me how he had convinced his stepfather to take a trip.

He and his brother gathered at his mum's flat in Maida Vale in north London with his step dad and mum acting as 'nurse'. Then all three popped a tab. After three quarters of an hour his step dad suddenly stood up, said this isn't working, I'm going home. That he was at home should have been a clue! He left the flat and went 'home' to his first wife and couldn't understand why his key wouldn't fit the lock. So much for Dave volunteering to guide me through the threshold of the unconscious.

We set up to film *Julia* one of three tracks from the album. A simple but a well crafted video.

It consisted of just Annie's face and bare shoulders with the camera making all the movement while she sat looking directly straight ahead. She told me she didn't feel entirely comfortable with the image as people might think she was semi-naked. I talked her round. The real problem was the tiny sore on her bottom lip. The more make up that was applied the worse it became. Finally she took me on one side and asked if we should abandon the shoot as it was clearly visible. She was right and we stopped filming. We decided to re-shoot it at their church in London. Sometime back they had acquired a church in Crouch End North London and converted it with a stage, small studio and offices.

When Branson found out we were going to need to re-shoot he really lost it. He figured I was out to screw him and Annie's problem was a figment of my imagination. I sent him a video of what we'd shot in Dublin with a note telling him not to be such a *putz.*

CHAPTER THIRTY EIGHT
CANCER AND WHAM

On May 26th 1984 Thomas came in to my world. That was it. There were now six of us. I remember holding him and thinking how Jewish he looked. When I got home I told Gideon and Elie that I thought their new brother looked Jewish and they replied almost in unison, 'But we're not Jewish, are we?' How to make dad feel good!

A few months after he was born Pearl discovered a tiny lump in her left breast. The specialist we saw thought it wasn't worth a biopsy as it was so tiny, but Pearl had an instinct about it and insisted he go ahead. The specialist called me two days after the procedure and confirmed it was cancer. He said it was the smallest lump he'd ever seen. We were devastated. Pearl went in to hospital and had a lumpectomy.

The treatment for breast cancer is so different today. The drugs that are now available offer most women a real fighting chance. The specialist felt that as long as she had regular check- ups, and with the lump being so small, the long-term prognosis was good. As a family, we dealt with it the best way we could and prayed the doctor was right.

Our lives would now be very different. Everything changed slowly. The dynamic of my relationship with Pearl altered subtly and a distance grew between us. She spent lots of time with the children, but it was now in large urgent chunks rather than steady and uniform as it had been up till then. It was if she needed to stuff it quickly into a bag and take it with her. She wanted to go out and spend all her spare time with friends, an activity previously shared, now done almost exclusively solo.

It was difficult for me to understand the changes she was going through and I began to feel lonely and marginalized. I guess I felt, rightly or wrongly, that it was a kind of payback for the innumerable times I'd spent away from home, often when I didn't have to.

My last video for Wham was *Careless Whisper*. George Michael was now a monster. A very brilliant and talented monster but a monster none the less. We filmed in Miami, using the helicopter shots and exteriors cut around his re-shot performance and everything seemed to be going well for a few hours until our hero saw the video playback. He hated the way his hair looked. He wanted it re styled. I pointed out that 1) we'd have to dump all the film we'd shot and 2) by the time he'd had his hair done we'd lose the day's filming. As we'd only budgeted for two days it was going to cost a great deal of money. Our lighting man who'd worked on *Close Encounter*'s hearing my conversation with Michael, sidled up to me and asked if he was serious. He'd not done many music videos obviously. A refrain I'd often heard from crews who'd worked in movies was 'I've never seen anything like it' when rock stars strutted their stuff.

I called Simon Napier-Bell in London and asked him who was going to cough up the extra twenty five thousand pounds. Not a problem he said, CBS will be picking up the tab. Knowing Simon I decided to check this out with CBS. They had a very different story. We will pay only the agreed budget. Any overages are all down to the band and Napier-Bell they told me. I was pissed. I knew that if CBS were paying I could continue filming and be entirely comfortable that the bills would be paid...but Napier Bell. No way.

I called him again.

'Hi Simon just had a very interesting conversation with CBS.'

'Yeah'.

'They aren't going to pay a dime for the extra day. They say it's all down to you.'

'Jon, Jon that's not right, someone's got their wires crossed.' The voice calm and persuasive. 'You know the corporate mind as well as anyone. Don't worry about it.'

'Simon I'm not worried about it but I'm not shooting one more foot of film till I know that the money is sitting in my bank account. The account details are with CBS. I've got enough to deal with out here without the bullshit. Let me know when the monies have been transferred.' I hung up. If I hadn't done it like that, I'd have ended up eating the entire overage.

Michael, true to form, hated the finished video and re shot his performance in London. The finished video used the helicopter shots and exteriors we shot in Miami around his re-shot performance and it wasn't at all bad. Perhaps he'd come of age and reached the time when he'd learnt enough about the making of music videos to impose his exclusive will on his work.

CHAPTER THIRTY NINE
WYMAN AND MANDY, HYPNOSIS, ANNIE AND ARETHA

A few days later I was off to Paris to meet Bill Wyman and Mandy Smith, his fifteen year old girlfriend. I'd been asked to make a long form video of *Willie And The Poor Boys*. This was a group of mega stars put together by Bill Wyman while Mick and Keith were screaming verbal abuse at each other, using the willing press to publish their invective. The group consisted of Ron Wood, Charlie Watts, Jimmy Page, Andy Fairweather Low and either Kenney Jones or Ringo. After my last experience with the ex-Beatle I prayed for Kenney Jones.

I arrived at Wyman's hotel room to find his manager, an assistant and Mandy Smith. I was introduced to Team Wyman. Mandy looked a million dollars which is probably the amount she received after their divorce. The few words she actually spoke included, 'money', 'clothes' and 'shopping'. Wyman thrust a hand in his trouser pocket, pulled out a wad of Francs, passed them to his assistant and told her to take Mandy shopping. Her face lit up. Nothing makes a girl happier than new shoes and a bit of jewellery even if you're only fifteen. It was good to see that rock and roll was alive and being practised by a middle-aged man who had a taste for schoolgirls. Viva the French Franc!

We shot the mini film in a hall in Chelsea. Wyman wanted to convey a fifties school dance feeling. What was it about schools and Wyman? We hired some professional dancers who jived their brains out. Girls swung high in the air only to be caught by male partners and then flung between their legs. A bunch of other kids added to the atmosphere of an end of term party. All this played out in front of the band performing from what looked like a school assembly stage. My abiding memory of this very amateur piece of work was that I didn't have to work with Ringo! The band were totally professional and Ronnie Wood, bless him, was the life and soul.

Pearl had been having her regular six monthly check ups and all seemed well. I was glad we'd moved out of London in 1978. I now hoped that living in the country would be kinder to us. Perhaps the pace of life would help see Pearl through the horrors of that terrible illness

While I loved living out of London I wasn't remotely big on country pursuits. I just enjoyed the peace and quiet. Many years later when everything was falling apart it was this very environment that helped keep me sane.

Gideon was eight and in primary school. Elie was five and the boys, Alex and Tom were two and one respectively. Gideon was a bright boy, but I'd have to wait nearly sixteen years to find out exactly how clever he was, though Pearl and I did get an early inkling. Our local restaurant kept a bunch of puzzles in reception, so waiting clients could ruin their appetites by trying to solve them. They weren't easy; I certainly couldn't do any of them. While Pearl and I were having a drink and chatting, Gideon stuck one of the puzzles in front of us having solved it in about ten minutes. We were amazed, hugged him, told him he was very clever and didn't really think much more of it. I wasn't sure if it was solved by more luck than judgement. How short-sighted that turned out to be.

1985 saw me become Jon Roseman, promoter. Why did I do it? Simple answer - it was something I hadn't done before. It was new. It was a challenge. It was a fucking disaster. Roger Cook had introduced me to Paul Goldin. Paul was a stage hypnotist. Coincidentally, I had seen him perform at the Brighton Hippodrome when I was fourteen. His act had made a big impression on me and it hadn't changed in twenty three years. He'd make his entrance on an empty stage and spoke in a phoney French accent and went through the following *spiel*:

'Good evening ladies and gentlemen. What you are about to see is not hypnotism but a meeting of minds. Now listen to me very carefully.' There then played, via a tape machine, Mike Oldfield's *Tubular Bells*. 'I want you all to stand up,' he continued. 'Now put your hands together and interlock your fingers. Push them tightly together. Now lower your hands to your waist keeping them firmly interlocked. My mind is now joining with your mind and you will find it impossible to pull your hands apart. Do *not* try and force them apart. It could be very painful. Those of you who cannot part your hands easily please come up on to the stage and I will release them for you.'

Good old' classical hypnosis. By forcing your hands together and suggesting that separating them would cause pain and getting you on stage allows Paul to choose the most susceptible punters for the show. And it really was a great show. All the normal stuff. You're Elvis Presley, the person next to you is speaking Martian and so on. He was a brilliant stage hypnotist.

Somehow I got persuaded to put him on in London at a theatre in Maida Vale for three weeks. Pearl reckoned he'd hypnotised me! She could have been right. My abiding memory of him was that he seemed to bathe in Paco Rabanne. After I'd booked the theatre, spent God knows how much on advertising and arranged a poster campaign, I found out that Westminster City Council had a ban on stage hypnotists. As sure as hell they weren't going to buy any of the 'meeting of minds' crap. Or were they? Paul and I met the appropriate council officials and persuaded them to allow us to put the show on. Perhaps he'd hypnotised them too?

He left the punters at the interval sitting at the back of the stage. Then he'd walk around behind the curtain putting them in a deeper trance. All jolly good fun. That is until he stuck a six inch needle through the face of one of them and drew it out the other side. I was standing backstage at the time when he performed this little routine. It was something I'd never seen him do before. After he retrieves the needle he takes a bow and announces, '*Voila*, look no blood!' And true to his word there was no blood. I went into meltdown. The insurance I'd arranged was never going to cover something like this. If the man had gone in to shock or ended up with septicaemia we'd both be done for grievous bodily harm.

For the dénouement of the show, Paul would give them all a post-hypnotic suggestion.

'I will shortly send you back to your seats. But when you hear me stamp my foot three times you will see a leprechaun holding a pot of gold. You will stand up and shout, *I can see a leprechaun,* then you will chase him, wherever he goes, to get at his pot of gold.' Unreal! He sends them back to their seats, stamps his foot, they all jump and chase the nonexistent leprechaun all over the theatre, out in to street, all the time shouting, *there's a leprechaun* and then proceed to run after said leprechaun. Heaven forbid the apparition decides to leg it across a busy road with a bunch of hypnotised people in hot pursuit!

The entire experience lost me thirty thousand pounds.

Dave Stewart called me a week or so after the show closed. He asked if I could hop on a plane and fly to Detroit to shoot *Women Are Doing It For Themselves,* a single from their *Be Yourself Tonight* album featuring Aretha Franklin. He told me he couldn't go himself as he was otherwise engaged and I could put his contribution on in post-production. I was immediately suspicious; he'd never missed a shoot before. Annie was working on some new material in New York and he suggested I went via Manhattan, meet up with her, and then we'd fly on to Detroit together. Detroit is home to Aretha, and as she suffers from pteromechanophobia (isn't Google wonderful?) she wasn't about to load her sizeable bulk on a plane and fly anywhere.

I checked in to the Algonquin in the heart of midtown Manhattan and after a quick shower took a cab over to see Annie in her rented apartment on Fifth and Broadway. She and her new boyfriend Billy Poveda were holed up in New York for three months where she was writing new material.

I liked Billy. He'd met Annie when he was a dancer on one of the Eurythmic's videos in the States. Not one of mine. The three of us had spent a lot of time together but I always respected his space. She insisted I stayed with them rather than the hotel. I was a little wary of this arrangement but since Billy had no problem with it, I agreed. He was spending a lot of time on his own while Annie was working and I was always good for a laugh or two!

I persuaded Annie to take some time out and we went to see Martin Scorsese's quirky movie, *After Hours*, a low budget film, shot in New York. The last shot shows our 'hero' being dumped out of a van encased in plaster of paris outside a huge ornate gold painted wrought iron gate.

We left the cinema and decided to find a coffee bar. After walking a few blocks we turned into a street and came face to face with the gates from the movie. That's New York! I looked around for anyone covered in plaster but saw only a fruit stall. Annie went over to buy some apples. As the woman weighed them she looked at Annie curiously and said, 'Has anyone ever told you you look like that girl from that English band, what's their name?' she thought for a second or two and said,' Yeah! That one from The Eurythmics!' Annie, smiling and offering a five dollar bill said, 'I get that all the time.'

Annie was fine with the fans when actually recognised. The only time I saw her get a little pissed off was when we were having dinner in a restaurant in London. We were seated a little too near the window and a small crowd had gathered. Annie didn't appreciate a gaggle of people watching her nibble her salad. Personally I don't even like my nearest and dearest watching me eat at all, but then I am a little weird! After words with the manager we moved to the back of the restaurant; he didn't help any by then playing *Love Is A Stranger* over the restaurant speakers!

A day later we flew to Detroit and headed to our hotel. Detroit is a god forsaken city. The motor industry that gave employment to its population had almost given up the ghost. With little other work available, the city was going downhill fast. It was reflected in the swathe of boarded up shops and restaurants. It still is.

My producer had already spent five days scouting for a suitable studio and crew and we settled on a large sound stage off Lincoln Boulevard. Set dressers tarted up the stage and hung a large screen on the back wall behind where Annie and Aretha were to perform. This is where I would superimpose Dave's guitar solos.

Aretha arrived in a limo large enough to carry the population of a small town. It was a relatively simple shoot. They stood on the huge stage and belted out the number. I soon noticed that Aretha kept her distance from Annie while performing and rarely spoke to her during the breaks. While this didn't necessarily affect the shoot it did make things a little uncomfortable for the rest of us. Neither spoke to me about any problem and I figured it best not to ask. Dave would no doubt fill me in later.

The lunch break was an eye opener. My production manager had arranged catering as is the norm. The food wasn't at all bad. Aretha had her meals sent in. Maybe we had something in common: maybe she didn't like people watch her eat either. Anyway, it seems she was a big fan of ribs. Lots and lots of ribs. I passed by her dressing room. Seeing her eat was an unsettling experience. She gnawed at those pork ribs as if her life depended on it. I'd never seen so many ribs stripped bare in such a short a time other than watching hyenas at a zoo.

I took the film back to London to edit after going via New York to spend a few more days with Annie and Billy. Billy and I mostly hung out while Annie was consumed by her writing. The world renowned engineer and mixer Eric 'ET' Thorngen who'd worked on the music soundtrack for *1984,* called the apartment. He was in town working on Robert Palmer's *Rip Tide* album. We'd got on well and he asked me over to the studio for a drink and dinner. Being completely ignorant of the reputations of music producers I had no idea how much respect ET commanded in the business. We'd met in Jamaica and had plenty of laughs together.

We were both enthusiastic marching powder fans and became mates.

He was a big man and always wore his trademark cowboy hat. The fact that he was revered by most of the world's top musicians left him untouched. He had a great heart. He hugged me till I thought my lungs would collapse and then introduced me to Robert Palmer. I can't say I was a fan. I'm not even sure I'd heard anything he'd done before. He considered himself a huge star and expected to be treated as such. But that was difficult for me as a) it's not my style and b) I couldn't have picked him out in a police line up, comprising the seven dwarves and a rock god.

I'd read in some tabloid that he was fiercely anti-drugs especially as he had young children. So I was a little surprised to be ushered in to a private room at the back of the studio where a large mirror covered in a mound of coke was the centrepiece on a table. ET, ever the gentleman, handed me a rolled up hundred dollar bill and invited me to partake. When I'd finished Robert and ET did the business. Robert had nearly finished his musical contribution for the day but ET had another hour or so to go, so Robert invited me back to his hotel for a drink and I do mean *a* drink.

ET didn't show up for nearly two hours and in that time I'd been offered one small bottle of brandy from the room's mini bar. A generous host he wasn't. He even limited me to just one line of coke while he took himself off to the bathroom with the regularity usually only reserved for people suffering from incontinence.

ET finally showed and we left Robert to his ongoing bathroom activities and went to dine in Little Italy. We both liked our wine and ordered a rather expensive bottle of Frascati. I tasted it and found it corked and asked the waiter for another bottle. He froze and stared at me as though I'd just asked him to give me a blow job, then left to get the manager. It turns out we'd stumbled into a mini mafia haunt.

The manager, wore a tailored bright blue suit, I knew it was handmade because even in New York you couldn't buy off the peg suits that required more material than a medium sized tent. This guy was huge.

Owning a restaurant must have been a godsend for him.

'You don't like my wine?' This, believe me, wasn't a question it was an outright challenge. Gazing over at the mountain of flesh standing before me I thought very carefully about my answer.

'I'm so sorry to have to mention this,' I said in my best British accent hoping it might deflect what might have been his natural tendency to have us both propping up some bridge and keeping company with Jimmy Hoffa. 'But I think the wine may be corked.'

He grabbed the bottle from the ice bucket, his hand so huge that it nearly covered the entire bottle and went to point at the label, but there wasn't one. He turned the bottle round a couple of times looking puzzled. Then he peered in the bucket and dipped his hand in it and began fishing around. No label. He looked at us and a huge grin enveloped his fleshy face. 'Hey guys, what can I say?' That's all he said and sent the waiter scurrying off to find another bottle. What not being able to find the label had to do with the wine being corked, I wasn't about to ask.

Over the meal I asked ET if it were true that doing a lot of coke took away what musicians call the top end. That's the ability to hear the treble to you and I. For a record producer I guess that's not a great thing to suffer from. He just shrugged and grinned and told me there were always ways to compensate if you suffered from some hearing defect. I guess that's true. Though after I had my eyes tested, and had to wear glasses, the quality of my work started to go downhill quickly. But then maybe it was because I was just getting old.

We left the restaurant and hailed a cab. The driver, an Israeli, wanted to know what we were doing in his city. I began to tell him when he tail ended the car in front. New York, because it was always on the brink of financial ruin in the 1980's, never attended to the enormous number of potholes that pitted their roads so they covered them with large sheets of metal. Our cabbie, seeing the car in front a little late slammed on his brakes at the very moment the front wheels came in contact with said metal sheet, hence the skid and destroyed fender. ET struck his head on the heavy duty perspex that separated us from the driver.

We exited the cab and crossed over to the sidewalk, me a little shaken, ET with a blinding headache. After the cabbie had words with the guy he'd hit, he ambled over to us and put his hand out. 'Twenty bucks?' he said with a straight face. We looked at him and shook our heads. 'Fifteen?' he asked. 'Ten?' We walked off to find another cab. I had to admire the guy. He wanted us to pay him for nearly maiming us. That's New York.

I returned to London to shoot Dave's segment which we did in The Church in Crouch End. When the crew arrived, I asked him what was going on. What exactly was Aretha's problem with Annie and why did he stay in London?

'Couldn't say anything at the time Jon,' he said, his strong Sunderland accent even more pronounced than usual. 'But when we were recording in Paris, Annie showed up with Annie Leibovitz. (a world renowned American gay photographer) and Aretha thought she was gay.'

'She is,' I said.

'Not Leibovitz, Annie.'

'Oh!'

'She's homophobic.'

'Annie,' I said surprised.

'No, Aretha.'

'Oh!'

'Anyway that probably explains the atmosphere between them.'

'And why you didn't show up. Cause you didn't want to have to handle it. Right?' No answer. We got on with the shoot.

In those wonderfully far off days there was a kids Saturday morning show called *The Multi Coloured Swap Shop* presented by Noel Edmonds. They used to play the latest videos and a have a guest pop star review them. Elton John was on that day and so was *Women Are Doing It For Themselves.* 'It doesn't look like they're together,' Elton observed, 'I think one of them was added on in the edit.' He was certainly right about the 'together' comment!

CHAPTER FORTY
AZOFF, BUFFET AND BLACK BANDS

In the time I spent in LA I had become a close friend of the wonderful Susan Markheim, then Irving Azoff's right hand. Irving was an iconic figure in the music business. A small man with a mighty reputation. He managed the Eagles and was credited with saving MCA from bankruptcy. Since those days Susan has gone on to run a hugely successful management company. I was having coffee with her one afternoon and Irving emerges from his office and shouts, 'Ready!' She nods and says, 'I'll get them all out to the coaches.' As Irving turns to leave he says, 'Roseman you're coming.'

'Susan, what is going on?'

'Jimmy Buffet doesn't feel we're giving him the attention he deserves. He's playing a gig in Anaheim and Irving is bussing the entire company down to see him.'

'Who's Jimmy Buffet?' I ask, perhaps rather naively. Susan knew me well. She was neither surprised nor disappointed. "All you need to know Jon, is that he's one of our biggest acts.' Ok then.

'Where is Anaheim?'

'It's about forty miles down the freeway in Orange County. It'll take us just over an hour to get there.'

I found myself on one of four coaches heading north west to a place I'd vaguely heard of with a gaggle (perhaps that should be a 'murder'?) of record company executives. On the coach I'm given a plastic badge emblazoned with the single word BUFFET to stick on my T-shirt. The coach took Whittier Boulevard for miles and passed under a railroad bridge over the San Gabriel River. Beer was passed round and Irving held court at the front of the coach.

We arrive at the Arena and Irving herds as many people as he can squeeze in to Jimmy's dressing room. The man is astounded to see the boss of his record company and his retinue pouring into the small room.

An hour later, having had no lunch, while watching the man perform, I'm starving. I ask Irving where the food is. He shakes his head, 'There's no food,' he says. 'But', I protest, pointing to my badge, 'it says there's a buffet.' I wasn't joking but he thought I was.

MCA looked after a then unknown black band called Ready For The World. At around this time MTV were getting some bad press when it came to showing the videos of black artists. They claimed that their music didn't fit the main stream saying they (MTV) reflected only the Billboard's top hundred. The late Michael Jackson was one of the very few exceptions. Whether he was black, white or pink at the time I can't remember.

Susan asked me, as a favour, to nip over to New York and do a cheapo video for Ready For The World's new single, *Oh Sheila*. Record companies didn't want to spend much cash on videos for black bands because they reckoned they wouldn't get any airtime on MTV. It became a sort of self-fulfilling prophecy.

I sent my producer Robert Lombard, on ahead over to prep the shoot and followed on a couple of days later. Robert has since gone on to become something big in the porn industry. I'd known him for quite a while and his new career came as no surprise to me. When I shot in America, he'd always make sure there were girls around to 'look after' the key people!

I check in to my hotel and he's arranged a meeting with the crew to meet me so we can discuss the shoot. I'd suggested to Robert over the phone from LA that we film it fake/live in a club; nothing special, to reflect the limited budget. The meeting seems to go well, but Robert appeared to be holding something back. I smell something but decide, as always, to go with the flow.

He's arranged a limo to take me down to the club on the afternoon of the shoot. We were going to film until nine or ten that night and then let in an audience to give it that 'live' feel.

The club's in Harlem. Harlem could be a scary place for us white folk back then. Now I begin to understand what he's been keeping from me. The club was dirt cheap to hire he told me with a wicked grin. I found out some months later it was given for nothing though Robert's budget reflected a five hundred dollar facility fee! He hustled me in to the club and threw his arm around my shoulders as if he was working for the secret service. Another thing I later found out was that two white guys were shot dead outside the club the previous night!

The club is run by some heavy dudes who look at me as we pass them as if I'm a piece of takeaway fried chicken. I notice for the first time our entire crew bar one is white. The token black guy is the runner. How could Lombard stick me with this? Money!? He made more than me on the shoot. I flew back to London and edited the track and sent it off to Susan in LA.

Three weeks later she's on the phone.

'Jon, Jon you've gotta come straight over. It's gone to number one.'

'What's gone to number one?'

'*Oh Sheila*!' MTV want a copy of the tape but we don't think it's good enough.' Gee thanks!

'What did you expect for fifteen thousand dollars, Michael Jackson's 'Thriller'?'

'I'm not saying you did a bad job for us it's just that.....' Her voice trails off. Bottom line they were a black band and there was no reason to give them a decent budget. Now it's gone to number one it's all hands to the pumps. My hands. I had to fly over to LA, hire an edit suite, and re-cut the bloody thing with some 'special' effects to give it a more 'expensive' feel. It still looked cheap to me though everyone seemed to like the new version.

CHAPTER FORTY ONE
DAVE STEWART, TOM PETTY AND PHONE SEX AND BOB DYLAN

Before I could fly back to London, Dave Stewart called me. He's in LA.

'How's it going?' He wanted to know.

'Why?'

'Your office says you're in LA so I'm calling you.'

'Ok.'

'So I'm working with Bob Dylan and we want to make some videos. Interested?'

'When?'

'Next week or two. Why don't you come on over?'

He gives me the address of Jimmy Iovine's home in Brentwood. Iovine has produced for the likes of John Lennon, Bruce Springsteen and Tom Petty. I'd never heard of him either. He turns out to be a great bloke and married to an ex-Playboy bunny. They are a lovely couple. We have drinks by the pool and Dave explains he's producing Dylan's new album and also working with Tom Petty. Putting my cards on the table at this point I'll be absolutely frank. While working with Dylan may have been some childhood fantasy of Dave's I was never particularly a fan. Not that I didn't appreciate his iconic status. It just didn't mean that much to me.

Dave's very excited as is Jimmy. As is Fergal Sharkey who shows up. For those of you who remember him and for those of you who haven't heard of him he'd had a major hit that year with *A Good Heart*. He was over in LA working with one of the members of Tom Petty's band. Confused? Me too.

The following day Dave asks me to drive him down to Tom Petty's house which is a forty minute drive out of LA. Petty has a recording studio in his garage. I liked him immediately. He treated me as guest in his home and couldn't do enough to make me comfortable. It made me feel very uneasy. It's always been the case that whenever people take care of me I feel a terrible Jewish guilt.

I sat in on the recording for a couple of hours. Previously I'd arranged to meet my American lawyer for coffee, so I told Dave I had to get going and arranged to have dinner with him and Sharkey that night. I asked Tom for directions back to Beverley Hills telling him I had to leave to meet my lawyer. It turned out we shared the same attorney. He drew me a map but I'm useless at directions. The more he explained the more confused I became. I'd probably end up in Tijuana. Finally he said, 'Jon it's easier for me to show you. If I take you as far as Laurel Canyon can you find your way from there?' I could.

He tells everyone he'll be back in twenty minutes and I follow his car to Laurel Canyon. Just like a real person. No rock star pretensions at all!

That evening Bob Dylan also turns up for dinner with Dave and Sharkey. I had no preconceptions of the man though people had told me he could be very difficult and didn't suffer fools gladly. When I spent time with him he was none of these things. The conversation ranged over dozens of topics from American politics to baseball. I didn't much like Sharkey though. I got the feeling that his recent number one in the UK charts made him feel up there with Stewart and Dylan which was patently absurd.

Dave and Bob had decided to shoot all three promos as fake/live in a hall reminiscent of a prom night. The band Dave had put together to back Dylan included Clem Burke, the drummer from Blondie, Phil Chen, one of the worlds' leading session guitarists, Tina Weymouth from Talking Heads and the wretched Sharkey on tambourine. We needed to find a venue so Bob decided we'd drive round LA the following day to do a recce.

We drove for bloody hours and finally settled on a hall attached to the First Methodist Church in Hollywood. On the way back, we pass an old bus depot and Bob catches a glimpse of a dilapidated fifties coach.

He decides he wants to add more colour to the promo and suggests we hire it and film the band getting on it as though they were heading for a real gig.

The following day we all meet to finalise what we're going to do. Bob has brought his manager/lawyer along. After we take a break for a couple of beers his manager pulls me to one side. 'You're not seriously going to drive that old coach round West LA (a pretty dangerous place at the best of times) with all those guys?' he asks me. I told him to take it up with his client. It wasn't my idea and I didn't care whether we did it or not. We did it.

We shot in the coach for a few hours, then a mile away from the church, it breaks down. Some of the biggest names in rock and roll have to walk through the streets of West LA to make it back to the Church. No one gave us a second look!

Dave or Bob wanted to make the video more authentic by having an audience. I call the local radio station, tell them what we're doing, and who we're doing it with, and say we want a hundred people by five o'clock, first come first served. I arrange security for the expected hoards. Four thirty floats by, no audience. I call the radio station again. They tell me they thought I was joking! I told them I needed the audience in an hour. We got our audience.

The shoot went smoothly other than Sharkey jumping up and down slamming his tambourine into his thigh like a man who'd taken intravenous speed.

The next day Reed drops by my hotel to say hi. I'm on my way to Iovine's to meet Dave. Reed tags along. On the way over he tells me he's set up a new business. Phone sex. He's put some of his ill gotten gains into it and apparently business is booming. We arrive at Iovine's house where Bob's 'back up' band are hanging and Reed tells everyone about his new venture. As ever, Dave wants to try it out.

The house has about eight extensions so we all grab a phone and listen to him as he gives his credit card details and is then put through to one of the girls.

'Hello,' he introduces himself.

'Hi. What would you like today?' a sexy girly voice asks. Reed, who's listening next to me, tells me that it's Daisy one of his best girls.

'I like rubber,' Dave says.

'Ok. I'm wearing a rubber dress. It's real tight and clings to.....' Dave interrupts.

'No I mean I like a rubber diving suit.' We all start to laugh.

'Is there anyone else with you? I thought I heard someone laugh.' She's not happy at sharing the call. Dave, who's standing about ten feet from me shakes his hand and puts his finger to his lips as in 'everyone shut the fuck up.' He continues with the call.

Tom Petty arrives. He's gazing around at a bunch of guys all with telephone receivers glued to their ears. I grab him and whisper what we're doing. He rushes off to find an extension. Guys can be so predictable! By all accounts Daisy was a great talker.

CHAPTER FORTY TWO
ALLEN KLEIN AND UFOs

The late Allen Klein, a man of diminutive stature and a shark's appetite, was one of rock and roll's legends. People either loved or hated him but as sure as hell on earth no one could ignore him. He was Lennon's choice to manage the Beatles and Jagger's for The Rolling Stones. I first met him in the mid seventies. A client of the Agency, John Fielding, who'd known Klein for several years, had been asked to do a major documentary for his company ABKO on UFO's. Fielding was a serious journalist, so I was surprised he'd even contemplate the job. As I'd said before, he had been an important member of the Sunday Times Insight team and helped expose the Thalidomide scandal.

I first met him on Weekend World where he taught me the finer things in life. He introduced me to good wines and expensive restaurants and always paid. Some weeks later the receipts for our gourmet life style always ended up on my desk for authorisation as part of his expenses. Fielding asked me to go to New York to cut his deal with Klein.

I was a little in awe of the man. I was aware of his reputation as a deal maker but went in with a firm figure in mind. I needn't have bothered. His office walls were covered in the paraphernalia of a music mogul. Gold and platinum discs covered the walls of his office occasionally making space for photos of him with his various artists past and present. Klein with Lennon/Harrison/Jagger and so on. His desk was a vast mahogany affair littered with even more framed pictures.

He spent an hour talking about the Beatles and how well he'd done for them after taking over from Brian

Epstein. I thought McCartney may have had a different
perspective on his achievements. It was common
knowledge that he hated Klein. Strangely he went to
great pains to tell me how fond he was of the ex-Beatle
and that their rift was much exaggerated. As fascinating
as all this was, I kept wondering when we'd get to
Fielding's deal. Finally he got round to it.

'It'll be three months work and I'll pay a hundred
and twenty thousand dollars.'

'I was thinking......'

'Don't think. That's the deal.' He stood up, held out
his hand to shake on it and I did. Well that was a waste
of time.

'Have you plans for dinner?' he asked.

'Not really.'

'Come to my house in The Hampton's, say seven
o'clock.'

Why he'd invited a total stranger to dinner I had no
idea. The Hampton's were inhabited by the rich and
famous and were on the East side of Long Island about
an hours' drive from the centre of Manhattan. I called
Fielding to tell him of the great deal I'd done for him and
he was very happy! When I mentioned I'd been invited
for dinner he wasn't surprised. 'You'll have a great time'
he said, 'enjoy!'

The house was, as I'd expected, a mansion, costing
back then a few million dollars. Today its value would
be more like fifteen million plus change but with the
global meltdown who knows! It was a warm evening and
he was sitting outside with a diet coke, wearing jeans
and an open neck check shirt. He was all smiles and
quite unlike the rottweiler everyone knew him to be. I
walked up a series of stone steps to be greeted by his
wife Betty. She was in her mid thirties and very
beautiful. She was also a gracious hostess. I sat
opposite Klein and Betty handed me a glass of
champagne. 'I'll leave you two to talk while I get on with
the dinner.' She left us and it was only then I noticed an
ornate chess set on the table between us.

'You play Jon?'

'Yes.'

'Any good?'

'I've had my moments.'

'Then let's play.'

I'd travelled across the Atlantic to negotiate a deal with one of the music business's legends and now I'm sitting outside his palatial home on his veranda playing chess with the man himself. The evening could only get odder. It did. While we played he talked about his foray into the movie business.'

In 1962 he'd made a completely forgettable movie called *Without Each Other*. The film is an utter disaster and having spent millions of his own money on it he can't find any interest from a distributor. He decides to gamble on hiring the world famous composer and conductor Dimitri Tiomkin to write the theme music. He figures that a soundtrack by such a renowned composer would at least guarantee distribution. No distribution meant no money.

Dimitri demands a suite at the Beverly Hills Hotel in LA and three hundred thousand dollars to write the score. Allen agrees. Dimitri moves in to the most expensive suite available and uses room service relentlessly. Having not heard anything for two weeks Allen calls him and is told 'it's coming along nicely.' A month goes by and now he's haemorrhaging money to the hotel and still no finished music. Finally after thousands of dollars he's got his soundtrack and it's dubbed into the picture. Still no distributor wants it. He decides to enter it for the Cannes Film Festival. When he doesn't hear anything from them after a fortnight he calls them.

'What are you doing with my fucking picture?' He demands. When they find out who they are talking to, they offer profuse apologies and say they've never received it.

'Come on Allen you never sent it in the first place,' I say. He looks at me as if to say 'are you suggesting.....' What he says is, 'Jon I promise you I sent it.' Neither of us is really buying into that. Anyway they are so full of remorse because he managed to persuade them they must have lost his magnus opus that they tell him they'll open the Festival with the movie, sight unseen.

The sheer *chutzpah* of the man. So it opens the Festival - and he still can't find anyone to distribute it!

I lost the game of chess and that really pissed me off but delighted Allen. The three of us had dinner around a table that could seat thirty people. As the main course arrives, some salmon concoction, served by their Mexican maid, a beautiful woman drifts in and sits down at the far end of the table. She doesn't speak and I'm not introduced. She's served a little salad, nibbles at it and then stands up and drifts away. Neither Betty nor Allen mention the visitor, it was as if it never happened. I found out later she was an Italian actress who Allen 'knew' well. After the meal Betty and I sat on the veranda and chatted about nothing in particular. Then she steered the conversation round to my client John Fielding. She began asking a lot of questions about John's personal life. I was getting more uncomfortable by the minute. After an hour of this cross-examination I'm looking around for Allen but he'd gone to bed! I made my excuses and fled back to my hotel. I was woken at eight thirty by Betty asking me out to lunch. This was getting weird. I told her I had to fly to Miami. When I got hold of Fielding I asked him what was going on, although I had my suspicions. He confirmed them. He was shagging Betty!

CHAPTER FORTY THREE
LIVE AID, ANNIE LENNOX, KLEIN AGAIN AND BOBBY WOMACK

Live Aid hit us in July 1985. A few months or so before it burst on to the world's television screens I was in New York visiting a friend at CBS Records. The receptionist told me that Bob Geldof was in one of their conference rooms and would I like to say hi. I've no idea how she knew I knew him, perhaps she thought that England being such a small country everyone knew everyone!

I popped in to the conference room, Bob feet up on the table, was in animated conversation with one of the other Rats. He waved for me to sit down.

'So listen we've got to do it.' He was saying, 'I'm not doing all this for nothing. It could be the way back for fuck's sake.' It was obvious to me that he originally saw Live Aid as the chance to revive the career of his band. No one, least of all Geldof, had any conception what a major iconic event it would turn out to be.

Annie Lennox and her boyfriend, Billy Poveda, were staying the weekend with Pearl and I in Sussex. Billy was one of the good guys. Being with Annie couldn't be easy. In all relationships that involve a star and a non star, various pressures built up. After a time the non star starts to be treated like a minion and unless they are very secure, with a career of their own, the cracks begin to appear and widen and deepen. They are rarely filled and smoothed over satisfactorily. Billy held out, I guess, for as long as he could.

My kids were watching Live Aid on the TV and it soon became obvious that this was no ordinary event. After twenty minutes I could see that Annie's expression was saying, 'Shit! why didn't we do this?' She went very quiet. I finally asked why the Eurythmics weren't there. She didn't reply. They'd been invited, but had said no. Normally Dave and Annie have good instincts; this time those instincts let them down.

I suggested she should call in and speak live to the studio presenters saying how sorry Dave and she were for not being able to perform and wishing them every success. She mulled it over and passed and we left the kids watching the show and went out for dinner. The concert was still on when we got back. She had been fine over dinner as we engaged in our normal student like debates, but she became quite upset when she watched what we all knew was going to become an historic uber-gig.

She was prone to many moods and the people who surrounded her let her get away with some bad behaviour. I wouldn't. One day after editing *Who's That Girl* Dave and I turned up at their converted church in Crouch End where Annie, the band and backing singers were rehearsing for their upcoming tour. They had built a large stage in the well of the church which was big enough to contain a lighting rig as well. As we passed by the stage during a break I said 'hi' to her. She completely blanked me. I stood and looked up at her and said, 'That's just unnecessary Annie.' She suddenly looked down and apologised. The rest of the band turned away in embarrassment whether for me or her I didn't know. All successful artists are prone to fits of tantrums and bad manners mostly because they can get away with it. Their entourages or hangers on make it so easy for them. If us mere mortals acted like them, most of the time we'd get a smack.

None of this explains her deep sensitivity, particularly to her critics. Annie and Billy picked me up one evening to go out for dinner. She was upset and sat in the passenger seat not saying a word. So I asked Billy what was wrong. Apparently Julie Burchell had reviewed their latest album and wrote, 'Every time I look in the sky and see a shooting star I imagine it's Annie Lennox coming crashing down in a plane.' I can't recall which album she was referring to but as I said to Annie, 'Who the fuck is Julie Burchell anyway?' All performers get their bad reviews, most, admittedly not as vindictive as Burchell's, but artists have to inure themselves against such things, otherwise they'll stop creating anything, for fear of what might be written or said about them.

John Knowles, an old mate who was running the marketing division for MCA, called me to tell me Allen Klein was in town and wanted to meet me. He'd remembered me even though ten years had passed since our dinner in The Hamptons. I met him at Claridges hotel. He was representing Bobby Womack and as I was, as he put it, 'family', he wanted me to direct his videos and a live concert at the Hammersmith Odeon where he was doing three nights. How or why I was 'family' was utterly beyond me. Apparently Allen felt we were similar characters, and that I wouldn't take any shit from his artist. Womack had an edgy reputation. He liked his substances and could be extremely difficult to work with. By this time I'd worked with so many artists that 'difficult' had been eliminated from my vocabulary. I shot the concert first. Klein gave me *carte blanche.*

As Womack was doing three nights I hired one of the best lighting cameraman in the business, John Metcalfe, to go with me on the first night to check out the band's lighting and to use his experience for camera positions. I was going to use thirteen cameras. It was all shot on film but each camera would provide a video feed to their own monitor situated at the back of the hall allowing me to see what the cameramen were seeing. That way, over radio links, I could direct them to give me the pictures I wanted. Having *carte blanche* was exceedingly rare. I was given the authority to change the band's lighting in any way I wanted. That meant Metcalfe could not only change the gels (the coloured filters that cover the lights) but also augment the rig with additional lights if he found it necessary. This was almost unheard of in the annals of a touring band's lighting crew. None of the lighting guys however were tempted to take up this sacrilegious interference with Allen. In any event Metcalfe decided that the lights were fine and no twiddling was required. If only I'd had him blood tested for coke the disaster that descended on me might have been avoided. I suggested to Womack we do a dress run on the afternoon of the shoot. He was more than happy to go along with this.

On the day my crew arrived and everything was set up he went through his set. This was a luxury very few directors would ever enjoy. It wasn't just the cost of paying the crew, but no artist/band I'd ever heard of would go through such an energy sapping performance immediately prior to a live gig. Bobby and I worked really well together. I asked him to alter slightly some of his 'routines' to accommodate our cameras and he never objected.

I had dinner with Klein and his daughter the night before the shoot. He was in fine form and the wine flowed freely. I had to take it easy as I needed to be clear headed for the concert. It was over the coffee that he told me, almost in passing, 'By the way if when you're filming tomorrow and you want Bobby to redo a song it's not a problem.'

'I'm sorry?' I said.

'If you don't like what you've shot just let the backstage crew know and he'll redo the song for you.' Redo? This was unprecedented but it only went to show the hold Klein had over his artists.

The shoot was exhausting but I felt we'd got everything we needed. The film was sent to the labs for processing.

Two days later I had to shoot two Womack videos. One of the tracks, *I'll Still Be Looking Up to You* featured one of the world's great saxophonists, Wilton Felder. As soon as I arrived at the studio, Allen was on the phone.

'Jon don't forget you're paid to film Womack.'

'I know that Allen,' I said.

'Don't fuck with me Roseman, you know where I'm coming from.'

'Allen *where* are you coming from?'

'I don't want Felder all over it. Ok?'

'Allen if you don't trust me, direct it yourself.' I hung up.

The filming went well and we had a great day together. Klein turned up late in the afternoon and even he was seen enjoying himself.

I filmed some location footage for one of the clips in Brixton and everywhere we went Womack was besieged by an army of fans. It was an unusually warm day and we took a break in a local park. We were sitting together smoking a cigarette when he suddenly turned to me and said, 'Jon you're the only person who's ever told me what to do. When we were rehearsing you asked me to move here and there and it felt real good. I'd like you to manage me.' This was not what I should be listening to. If Allen ever found out about this conversation I'd be wheelchair bound for months. I told him he had the best manager in the world and changed the subject round to who were better fucks, black or white women.

A week later I turned up at the film edit suite to view the rushes. It was then that I saw the catastrophic damage the drugs had done to Metcalfe's judgment. More than a third of the pictures were so dark I may as well have filmed with no light at all. He'd fucked me big time.

Allen had given me every opportunity to change anything and everything but Metcalfe had taken the view that no changes were required. I had to tell Klein it was a write off. He wasn't a happy man. He didn't want to hear excuses and blaming Metcalfe would have been a total waste of time. I was the director and rightly it was down to me. I managed to get the record company to pay the crew, that is everyone but Metcalfe.

A few days later I get a call from the ACTT, the technician's union, telling me they've had a formal complaint from a Mr John Metcalfe that he hadn't been paid! I explained that Metcalfe was a coke abusing asshole and that he had solely and exclusively destroyed the entire shoot as well as my relationship with Allen Klein and MCA Records. Finally I invited them to view the rushes. They never took up my offer and Metcalfe and the ACTT vanished from my life.

CHAPTER FORTY FOUR
PEARL AND LIBEL

It was 1986 and Pearl's breast cancer had reappeared. She was thirty nine. She was now being treated by Professor Baum who was then at Kings College London. He was the best of the best and one of the world's leading oncologists. At that time he only treated national health patients and we visited him at his office in the East End of London. What always struck me about him was his voice which exuded calm and optimism. He advised an immediate mastectomy. The feelings we were all going through at this time are difficult to describe. It seems almost prosaic to write that you have to have been through it to understand the deep emotions that swarm through your mind. The surgery went well and we visited the Prof every few months for checkups.

We would travel up from Sussex to his clinic at King's College Hospital in Denmark Hill in South East London where a member of his staff would examine Pearl for a few minutes then head back home. A year or so passed before I asked the Prof how beneficial these visits actually were. His answer came as no surprise. It appeared it was more a comfort gesture than anything else; a physical examination unless further lumps were actually found was a waste of time. I never mentioned this to Pearl.

Like many people embroiled in the battle with cancer, you try any avenue, no matter how bizarre, to fight it. Professor Baum was dismissive about alternative therapies. He was particularly against diets that claimed all sorts of almost magical success. His view was if you liked a steak and a glass of wine, enjoy. This didn't stop us from pursuing some pretty weird stuff. We tried special massages, crystals and Chinese herbal medicines. Pearl would mix the herbs in a large saucepan and stir them for hours, then pass the mixture through a sieve and drink it twice a day. The after taste of boiled twigs lingered for hours. Desperate times called for desperate measures.

I decided to hang up my pop promo boots. With Pearl's illness and four young children, I needed to be a constant presence at home. John Willcocks, who had been running the agency with little or no interference from me, wasn't too happy I'd returned to what he, understandably perhaps, had come to consider his own domain. Tensions ran high. Also I was able to spend more time marketing the video editing company where business was slow.

It would only be in retrospect that I would become aware that my life had changed irrevocably with my retirement from making videos. I had been living the life of a single man. I travelled and stayed where and when I wanted to, never having to make allowances for anyone else. Pearl being the earth mother she was had looked after our children brilliantly allowing me to float around without having to worry about the wellbeing of my family. I'd missed so much with this wayward life style and it's one of my life's most serious regrets.

Mike Hollingsworth, Anne Diamond's husband, called me to set up a meeting with the intention of the Agency representing her. She was then a major face on television via TVAM and he was running Music Box the first European music station.

I'd always got on well with Mike. Like me, he has his detractors. Our meeting went well and the Agency took her on much to Willcocks' chagrin. It seemed *any* involvement I had irritated him. His attitude began to wind me up to the extent that I started to feel one of us had to go, and that one wasn't going to be me.

I was still in the middle of litigating with Howard Kruger. After we'd parted company he'd gone on to represent snooker players. Image is all important in the media business. No client wants to be represented by an agent who has worn shirt cuffs, wears a threadbare suit and lives in a council house. Kruger took it all a bit too far. Barry Hearn told me that at one Embassy World Snooker Championship in the Crucible in Sheffield, he was paged and told his driver was waiting in reception. Seconds later the tannoy burst in to life again announcing that Mr Kruger's helicopter's pilot was waiting for him!

Image was always a major issue. This was my ongoing undoing. Presenting an image I neither really wanted and could rarely afford. It wasn't as though at this particular time I was penniless. I had a reasonable income from both VEC and the agency. While the production business provided a good life, it mostly lost money, but the losses were manageable.

People were always under the impression that if you're filming all over the world, staying in nice hotels and drinking the occasional bottle of fine wine you're loaded. I think the history of the so-called "successful producer" paints a far different picture. The number of film producers who went belly up, on more than one occasion, is considerable. While not in the same league, nonetheless we all suffered from the same problem - hunger. Not money hunger but next-project-hunger. We were always planning the next two or three projects when we had no idea how the current ones were playing out. We thought that no matter how good the existing projects were, the next would always be the *one.*

I have always maintained that success is sixty percent luck, twenty percent recognising you've had the luck and the final twenty percent having the intelligence to use it to your advantage. I've never bought in to the saying, *you make your own luck.* If you're lucky, you're lucky. We have all met or read about people who have exceptional talent but achieved nothing. Others, who offer little, have gone on to enjoy fame and fortune. The TV business in particular is littered with examples.

A friend rang me to ask if I'd read the latest monthly edition of *Direction* Magazine. Not only had I not read it, I'd never heard of it. It was soon to take over my life. The magazine in itself was totally harmless and normally printed nothing more contentious than some piece of technology might be better than one of its competitors. Stuck in the middle of this issue of the magazine however is a two page article about me. Claiming amongst other things that I was a major distributor of cocaine. It was a little like opening The Times and finding a naked girl, legs akimbo, staring back at you with a smile that says, let's fuck!

I rang the editor.

'My name is Jon Roseman. I couldn't help noticing a story you've just written about me.'

'Yes.' As in 'your point is?'

'Did you leave me a message that I somehow missed asking me to comment on the story before you published?'

'No.'

'You are aware of the law of libel?'

'Yes.'

'Well it's coming your way.' I met my old friend and lawyer Ian Bloom and showed him the piece. The fact that a publisher doesn't give you the opportunity to comment on a highly poisonous article increases your chances of winning serious damages which can double your award if you win. A big "if". In those wonderful olden days there weren't any "no win no fee" deals with lawyers. You actually had to cough up real money to sue for libel. Legal aid didn't cover it. Ian, friend or not, had obligations to his partners and the barristers he instructed on my behalf. And while he could be a little flexible, he still required my cheque for five thousand pounds. That was just the beginning...

Direction Magazine was owned by Haymarket Publishing, which in turn was owned by Michael Heseltine, then deputy leader of the Conservative Party. Ian took me to see one of the country's leading libel barristers, David Eady QC, now Judge Eady QC, the senior High Court libel judge. There was no doubt we had a good case in that most of the article was a total fiction.

Letters were written. Battle had commenced. It took just over a month for my five grand to disappear. I had to come up with more. I've often had skirmishes with the press over the years about unfounded or totally fabricated stories of clients. I rarely advise suing for libel. The best way forward is to speak to the respective editors and try and negotiate an apology and never be greedy when it comes to damages. Over the years, I've gone out of my way to wine and dine media journalists and editors and forge relationships with them. It's so much easier if there's a mutual respect to settle things amicably. But this was different. There was a hidden agenda. Why would a fringe magazine that normally published bland pieces for the advertising industry print a character assassination of me?

Kruger!

In my experience, it takes at least half a dozen letters to be exchanged before things get moving. After a couple of months Haymarket paid ten thousand pounds into court. This is meant to get you off their back. A tidy sum which you're free to accept or ignore. If you actually end up in court and win but the award is less then the other side's payment in, you end up forking out their costs as well as your own from the time when the payment was made. In a major libel action that could be the best part of hundreds of thousands of pounds! As it is written, the lawyers never lose. The case ran into 1987.

David Eady QC told me to consider taking the money, the apology on offer and the costs to date. Years of drug abuse probably addled my brain and I refused. I wanted more, a lot more. The way I'd figured it, Heseltine was angling to be party leader at the time and this libel action could be used by the Labour press to show his company as a bunch of negligent lying shit-heads. Trust me, it takes a pretty addled mind to come up with that ridiculous scenario.

Pearl took the whole libel thing badly probably because she could see the effect it was having on me. I went to bed gnawing at it and woke up thinking of little else. I went to watch Brighton and Hove Albion play football and realised I'd lost twenty minutes of the game. My mind kept wandering everywhere but on the Seagulls. That, together with the ongoing litigation with Kruger, made my life hell.

Not much happened for six or seven months other than Ian secured a fixed trial date for the actual trial. Then, suddenly, *Direction* increased the payment into court to forty thousand pounds. My lawyers repeated their advice about the costs consequences of rejection. I still wanted more, much more. I'm not sure what my lawyers thought of my refusal to settle on these terms, other than they probably thought me a sandwich and thermos flask short of a picnic.

A couple of months later they paid in another thirty five thousand. I had, if I'd accepted it, seventy five thousand tax free pounds. Libel damages are tax free. Still I didn't budge. It's not incumbent on the plaintiff to decline a payment into court, so we just ignored it.

None of this was going down well with Pearl. The stress of the litigation and her own private nightmares may well have been aggravating her condition. She'd just decided to have plastic surgery for a breast reconstruction. Professor Baum was fantastic. He'd become very fond of her and I believe respected her bravery and wry sense of humour. He contacted one of the country's leading plastic surgeons who had a two year waiting list, and using his friendship with him, Pearl was operated on within three months. The following year she felt comfortable enough to sunbathe, topless, on holiday in Spain.

The libel case was trudging on as was my litigation with Kruger. Running both actions simultaneously was crippling me financially and emotionally. I spent some time investigating why the writer of the Direction article, Mathew Gwyther, would have been motivated to do such a piece in the first place and what, if any, was his connection with Kruger. To my knowledge I'd never heard of him, let alone met him.

A chance meeting with an old producer of mine made things a little clearer. Gwyther had been put up to it by Kruger he told me. Confirmation of sorts. He felt that if he could discredit me, it would force me to back off from the lawsuit I'd brought against him, because if you have no reputation to defend it becomes mighty difficult to win a libel action. I wasn't sure how sound that theory was until I thought back to a curious incident the year before.

I was still renting my tiny apartment in Conway Street. Some time back, soon after I'd begun the libel case, I'd had a break in and a few items were stolen. I didn't think any more of it. At this time I'd put on a few pounds and joined a gym yet again. As the weeks passed, the weight shifted and I was able to wear some clothes that had lain somewhat dormant for a while, a long while. Different clothes meant different shoes. As I slipped my foot in to one particular shoe I hadn't worn for a while I came across something small and hard. I removed a two inch block of cannabis. I don't smoke dope. It wasn't mine so consequently someone must have stashed it there. I didn't consider the find particularly suspicious at the time as I had some pretty odd visitors to my flat.

Two weeks later a friend, Jack Steven, who had been staying there while I was in Sussex, emerged from my temporary semi-basement abode to pick up his car. Suddenly a dozen policemen converged on him from two different directions. They asked him if he was me and despite his denials, they forced him back inside the flat waving a warrant to search for drugs. They found nothing. I have a canny suspicion that the "burglars" apart from removing a few items, left one behind. Had I not been so weight conscious I'd almost certainly have been done for possession. It's not rocket science to assume whoever planted it had every intention of calling the drugs squad.

I decided that the time had come to look Haymarket Publishing in the eye. The trial date was fast approaching. I asked Bloom to arrange a meeting with the other side's lawyers, who were Farrers, the Queen's solicitors, and a director of Haymarket. They agreed to a meeting and Ian rang me to say they wanted to know if their barrister could attend. I told him to tell them that, 'It wasn't a fucking peep show.' Their intention, no doubt, was to see how I would conduct myself under future cross- examination.

We all went to Farrers' Lincolns Inn office for the without prejudice meeting. By "all" I mean my solicitor, Ian Bloom and his articled clerk. We were ushered into their boardroom to be met by four Farrers' lawyers and a director of Haymarket. The room was a plush affair with deep pile carpets and paintings of their founding fathers all long dead and in lawyer heaven - if there is such a place.

Ian told me later that, even though the meeting was "off the record" and no barristers were present, he was still concerned about what I might say. He decided that, since I was determined to speak, and speak about the impact this stress was having on Pearl, he would unleash me. I told him that I doubted that he could have stopped me anyway, but it is always risky hiring a lawyer and yet wanting to bark yourself.

I kicked off the meeting by explaining to the director of Haymarket how I felt about the lies that Gwyther had printed about me. I explained how it was affecting my wife to the extent that it was aggravating her condition. I noticed a woman, who later turned out to be one of their senior solicitors, Mary Turbeville-Smythe, shake her head in disbelief. That was it for me. I reacted automatically. 'Don't shake your head like that, you fucking bitch!'. I doubt if those words had ever been uttered in the hallowed portals of Farrers. I continued to develop my *raison d'être* for pursuing the case to the elderly gentleman from Haymarket - I think I saw some sympathy in his eyes.

Ian Bloom got a call from Farrers that afternoon. 'Nice try from Roseman but we're not going to pay any more money.' I told Ian that I wanted a quarter of a million plus costs and that was my final and only position. I think he thought I'd truly lost it.

By now I'd borrowed close to a hundred thousand pounds to fund both this and the Kruger action. There was no way I could afford to go to court for either. Ian Bloom had cleverly set the Kruger trial date to coincide with the Embassy World Snooker Championship. As the trial date approaches, Kruger and his lawyers realise what we've done. They immediately apply to the High Court for a postponement.

The judge noted that the date was set nearly a year earlier and isn't best pleased to consider any delay. The Courts at that time were full over a year in advance. Kruger's barrister argued that he needs to be at the Crucible in Sheffield to advise his players. In all the years I'd known him, I'd never even seen him pick up a cue so what valid advice he could give his clients like Hurricane Higgins and Jimmy White was a complete mystery to me.

The judge however was thinking laterally. 'Perhaps you could ask Mr Kruger,' the judge suggested with just the hint of a smile, gazing down at the barrister, 'what advice he would be giving if two of his clients were drawn against each other?'

It was thrown out and finally Kruger was forced to settle. He agreed to pay the Company one hundred and sixty thousand pounds, this despite his accountants pleading with us that he was broke and had no assets. I guess the helicopter was rented. Still he tried to avoid payment. We applied to the court to serve him with a bankruptcy notice.

I travelled down to Brighton with the process server. Gary was in his early twenties, but had been doing the job for a few years. I'd decided to go with him as I knew Kruger would do anything he could to avoid getting served. We waited in a pub across the road from his office and at around one o'clock he emerged in the company of another man. They got into a car and sped off.

Gary, the calm operator that he was, crossed the road, walked in to Kruger's offices, asked for him, told he was at lunch and managed to catch a glimpse of his diary and noted he'd be back for a meeting at three.

We waited. When the pair of them returned I made certain Gary knew which one was our man as they were both of similar build. He strolled over to the two of them and asked Kruger to confirm his identity. Kruger coolly pointed to his friend saying that he was in fact Kruger. Gary held out the document, and as he went to serve it on his friend, he suddenly swung round and stuffed it in Kruger's hand. Job done! Kruger coughed up within the week.

This seemed to have a knock-on effect with Farrers. Within weeks of the Kruger settlement they topped up the payment into Court to one hundred thousand pounds. It would appear that some of Farrer's witnesses had done an about turn after Kruger's demise.

We're now getting ever closer to the trial date which was about ten weeks away. My life had been totally consumed by all this legal manoeuvring and I spent little time on either VEC or the Agency. Thankfully Pearl was feeling better and I did my best not to appear to be too preoccupied or aggravated by it all.

Two more weeks went by. Direction increased their offer to one hundred and fifty thousand. Things were looking up. I'd never heard of 'brief fees' before having never got so close to a trial before. Ian Bloom calls me to tell me that David Eady's clerks want the formal brief which would, automatically make Ian's firm liable for the brief fee. That's the system. So Ian needs financial cover from me. If I wanted the QC to sit down and start to work on trial preparation I had to find thirty thousand pounds. I'd never conveyed to Ian that I couldn't fund the trial, because I felt the other side might pick up on it, in their conversations. I found the money but that was it, I would not be able to find another penny.

I guess Farrers now knew, with absolute certainty that battle was about to commence. In those days, libel awards could be very substantial, and they knew that their client now faced paying serious money because the sting of the libel was not only totally fictitious, but plainly incapable of being proved by the magazine. To make matters worse for them, I was never given the opportunity to comment on the article prior to publication. This meant, if I won, I'd be almost certain to be awarded pretty substantial damages. Another payment into court was soon made. It brought the total to two hundred thousand. We never acknowledged it. Much more of this bluffing and I'd end up being sectioned.

Three weeks from the trial they make their final offer two hundred and twenty thousand pounds. Every-one's congratulating themselves except me. Ian calls me and says that Farrers have told him it's the end of the road. No more money. They'll take their chance in the High Court.

I'm driving down to Hove with Pearl to visit her mum who has had an accident and is in bed with a badly sprained ankle. I tell Ian that my bottom line hasn't changed and we'll see them in Court. At this point I really should have been locked up in a padded room. I have no coherent explanation for my bravado. I now owe a hundred and thirty thousand pounds and had absolutely no chance of finding the money to fund a trial. Ian explains calmly but with some force, that it really is all over and that it really was their *final* offer. I tell him to tell them 'to go fuck themselves.'

Pearl and I are standing round her mum's bed when the call comes through from Ian. I don't know what he had said to them, but they had surrendered. They will pay the money - plus costs of course. It had been nearly two years of hell; it had taken over my entire life and I felt nothing. Nothing at all. No sense of victory, no lap of honour, just a numbness. I told Pearl who was both relieved and ecstatic and we hugged and kissed as though I'd scored the winning goal in the Cup Final but it was all an act on my part.

We drove back home to Hayward's Heath in near silence lost in our own thoughts. Many years later, Tom Crone, who's still News International's in-house lawyer, told me over lunch that I had the last big pay out that was made in an out of court libel settlement before the Court of Appeal reduced libel payments following the absurd jury award to Jeffrey Archer, and he was well aware of the role I played. If true, I still didn't feel like celebrating.

CHAPTER FORTY FIVE
SIMON DARLOW AND SPITFIRES AND PEARL

I was back! It was 1988. Libel and Kruger over, I was ready to kick ass. Not that there was much ass to kick like in the good old days. Looking after Anne Diamond took me in to the heartland of the Agency. Willcocks was getting more and more unhappy about my presence. I understood his feelings but the bottom line was that it was my company and not his. He decided to leave and set up on his own. He'd expected the majority of the clients to follow him. None did. As a consequence he haunted me for the next ten years. Phone calls to me, the clients, to anyone who'd listen. I could understand his anger and frustration but ten years...?

When I took on Anne Diamond, she was involved in a plethora of libel actions. I told her we really had to get rid of them as it affected her image. Not that there were any that were frivolous, but it just took up time and money.

The first action I put to bed was a front page story in The Sun. The front page headline declared, *Anne Diamond Killed My Father* and just below it a caption that read, *In Her Sports Car*. The impression given from the article was that Anne was guilty of causing death by dangerous driving as told by the man's son. Turning to the last column on page two the story unfolded. Half way down the piece, it explained that the elderly gentleman had stepped out from behind a parked car in to the path of Anne who couldn't have seen him and was travelling well within the speed limit. He was taken to hospital and was doing well but after a few days he died suddenly. Most of these details were a little hard to read as the print mysteriously became smaller and smaller the further down the column you read. It cost The Sun sixty thousand pounds plus costs.

News International were not over fond of Mike Hollingsworth, and by association Anne. This stemmed back to the days when they'd just started going out, Mike was married at the time. After a few months they decided to take a break from each other. But it was then that The News Of The World ran a story linking them. Strictly speaking they were on a break and therefore not together. Mike sues and, much to Tom Crone's ire, they were forced to settle and pay damages and costs. Tom never forgave or forgot. Years later we had reason to do business together and I thought him tough but reasonable. All Anne's libel actions bar one were settled over the next eighteen months.

Pearl seemed to have an instinct for her cancer. One February morning in 1989 she tells me she doesn't feel right and we head straight for Professor Baum. Tests reveal it's back. All the checkups we'd attended proved to be a waste of time. She had her own in built sensor system. Chemotherapy came into our lives. It was terrible for her but she was incredibly brave. She was now a regular in-patient at the Royal Marsden Hospital. After ten days we returned home and she spent a lot of time in bed dealing with the after effects of her treatment. The children, aware things were not great with their mum, did what children do. Got on with their lives.

I'd given up my role as the Methuselah of the pop video and was now focusing on the Agency and VEC when I got a call from my mate John Knowles now at Magnet Records. He has an artist who is a problem. He wants him to 'look' rock and roll.' Could I help? No I can't, I'm retired. Just listen to the song. No. Please. Ok.

He couriers me the song and a video. The artist is Simon Darlow who has a great track record as a song-writer. He co-wrote Grace Jones *Slave To The Rhythm* and Toyah's *It's A Mystery* among other best sellers. I listen to the song. It's a ballad. I watch the tape. He looks to me like a young John Denver, no help there then. I can't think of a single way I can make him 'rock and roll.' I'd never worked from home when thinking up ideas for videos and maybe that's what was blocking me. I did something I'd never done before, I took the tape upstairs to Pearl who was now having to spend much of her time in bed, told her the problem, and asked her, if she was up for it, to give it a listen and come up with ideas. It might help to take her mind off things for a bit, which was no bad thing. She perked up, and the creative juices started flowing that had been absent from her life since her 'fashion' days.

When I took up her dinner that evening she told me I should make him a wartime Spitfire pilot. The lyrics had sod all to do with Spitfires or the war but then I'd made God knows how many videos with story lines that had nothing at all to do with the lyrics. I liked the idea. I wrote a treatment and sent it to my mate at Magnet. He calls me the moment he receives it. He tells me I have to meet Darlow. I tell him, again, I'm retired and he can have the treatment with my compliments. That's not good enough for Knowles. He pesters me to come up to London and meet the artist. I agree.

Simon Darlow was twenty eight, looked ten years younger, blond, slim and handsome. John Knowles is none of these things. He is in fact a big, strong, bearded maniac.

We chat for a few minutes then Darlow plays me the second track from his album called, *Flying Over England*, a song about a Spitfire pilot! This turned out to be the cause of their excitement. Pearl had seen the future! Or at the very least the second track. They were desperate for me to direct the treatment. The process which record companies go through to pick singles from albums is beyond me. In many cases it's also beyond the record companies. But *Flying Over England* was not on the short list of possible singles. I told them it wouldn't be cheap. I'd need an airfield, a Spitfire and a bunch of extras to play pilots and ground crew. They agreed. Not having shot in a while I needed to find a producer.

An old friend, Jackie Adams, came to my rescue. I also needed a production company to put the job through. Tommy Vance had become a client and had been a close friend for years. He'd also married Cookie, Stella Richman's daughter, so he was family too. Tommy wasn't just a great 1960's DJ who'd managed to prolong his career into the 90's; he was also a popular voice-over artist for commercials. If you are of a certain age and you watched ITV for more than ten seconds, you would have heard him. Even now if I mention "Gillette – the best a man can get", you can hear his voice. Tommy was also cute enough to run a successful production company. He offered to help. I, in turn, offered the vintage gravelly-voiced DJ a job as second unit director.

Costumes were an expensive part of the budget. I met Darlow and his fiancée, Danielle, at London's largest costumiers to fit him for his 'uniform'. Knowles had told me that Danielle was very much in charge and to be careful as she could be a bit of a dragon. She certainly didn't look like a dragon. She was petite with chestnut coloured hair and very cute. Later I found out she could be a feisty little thing!

We shot the video at Duxford airfield in Cambridgeshire. It was mid-February and freezing cold. Making the one Spitfire we had rented for the day look like a squadron was a little taxing but it worked out. It was the closest I ever got to shooting an action film. Extras dressed as pilots running for plane(s), ground crew sitting around waiting for them to come back from their sorties. Offices with flight crew chalking up the results of the missions on a blackboard. I had a fun old time. I even gave the classic Spielberg shot a try. Tracking and zooming in on the subject while the background remains the same. I shouldn't have bothered, it took up nearly two hours for six seconds of screen time! Simon and Danielle visited the edit and everyone seemed to like the finished version. I, in turn, liked them both - especially the cute dragon lady.

Pearl was now having to spend more and more time at the Royal Marsden and was often away for a week or more. We had a rule, I would visit her daily except at weekends which I would spend exclusively with the children. We had the support of a live in 'nanny', without whom I could never have gone to work in London or for that matter visit Pearl in hospital.

I often bumped into Professor Baum and asked him how Pearl was doing. He said it was impossible to give a prognosis and we would just have to wait and see.

With Willcocks gone from the Agency, I had to be more involved, but with Pearl often in hospital, and my need to be there for our children, it was very difficult. I was lucky to have Jules Bennett working for me to deal with many of the day-to-day tasks. She was a first rate agent. I've always maintained that the best agents are women or gay men. Though in my experience gay men could sometimes take a step too far and become real bitches.

About six weeks after I finished shooting the Darlow video, he rang me for a chat. Simon and I had got on well, both having a mutual regard for one another. He suggested we meet for lunch and just hang out. I rarely did this as most artists are not great company and, not to put too fine a point on it, are stuck so far up their backsides they can only communicate by farting.

On the shoot I'd mentioned Pearl's illness to him. Apart from Dave and Annie, I'd never had any real social contact with any of the artists I'd worked with. Simon had a great sense of humour and a true artist's sensitivity. After we'd had lunch he invited me to his house for Friday night dinner. I soon discovered this was a ritual he and Danielle shared.

Friday night dinner always consisted of smoked salmon, cream cheese and chips. We became good friends. Often they would stay over at weekends when Pearl was in hospital to help with the children and cheer me up. I was never one to show my inner feelings and people thought I was handling everything like a titan. Inside I was desperately afraid for Pearl and the kids.

A symptom of cancer, at least in my experience, is how selfish the patient can become. This is in no way implied as some sort of criticism or complaint but merely an observation. I've never really talked about these painful years. How the hospital visits would turn from a check up to a week's stay or longer. About the pain you feel in seeing someone you love suffer and being helpless to do anything about it and secretly fearing the very worst.

Pearl always managed to retain a sense of humour although it was sometimes black and often could shock people. Once we were out to dinner at a friend's home. They had a few guests who'd neither of us had met before. After dinner one of their guests who was sitting next to Pearl asked her if she minded if he had a cigarette.

'Actually I do,' she said, 'I've got cancer!' It was her way of dealing with it and it was said with a sly grin. The guest didn't know how to react and she touched his arm as if to say, 'It's ok I'd just rather you didn't.' If I sometimes slipped in a little black humour of my own, she'd respond by saying, '*I* do the jokes!'

CHAPTER FORTY SIX
LORD LITCHFIELD, GOODBYE EDITING AND DEPRESSION

Nik Powell and I were now seriously getting on each other's nerves. It was 1989. Business at VEC wasn't great but nor was it disastrous. I realised that the setting up was where the fun was. I was aware of my responsibilities to the staff and I'd built a pretty strong and happy environment but I was bored. I'd introduced it to the world, well Europe, but now I needed another challenge. This was never going to happen. New challenges required too much time spent away from home and that wasn't possible. For the first time in my life I'd become nailed to the ground. I was forty one. I hadn't missed a single element of the pop promo business, certainly not the endless travel and having to deal with overstretched egos. I missed the freedom of movement. I recalled the Thom Gunn line again, *you're always nearer by not keeping still.*

Sometimes though, an occasional gem turned up. Lord Litchfield called me. Could we have breakfast? We could. We'd never met before but it seems he'd heard of me and my involvement in pop videos and wanted to pick what was left of my brains. We met at my old stomping ground the Carlton Tower for breakfast and had a grand time. It was apparently never too early for champagne for the Earl and it gave me a flicker of my previous life. He asked dozens of questions about the pop video business as we guzzled back the champers.

'It's a shit game.' I told him.

'But much more fun for me at the moment' he said. I doubted that since this was the man who'd shot a few Pirelli calendars.

'Patrick, I find that difficult to believe.'

'It's true, I promise you. Though Chalkie and I had a bit of a giggle last week.'

'Chalkie?'

'My assistant. I'm doing a coffee table book on Soho strippers. We'd just finished shooting in some pretty dingy club in Archer Street when Chalkie fancied a pint. They had an upstairs bar which was quite empty. I found a seat by the window and asked Chalkie for a tonic water. The lady behind the bar was topless with the biggest pair of knockers this side of page three. When he asked for his pint of beer she said, 'with or without?' I glanced over and caught his eye. He seemed a little confused, after all what can you add to a pint of beer.' Lemonade I thought. 'He told her, 'without' and brought the drinks to the table. Five minutes later a gentleman came in and asked for a beer, and is offered the same choice. He selects 'with.' She fiddles behind the bar and comes up with two of those crisp hoola hoops. She places one on each nipple and the gentleman eats them both.'

'I guess that's 'with," I say.

"Probably!' We laugh.

I liked him. I think I heard that he went on to shoot a few videos.

What I didn't need was the daily grief both Powell and I put ourselves through. I'd had enough. I sat him down and asked him to buy me out. We talked around a figure of two hundred thousand pounds. He hadn't got the cash but said he might be able to raise enough if he could amortise the payment over eighteen months. I left him to sort it out. Even though the deal would take some time to put in place I effectively withdrew my energies from VEC. I was left with the Agency.

It was Jules Bennett who saw it first. She'd been with the company for over five years. Dealing with Pearl's illness was making me distant and indifferent to the Agency. I found it nearly impossible to give it any focus or leadership. There wasn't much I could do to change my perspective as most of the time I was unaware of how I was being affected. It would take a few years before I'd seek help to deal with it.

CHAPTER FORTY SEVEN
ANNE DIAMOND'S GOODBYE TO TVAM AND THE ULTIMATE REALISATION

For some time Anne Diamond was being marginalised by her bosses at TVAM. When she turned up at her office to find the desk, carpet, chairs and hat stand had been removed, we knew it was time to act. It was 1990. We discussed how we should deal with the bastards' attempts to intimidate her, booked a meeting with them and went along full of anger and venom.

Perhaps a cooler approach may have been better but neither of us was in a mood to take any prisoners. We arrived at two o'clock and were ushered in to the boardroom at TVAM's offices in Camden. There were four of them. All smartly dressed in dark suits and ties and all smiling 'welcome'. They even were allowing me to smoke in the non smoking building. We declined their offer of coffee and took our seats at one end of the long polished table. I started the meeting.

'You are treating my client like a cunt!' In for a penny! That didn't go down too well. One of them, the fat one with a ruddy complexion, the others slimmer and perhaps healthier, stood up and gasped for air. Anne couldn't wait for me to continue and went straight for the jugular.

'You're all a bunch of fucking misogynists!' she said standing up, hands on the table, leaning towards them. A woman on a mission. This vitriolic attack added to my foul language and set the tone for the rest of the meeting which didn't last too long. Anne left the company and battle commenced. It became a matter for the lawyers. Writs were issued and counter claims made. It went on for months. Anne found the leaving, her treatment by a company she'd worked for so loyally and successfully, deeply hurtful and depressing.

She called me one morning very despondent and told me to 'just settle it.' She didn't care about the money, she just wanted it out of her life. I intended to ignore the call putting it down to depression, when Ian Bloom, who was acting for her, called me minutes later. 'They want to settle,' he said. 'They want to meet tomorrow at my office.' I rang Anne to tell her and she instructed me to resolve it any way, but get it done and dusted.

My meeting with TVAM's executives was less aggressive second time round! We talked numbers and got to one hundred and eighty thousand. I said I'd need to speak to Anne. I left Ian's conference room to find a private office and called her.

'We've got to one hundred and eighty,' I told her. There was a long pause then she spoke. 'One hundred and eighty pounds!'

'No Anne, one hundred and eighty *thousand* pounds.' A whoosh of air travelled down the phone line. The deal was done.

Pearl had begun to feel some pain in her left leg and she was finding it very difficult to walk. We made an appointment with Prof Baum and she had a series of X-rays. He suggested she may need surgery as her left femur had been weakened by the cancer. He sent us to one of the best orthopaedic surgeons in the country at the Charing Cross Hospital, Professor Bryant, another top man in his field, with a long waiting list. But a personal letter from the Professor got us an immediate appointment.

After she was examined by him he said he wanted a new series of specialised X-rays but suspected she'd probably need a pin in her femur. I was given her notes to take to radiography. His senior houseman walked us through reception and on to the radiography department. Pearl mentioned she'd like to see the letter Prof Baum had written to Professor Bryant. I opened the large envelope containing her notes, found the letter, and we began reading. The houseman, who was standing directly behind us, suddenly took the file with the letter and said we needed to get to X-ray as soon as possible. Pearl asked, half jokingly, if there was something in the letter he didn't want us to see. His response was calm and professional. 'No, but the radiologist leaves at four o'clock and we've only got ten minutes.'

She was taken in to X-ray as soon as we arrived. The houseman handed me back the notes and asked me to give them to Professor Bryant when we were given the X-ray results. He left me sitting alone on a metal chair to wait for Pearl. I opened the large manila envelope and found Baum's letter. It was effusive in his praise for her bravery and sense of humour and finished with, 'I hope you can see her as soon as possible as a personal favour to me. I know that you will be able to give her some comfort in the last year or so of her life.'

I read the last sentence over and over. I'd known deep down for some time that it was inevitable, but our minds can so easily thrust all kinds of horror to one side. Denial is a shitty state of mind offering, as it does, a false comfort zone.

Pearl was admitted the following day. It was a terrifying time. I wanted to speak to Prof Baum about what he'd written but there wasn't time. The operation was a partial success. I spoke to the surgeon afterwards and he explained that her femur was so full of tumours that when they tried to insert the pin the blood loss became life threatening. Unfortunately they only had two sizes of pin, one was too short and the other too long. They had to use the larger one. Though she suffered some pain because of the wrong size, it still aided her mobility considerably.

Over the last few years the National Health Service seems to be targeted by the press as though the problems of poor care and overcrowding are only a recent manifestation. After Pearl's operation at the Charing Cross Hospital, which for some peculiar bureaucratic reason is located in Hammersmith, I visited her twice a day.

She shared a ward with four other women all in their late seventies. What I found shocked me. She was very weak after the surgery, having lost so much blood and was in terrible pain and could barely speak. Her prescribed pain killers were over an hour late. For maximum effect pain killers should be taken *before* the pain kicks in. She had lain on her bed suffering to such an extent, that one of the other patients, who could barely walk, was so concerned that she attempted to get out of bed to get Pearl some attention. The buzzer to call for help was only turned on at night!

I found the ward sister and, for me, calmly explained that my wife's treatment was unacceptable and if she wasn't helped immediately I would contact the hospital authorities and cause her and the hospital more grief than she could possibly imagine. The pain killers were never late again. This started me thinking about the other patients in the ward. They didn't have a Jon Roseman to fight on their behalf. I spent time with each of them when I visited Pearl to make sure they were being properly cared for. She spent a week in hospital.

One evening, on the third day I found her in tears. A male nurse who worked nights had forced her to turn on her side to change the draw sheet even though the slightest movement was agony for her. What kind of place was this? When someone I love is being bullied and treated like an in-patient of Dr Mengele I could lose it a little. I really went for the guy. I told him if he ever touched my wife again I'd rearrange several of his internal organs. He was a nasty butch queen and had all the qualifications for working the wards at Auschwitz-Birkenau. I found the ward sister and had words. By her reaction I could tell that this wasn't the first time a complaint had been made against the guy. We never saw him again.

I had been having some severe neck pains and went to our local GP. He had always been there for Pearl and received constant updates from the hospital. He was a lovely bloke. After he made his examination he took a long look at me and said, 'It's stress Jon. The problem you face my friend, is all your friends' and family's concerns are for Pearl and they don't really appreciate what you're going through.' He reached forward and put his hand on my arm. I burst into tears. When anyone offers me those little kindnesses I find it so hard to take. I'd rather give the present than receive one.

CHAPTER FORTY EIGHT
ANNE DIAMOND, THE BBC AND COT DEATH

It was 1991. Anne Diamond's profile had, understandably, dropped significantly after she left TVAM even though she had gone on to present a successful afternoon series called TV Weekly. Her husband, Mike Hollingsworth, had been working on confidential reports for the BBC to help address their disastrous morning schedule which would ultimately lead on to Anne and Nick Owen joining up together for one last time. Anne's deal with the BBC was one of the largest I'd done at that time for a client apart from David Banks and Nick Ferrari. The head of Pebble Mill, the BBC's studio in Birmingham where the proposed series would be made, was due to meet me at two o'clock at Anne's home in Camden, North London near Regents Park.

I arrived at twelve thirty and we went for an early lunch round the corner in Camden High Street. We talked about what we wanted from the deal. Stuff like a mobile phone, fax machine, a car to and from the studio and so on. When it got to the money she asked me what I was going to ask for. I said I didn't know. Always when entering a negotiation I rarely had a fixed figure in mind. I let the mood dictate the way I did the deal.

We returned to her home and waited for the man from the BBC. He duly arrived and after the briefest of introductions Anne left to go shopping.

'I guess we'd better get the money out of the way first,' I said as we sat opposite each other at Anne's dining table. He nodded. Jeremy Taylor was a big man who obviously liked his food. By the look of the veins down the side of his nose he liked a few drinks as well.

He'd been with the BBC for ever and had clawed his way up, no doubt leaving a few bodies behind, as one has to do in that organisation.

'If we can't agree the money, then everything else becomes irrelevant.' He nodded. 'Are you thinking of a two or three year contract?'

'Two years with an option for a third year.'

'Two hundred and fifty thousand for year one and two seventy five for year two and negotiate in good faith for the third year.' I said all this casually as if I was talking to the kids about their pocket money. He thought for a second.

'Agreed.' Well that bit was easy. It's an agent's worst nightmare when an agreement is reached without argument. The first thought that immediately occurs to you is, should I have asked for more? The answer is simple. No. If you spend your time worrying about it, you will take your eye off the ball when dealing with the other aspects of the deal. It's not always about the money. There are other important issues that have to be addressed. Can you get the client out of the series if it starts to turn into a disaster? If they want to get rid of the client, under what conditions can they do this? If the client feels they have a grievance, what is the procedure? Can you restrict the press office from doing anything without consultation and only publish or allow out those photographs that have been agreed with the client?

Having agreed the cash we went through the impromptu list I'd prepared while waiting for him to arrive. We ticked all the boxes very quickly. There was not a negative response to any of it until we got to moving expenses. Anne, and Mike as the programme's editor, would have to sell up and move to Birmingham. Jeremy pointed out that while fax machines and mobile phones were in his gift, moving costs fell in to an altogether different category. The rules surrounding such costs were very specifically defined and he'd have to get back to me on it. It does seem strange that he had total power to agree a contract that would cost the BBC well over half a million pounds, but the payment of a few thousand to get a sideboard up the M40 was subject to stringent policy regulations.

The series did ok. When you're up against *This Morning*, which had been established since before TV had been invented, it was always going to be a hard road to travel. While Mike has often been in the forefront of a lot of controversy over the years, few could deny his abilities as an editor. The fact that his wife presented the show didn't affect his judgment at all. Whereas Martin Frizzell's role as editor of GMTV when his wife, Fiona Phillips, presented for GMTV, was a constant issue among staff and presenters alike. They would often complain, though not to him, that they all had to be extra careful around Fiona. And problems that producers sometimes experienced with a show's presenter, when that presenter was Fiona, would rarely be taken to the editor. It didn't help that, unlike Mike, he was new to running a TV station.

Mike had no problem differentiating between his professional and personal life. Though he had been known to take things a little too far. Anyone who can argue with his wife about her contribution to the programme when in bed together, then fire her and turn over and go to sleep, deserves our highest admiration.

Mike called me early one morning on 12 July 1991, at about seven thirty with horrific news. Their baby son, Sebastian, had died. Their loss was unimaginable. I asked Mike if he wanted me to come up and he said he did. Living in West Sussex meant it would take a good hour and a half to get there. I showered, quickly put on a suit and drove to Camden.

When I reached Trafalgar Square it occurred to me that I hadn't spoken to Anne and perhaps she wouldn't want her agent around at such a terribly sensitive time. I called the house and the phone was answered by a male voice which I didn't recognise. I assumed, rightly, that it was a police officer. He put me on to Anne who sounded glad that I was on my way.

After parking my car I walked over to the large terraced house, apprehensive as to what I'd find and wondering how I'd deal with it. Mike opened the door and looked drained and hugged me. Anne came over and we kissed hello and I in turn gave her a big hug. As Annie was a staunch Catholic, they were trying to contact their priest to come to the house and say prayers for Sebastian who was still in his little cot upstairs. Anne finally spoke to him only to be told that he needed more notice and that he couldn't just drop everything! A close friend suggested an old pal of hers who was the Chaplain of Harrow School and who lived locally. He came immediately. So quick in fact that he'd forgotten his dog collar. He improvised by cutting a strip of paper and placing it around his neck!

As with all cot deaths, the police and the coroner had to be informed. The atmosphere in the house was oddly surreal. It was as though there was a collective holding of breath. I sat at their dining room table, trying to stay out of everyone's way. Mike looked like a man lost deep within himself. Anne was coping with their two other sons, Oliver, four, and Jamie two and a half. I wondered how a parent could even begin to explain to their children that their baby brother had died.

It was about eleven thirty. Mike, Anne and their nanny followed the priest upstairs. Mike stopped half way up and called down to me, 'Jon I know you're Jewish but if you'd like to come up.....'

We all stood round the cot, baby Sebastian facing away from us. It was very hot in the tiny room and I felt like an interloper who had no right to be sharing this deeply personal moment. After the brief service, we went downstairs each with our own private thoughts. The coroner arrived and Sebastian left the house for ever.

There are certain 'duties' I've had to perform over the years as an agent which have been emotionally challenging. This was certainly the worst. I took Anne and Mike on one side and explained that because they both shared such a high profile I needed to advise the media of their tragedy. They both reacted totally professionally and agreed. I wrote a brief one liner and called the Press Association. I asked for the news desk, identified myself and read the one liner. Bizarrely they never bothered to confirm my identity and put the statement out immediately.

Within two minutes the phone rang. We'd already agreed I'd handle all the calls. It was Eve Pollard, the editor of the Daily Express. She offered her sincere condolences but added, in a way only a journalist could, 'And if Anne would like to talk about it please, please ask her to call me'.

The police had left with the coroner. Mike and I sat down and had innumerable cups of tea. He was a lost soul, and Annie I could tell, was busying herself with the two boys, just to put herself, however temporarily, in another place.

After half an hour the priest also left. As we were drinking the sixth cup of tea the door bell rang. None of us had taken any notice of the activity that was growing outside the house. I opened the door to two reporters clutching a bunch of elderly daffodils, no doubt purchased from outside Camden tube station.

'These are for Anne,' one of the men said. There were now half a dozen other reporters gathered outside on the pavement. 'We all appreciate this is a very difficult time but would it be possible to get a quote from either Mike or Anne.' I said I'd see what I could do. I closed the door quietly and went back to sit with the two of them. 'I think we may need to give them something,' I told them. 'Maybe I should jot something down and show it to you.' They agreed and I took off for their back garden and sat on a bench and thought about what I'd say. Mike came out and sat with me for a while and we chatted over some ideas. It took me forty minutes to come up with eight or ten lines. It was innocuous but necessary.

When I opened the front door, I was met by about thirty reporters and two OB trucks, one from Sky and the other from BBC news. A couple of photographers busily snapped away, the flashes from their cameras making me feel even more disoriented than I already was.

I read the statement, apologised for ignoring their questions and went back inside. I was shaking. Sure I'd dealt with a huge variety of situations before but a baby's life being snuffed out like a candle, a baby who would now never have a life, go to school, grow up, have a career, get married...a baby for Christ's sake. I'd never believed in a God, any God. This just confirmed for me what I remembered Camus had written, 'we are all born condemned to die'.

I took myself off to the garden and walked up and down smoking. I suddenly became aware of a house that overlooked their property and what looked distinctly like a photographer standing on a balcony. Anne and Mike took that moment to come in to the garden, I put my arms around them, gently turning them around, and told them we had company. I guided the pair back into the house.

My own life was given some perspective by what was going on around me. My wife's cancer was getting worse, and it might well soon end her life when she should have so much to look forward to. I had four children to bring up, perhaps alone, in a treacherous world. I'd both made and lost a lot of money and had been living a life that I now viewed as feckless in the extreme. I wanted a magic wand to make things right, but by this time I had even less idea what the future would hold than usual. But I knew it would get worse.

The press have different values from us normal folk. They need to tread where most people either fear to step or don't feel they have a right to step. Two hours after I'd made my appearance on the doorstep, their numbers had doubled and so had the OB trucks. Things were getting a little out of hand. Anne and Mike, being experienced media folk as they are, were both understanding of the mêlée, but it was down to me to put an end to it.

I edited my initial statement adding nothing new but merely changing the order of what I'd said before. I revisited the doorstep, read the 'new' statement, folded it up and shoved it in to my trouser pocket. The questions rained in. I stood for nearly a minute gazing around at the assembled flock and finally said, 'Ladies and gentlemen, today is Oliver's birthday. Anne and Mike were expecting to have a birthday party today. We all understand why you're here and that you have to cover an important news story, but try to imagine what Anne and Mike are going through. I have nothing further to add and I beg all of you to call it a day so they can have time for contemplation and privacy.' I went back inside. To their credit within twenty minutes they were all gone.

Sebastian's funeral was to be held in a little church in Ewhurst near Bournemouth where Anne's parents lived. They were both concerned about the possible press attendance at the funeral. A couple of months before, Eric Clapton's son, Connor had died, and the funeral became a free for all, with photographers stomping all over the little grave to get pictures. I wrote to all the editors of the national papers asking for an embargo. Their response was both respectful and positive.

CHAPTER FORTY NINE
FRANK BOUGH

A client I'd long admired was Frank Bough. When I started to represent him, he had about six or possibly seven agents! He didn't require anyone to negotiate with the BBC. He managed to do that very effectively himself. The agents were there to supply him with a steady stream of lucrative corporate work. After the first scandal a couple of years before, the BBC turned their back on him. I suggested to him at the time, that he would be better off being represented by a single entity. He agreed and decided it should be me.

He worked at LBC for a while and Sky offered him a series called the Frank Bough Interview. He wasn't too sure at first whether he wanted to work for a Murdoch company as one of his papers had effectively killed his great career. But while he had been devastated by the revelations, time had managed to plaster over some of the more painful cracks. I remember lunching with Kelvin McKenzie soon after the *News Of The World* article, and perhaps a little naively, decrying the piece.

'Come on Kelvin, he's a fucking TV presenter not a scout leader or public servant. Turn over the politicians, I'm all for that, but why Boughie?' The reply was Kelvinesque in the extreme. 'If he wears those bloody cardies, what does he expect?' Irrefutable logic from the then editor of Britain's biggest selling daily.

In 1991 Frank scored big time by being offered ITV's rugby world cup coverage. Perhaps, I thought, things were looking up. In the interim he'd suffered the inevitable barrage of piss taking by every cartoonist, comedian and columnist in the UK. To attempt to repair some of the damage, he bravely appeared on *Have I Got News For You*. While Merton and Hislop made gentle, for them, references to his earlier indiscretions, Angus Deayton and his script never alluded to them at all. Now we probably know why! Mr Deayton's own indiscretions would soon hit tabloids.

Some time later, in 1992, Kelvin called me.

'Jon we've heard that Frank's up to his old tricks again.' I guessed "we" meant the papers in the News International stable. 'We're not going to do anything; Murdoch has put an embargo on any stories about him. So I'm just giving you the heads up.' For that I was extremely grateful.

I had to decide what to do. If Kelvin and co knew about it, it wouldn't be long before some other tabloid would be on the case. I called Boughie and said I needed to talk with him about a matter of some sensitivity and suggested we meet in a small hotel in Charing Cross Road near my office. I paid for a small suite, some sandwiches and a bottle of Chablis. It was January 26th.

'I'll come straight to the point,' I said, then proceeded to tell him about Kelvin's conversation with me. I was surprised by how calmly he took it. 'Look mate I'm not here to judge you, 'cause what I've done makes the revelations about you, vicar tea party stuff. But no-one's interested in little ole me thank the Lord, but you, you're big news. I don't want you going down that same road again. Shit! Frank we're nearly back on the straight and narrow.' Which was certainly true. Even the BBC was making positive noises.

'Jon, I promise you, I've not wandered for some time.'

'When?' I asked.

'The third or the fourth...'

'Of ....?'

'January,' he said without a trace of irony.

All I could do was let him know the score and hope discretion would be his byword.

I left for a family holiday in July. Months had rolled by and whatever information the News International bunch had, had not leaked to any other papers. I was very fond of Frank and his wife Nesta. He'd put his family through a lot and they'd stood by him because, simply, he's a fantastic bloke and a brilliant presenter.

After Kelvin's warning, and with a deal from the BBC on the table, I'd hoped we were on the same page.

Ten days later I returned from my vacation and went directly to my study. It was a charter flight and the time was close to three am on a Monday morning. My fax machine showed a message from Boughie saying simply, 'Sorry about today's papers. I'll call you in the morning.' All the Sundays were piled high in my study put there by our nanny. I went through them. The Sunday Mirror had the exclusive. He had been caught again.

All this was in the wake of Major Ron Ferguson getting turned over. Much later I called a psychologist client of mine and asked WHY? Why would a well known public figure think that paying a bunch of hookers buys some kind of confidentiality, when in our culture selling salacious stories to the highest bidder is now *de rigueur.* He implied that that was the whole point. The excitement of getting caught was part of the process. Obviously it marked the end of one of the greatest presenting careers in television.

Some years later Boughie and Nesta were invited by the BBC to celebrate the Beeb's seventy fifth anniversary. Normally he'd never attend such a high profile event, being fearful of what the press would write about him, but having been invited by his old friend and colleague Will Wyat, then Managing Director of the BBC, he took the unprecedented step to attend.

I watched the programme. There was footage of all the celebrities and guests arriving, the camera swept over them throughout the programme as they celebrated the major achievements of the last seventy five years. There was a compilation of all the great programmes the BBC had made over three quarters of a century including of course, Grandstand, Nationwide and the birth of Breakfast TV. Not one single shot of Frank in the entire extravaganza. He'd been air brushed out like so much Soviet revisionist propaganda. I was incensed.

I called Will Wyat the following morning and asked what the fuck was going on? If they were going to excise Boughie from their history why invite him and his wife to suffer the BBC's contempt. He tried to tell me that the programme was full of contributors over a very long period and they couldn't fit everyone in. What a crock of shit.

CHAPTER FIFTY
TRAGEDY

I was having real difficulty sleeping at this time. Looking after Pearl and the children was taking its toll emotionally. I took myself off to our local GP. He really was one of the calmest, most caring people I'd ever known. He listened to what I had to say and, as before, pointed out that I was living under severe stress. He suggested he approach someone he knew from the local hospice, not to have Pearl admitted, but to help us both come to terms with what might happen.

I knew she'd hate that. The mention of a hospice to most people meant death was inevitable. That's what I thought and I'm sure that would be the impression Pearl would have. He told me that wasn't the case. They could be very supportive and help put things in a better perspective. I said I'd speak to her but not to hold his breath.

After a few days of gently bringing the matter up she reluctantly said she'd give it a try. I sat on the bed with her while the man from the hospice and our GP sat on chairs next to the bed. He was a kind and worldly man in his late fifties. After some preliminary chat he got down to the nitty gritty.

'Pearl three things are going to happen. You are either going to get better, or at least you won't get any worse, or the illness will become more advanced.' She seemed to think about this for a moment, then looking him straight in the eyes she said,' Well you can fuck off with the last two that's for sure!' It was this ability to fight that had made her survive as long as she did. Needless to say they both left not long after.

1992 was the Queen's *annus horribilis*. It wasn't that great a year for me either. I had now extricated myself

241

from Nik Powell and VEC, but Pearl's condition had put me in such a state of depression that I was a useless add-on as far as Jules Bennett and the Agency were concerned. It was round this time that we took on Jill Dando. She was, even then, everybody's favourite presenter. If I knew what she had, I'd have bottled it and made a fortune. She could have a twinkle in her eye, gravitas, a sharp journalist's mind and look a million dollars. There's not been a female presenter since she left us, who has come even close to her.

Pearl had an appointment at the Marsden and we drove up early one February morning so I could take a meeting with Jill prior to driving on to the Marsden. When we got to the office, which was now in Charing Cross Road, Pearl felt very unwell and laid down on one of the sofas in reception. I went to my office to take a quick call when Jill arrived. She'd met Pearl before and sat next to her on the sofa and chatted to her. Pearl told me later that the brief chat had really perked her up. It wasn't a Mother Teresa moment but Jill had an amazing ability to bring out the positive in everybody.

The hospital appointment turned into another three day stop over. I stayed with her till around eight then left to go home. As I walked down the long winding staircase from her ward to the front door, my head full of dark thoughts, my face felt wet. I put it down to perspiration as it's always so hot in there. When I dabbed my face I was shocked to find tears. I'd never experienced anything like it before or since. I had been crying and hadn't known it. Often over the last few months I'd park the car a hundred yards or so from the house and have a good cry. I was already starting the grieving process.

One Wednesday afternoon, toward the end of May, Pearl suddenly decided she wanted to go out for dinner on Saturday night with two of our friends who lived locally. I hadn't been out on a Saturday night for over a year. She surprised me again when she asked me to contact her hairdresser to pop over to the house to 'do' her hair. On the rare occasions when she left the bedroom to come downstairs she needed a walking stick. So I found all this sudden activity rather disconcerting.

Her one big luxury was bath time. The hospital had lent us a device that allowed her to raise and lower herself into the bath. Without this she wouldn't be able to take a bath at all. The hot water provided additional relief for her. Our daughter, Elie, spent every bath time with her and they talked for hours.

That Saturday night we had dinner at a Chinese restaurant in Hove which we used to eat at regularly in the old days. We hadn't been there for a long time and the owner, Mr Li, made Pearl feel like the Emperor's daughter. He was very fond of her. She always had great legs and had chosen a mini dress to wear and looked fantastic. We had a great meal and on the way home we had a bit of a row about something to do with the car. Things couldn't have felt more normal!

The next morning Pearl experienced severe pain in her back and rib cage. I called our local doctor who came by and gave her some morphine. Time was running out.

I spoke to Prof Baum on Monday morning. He suggested I take her into the Marsden on Friday. Friday came round all too quickly. I'd hired a private ambulance to take us to the hospital. Our family doctor was on hand to give her some more morphine for the journey. As we passed through East Grinstead heading towards the M23 she looked over at me and said simply, 'This is it.' I held her hand and made the 'don't be silly' noises but I wasn't fooling any one, least of all myself.

As soon as we arrived at the Marsden she was whisked straight to X-ray. I wandered up and down the reception area, my mind a complete blank. I could have been waiting five minutes or two weeks, time had become a shadow.

She finally emerged after half an hour and was taken to the ward. She was obviously in a lot of pain and my heart was breaking. The ward consisted of ten or so small rooms around a central nursing station. The rooms contained just two beds. We both knew most of the nurses by now having spent so much time there. They were totally dedicated people whose compassion and skill in having to deal with the lives of patients and their families would match any saint.

I was asked gently if I would leave her for twenty minutes so the staff could insert a drip. I sat with her for a few minutes and we spoke about what, I can't remember. As I left the room I turned to smile and said, 'be back in a min.' She smiled back, 'Ok.' It would be the last time we ever spoke.

The nurse told me that Pearl's X-rays revealed that three of her ribs had literally dissolved due to the cancer and a large part of her left femur was gone. It was now all down to pain control for her final days. When I returned to the ward she was on a morphine drip and in a deep sleep. I talked to her not knowing if she could hear or understand me. I think I was completely numb inside.

How I managed to drive back to Sussex without incident is a complete mystery to me. I slept fitfully and woke at six. I called the hospital and was told Pearl had had a quiet night.

I knew the weekend was going to be very difficult and phoned Cookie, and asked her if she would come down the following day, Sunday, to help me with the children. We had someone living in, but I wanted to have Cookie there. She was 'family'. Gideon was fifteen, Elie eleven, Alex nine and Tom eight. The strain of the situation was starting to overwhelm me.

I stuck to our rule about not visiting on weekends, though now I wasn't so sure it was the right thing to do. At least on Sunday I would see her. Gideon had been staying with friends in London and I had to drive up to collect him.

Cookie turned up in the morning with her husband Tommy Vance and their two children Daniel and Jessie accompanied by Danielle, who had recently broken up with her fiancé, Simon Darlow. My children had known Cookie's family all their lives and we'd shared some great summer holidays together, so they provided a huge comfort zone. It took only a few minutes for Cookie and Danielle to take control and I left to drive to London to pick up Gideon.

I stopped off at the Marsden to see Pearl. She was now in a coma. The person I'd known for twenty six years was lying in bed in the little ward and had begun to look like a stranger. In thirty six hours the woman I loved had begun to disappear. The physical features that define who we are, are so fleeting, so meaningless, in the scheme of life.

I left the hospital to collect my son. As I drove, holding back my tears, I told Gideon that his mum wouldn't be coming home. That's a lot for a boy of fifteen to take in. His reaction was that of someone who had known the truth for a long time. I said that when we got home I would have to tell the other children and asked him where he thought the best place was for me to speak to them. He said, 'not your study', and added, 'I just don't want to be there when you tell them.' I probably shouldn't have asked him but I needed all the help I could get and for all his young years he was nobody's fool. We drove back to Sussex in silence.

When we arrived at the house I took Tommy, Cookie and Danielle to one side and told them what had happened at the hospital, and that the time had come for me to speak to my children. All the kids were playing in the garden. I remember it was a beautiful sunny day. Gideon had already taken himself off to his room when I called them over. We sat round the garden table and I began the most difficult talk of my life. Much later Elie told me she thought I was going to tell them something 'nice'. If only.

Their reaction was to sob and scream; somehow they'd amalgamated both into one horrendous wail. It was the most heartrending sound I'd ever heard. The three of them ran off to the boys' bedroom. I followed and we all ended up on the floor hugging and crying. After a few minutes Cookie and Dani came upstairs and we all hugged together.

Cookie suggested we should stay at her home in St John's Wood, so we could be nearer the hospital. We hastily packed a few things and drove to London. I took the kids to the hospital first and we sat round Pearl's bed holding hands. Elie asked one of the nurses what the small foam squares with a collection of tooth picks in a bowl by the bed were for. She explained that it was the only way her mum could take water. She pushed a tooth pick in one of the tiny foam squares put it into a glass of water and then placed it next to Pearl's mouth. We watched as she suckled at the foam. Then Elie took it from the nurse and continued to do it herself. My heart was broken into a million pieces.

That night, after Cookie and Dani helped to put all the kids to bed, I called the hospital to check on Pearl. I didn't know that a patient, who is effectively unconscious, receiving large doses of morphine, had to be disturbed every now and again to ascertain if they could feel any pain and additional relief supplied if they could.

I don't recall sleeping that night.

April 6th 1992. I called again at about seven thirty in the morning to be told she'd had a fairly peaceful night. I decided we'd all go back to the hospital around ten. While the children were getting ready the hospital called me. When they had moved her gently to wash her, her breathing had changed. They suggested we should come straight over. We all bundled ourselves into two cars and sped off to the Marsden.

While Cookie, Tommy, Dani and the kids were in the waiting room, I went to see Pearl with a nurse. I was totally unprepared for what awaited me. My wife had vanished. What I saw was a tiny, emaciated figure lying in the foetal position, her long red hair lying lank across the pillow. I stared at her for a long time. We'd been together for so long and whatever grief we'd put each other through, and there was plenty, we were still inexorably part of each other. I asked the nurse if we could make her look a little better for the children's sake. She gripped me gently by my arm and looked into my face and said, 'Jon she's going, she's going now.'

I went to fetch our family. As we gathered around her bed at exactly one minute to ten she took her last breath. She was gone. She was 45 years old. Our nurse checked her with a stethoscope and shook her head. We'd known her for a long time and she cried with us. I told the children that perhaps they'd like to pray. We were never a religious family, but praying seemed the only thing to do. The sight of the four of them kneeling by the bed, hands together, was the most moving experience of my life.

As Pearl and I had never talked about death, I sat down with the children and let them plan the funeral service. She was to be buried in the cemetery of the church of the Holy Trinity in the village of Cuckfield in West Sussex. It was a beautiful old building built on the remains of an eleventh century church. The local vicar was on holiday so his locum paid us a visit. He was a young man not long having taken up holy orders. The children told him what they had in mind which included playing Beverly Craven's song, *Promise Me* at the end of the service. He had no problem with any of their suggestions. He asked me if I would like to say a few words. I wasn't sure if I'd be up to it, so I asked him to give me a nod at the appropriate time and I'd make my mind up then.

On Saturday, two days before the funeral, Cookie and Dani took the children shopping for new clothes. Elie insisted on wearing her new dress when we took a walk the next day in the tiny village. Two elderly ladies walking their dog stopped to admire Elie in her dress and asked if she was off to a party. 'No,' she said, 'my mum's funeral.' So calm and assured. A lot more than her dad was.

On the morning of the funeral the children went off down the lane where we lived and removed vast numbers of daffodils that lined the small banks.

At two pm we left for the church which was a two minute drive from the house. I parked at the far end of the cemetery and the five of us walked along the path set between the ancient grave stones towards the entrance. Both sides of the path were strewn with wreaths. Elie, clutching a huge bunch of the illicit daffodils, asked me who the wreaths were for and bent down to examine the messages. They were all for Pearl. I was astonished at the sheer number of them. I noticed one from Dave Stewart and his wife Siobhan. I hadn't spoken to Dave in years.

I'd told no one about the funeral other than family and close friends so I was amazed to enter the church and see it filed with all my clients, a smattering of ex-clients and many others from the world of TV and the press. I found out later that Cookie and Dani had been hammering the telephones in order to let people know what had happened and letting them make their own decisions whether to attend. I was surprised and delighted to see Mr Li from the Chinese restaurant in Hove. How he'd heard about Pearl's death remains a Chinese puzzle. It went to show how many lives she'd touched.

We took our seats at the front and the service began. It would need the skill of a poet to describe what I felt at this time. Looking at our children and seeing the great affection all these people had for my wife was beyond anything I could have imagined. The part of the service arrived when I had to decide whether to say something. The vicar, bless him, decided for me. He looked down at me and said, 'I think Jon would like to say a few words.' So much for a nod and a wink then!

I walked up the three or four steps to the lectern and gazed out at the sea of faces. I had prepared something the day before in the unlikely event that I'd actually need it. And here I was. I looked down at my children. What could I say that would give them any solace, show them that I knew what they were going through. Showing how much love I had for them. It was an impossible task but I had to give it a try.

I addressed myself just to them. I told them that each of them carried some intrinsic part of their mother. Tom the artistic side. Alex the sensitive side. Elie the sense of humour that had so helped her mum in the last year of her life. Gideon the bravery and intelligence that had been so vital to the way she had dealt with her illness. And then it was over. We walked together up the aisle, Alex and Tom clutching my hands to the soulful sound of Beverly Craven singing *'Promise Me'*.

Anne Diamond told me later that she had just about managed to get through the service without crying until Beverly's voice flowed out of the speakers that Tommy Vance had installed that morning. She said she couldn't stop blubbing. I think we all felt something similar.

As the days, weeks and months passed I kept an eye on the children to ensure, as best I could, that they were dealing with this tragedy as well as was possible. I sought counselling for all of us. Somehow we got through it. Each in our own special way. But it took a very long time. And even now, I know that having a wife and mother whose life was cut so short still affects me and the children. And it always will.

CHAPTER FIFTY ONE
BACK TO LONDON, IMRAN KHAN, THE AGONY AUNT AND ROGER COOK

In 1993 I had to make a very difficult decision. All the children went to local schools and with their mum gone for just over a year, I was finding it exhausting taking all four to different schools in the morning, and then taking the train to the office. I had to leave the office at three so I'd be on time to collect them all. We did have a live-in nanny, but I thought it was vital for me to be as ever-present as was possible.

It was a tough time for all of us. I wasn't paying much attention to the office which would have dire consequences. I couldn't focus on my family, deal with my own trauma and run a business. I discussed with my children the idea of moving to London. I think they could appreciate what all the travelling was doing to me and we all agreed a move was for the best. Leaving behind their friends, who were obviously an important anchor for them so soon after their mum died was immensely difficult for them all. I sold the house and we moved.

I rented a house in Chiswick.

Pearl had always done the school thing. Finding the right schools was an art form, an art I did not possess. But needs must. Any parent who has been in a similar situation will know just how stressful such a move is. But we got through it with the help of friends. Cookie, Dan, my sister Jane and her husband Tim, who lived in nearby Kingston-upon-Thames, Toyah Willcox, an old friend of Dan's, and now a client, all provided help and support without which I'd surely have had a nervous breakdown.

This time we had no live-in help but we went through a few housekeepers. The school run was now a doddle and, after a few hiccups, we all settled down to our new way of life, or so I thought. But all the stress and strains of the previous years began to surface and hit me hard. Pearl's death, the additional responsibilities in looking after my family, the libel action, the tedious fight with Kruger for compensation, the day-to-day dealings with clients, all put together had sucked the life out of me. My Agency went into administration. The DTI tried to ban me from being a director. It was a very bad time. I started again, not a rare occurrence for me, but it doesn't get any easier. I managed to retain all the clients and hired some new staff, using up most of my savings in the process.

MTV Europe had been on air since late 1987. It wasn't a station I'd ever had much interest in and rarely watched particularly since I'd retired from the music video business. That changed when I received a call from Kristiana Backer. She was what was called in those very un-PC days an MTV babe. She was German and had a huge following back home. She was an ex model, sexy and beautiful. Tall and slender, legs that didn't know when to stop, and immaculate sleek dark brown hair. Then she spoke. For me there was always something about the German accent that caused anxiety. Perhaps my DNA contained the sound of marching boots or perhaps it was their way of beating us on penalties every bloody time we played them. Through Kristiana I met and became friends with Brent Hansen, a Kiwi and the head of MTV Europe.

A DJ's (video jock) work is not particularly onerous. You read forty links from an autocue in six hours, four times a week and then your links are inserted around a bunch of video clips and they pay you forty thousand pounds a year. Nice work if you can get it. Kristiana's problem was her delivery. Though she spoke English fluently, she found it very difficult to get the cadences right. I spoke at length with Brent about this and I told him I'd spend a couple of afternoons working with her. No matter how many times we went over her links, she would keep pausing in the wrong place. I gave up.

251

Whenever we were out walking together she always received a lot of attention from the guys! I have probably spent half my life going intermittently to the gym and bored the world to death talking about my weight. During the time I'd been spending with Kristiana I'd put on a few pounds and wasn't happy with myself. We'd just finished a voice coaching session and I was walking her to her car when we passed a bunch of teenage lads clutching their football kit bags. They stared at her and made the normal remarks you'd expect as they walked by. As we got to her car, I heard one of them say, 'Don't get a heart attack mate!' I felt so fucking old! I strolled miserably over to my car and saw a small black boy, about six years old, playing on a garden wall. As I passed him I warned him to be careful as the brick wall looked like it had seen better days. The response? 'Piss off baldy!' I wasn't having a good body image day.

Dan and I had just started going out and she got on well with Kristiana who invited us round for dinner. She was dating Imran Khan at the time. I liked him. I've never been a big cricket fan. Rugby and football were my sports of choice, but I certainly knew that he was a great all-rounder. I'm not sure what I expected having read so much about him in the press, both in the sports and gossip pages. As an agent your mind grows calluses over the years when it comes to the tabloids. He'd recently had an operation on his nose which made his voice sound very nasal and sometimes difficult to understand.

The dinner conversation covered a myriad of topics including a Pakistani charity he was deeply involved in. I was scoffing back the curry, not my usual fodder, but it was excellent. He told me he wanted to auction his car, a Mercedes, to raise money. His intention was to sell raffle tickets from local Pakistani corner shops. I suggested he got a national newspaper behind it like The Daily Mirror. He liked the idea, the bigger the exposure, the more money for the charity. I said I'd set up a meeting with the Editor, which I did first thing the next morning. I picked up Imran and drove him to the paper's office.

They were under the impression I would be on my own. The receptionist called up to say I'd arrived and a reporter came down to meet us. She took one look at Imran and fawned over him like a teenage pop fan. I heard her call the Editor's office from a phone in reception, 'He's only brought Imran along hasn't he!' The meeting went well and the Mirror was up for it, but Imran felt that his image would be best served by promoting the lottery idea via local Pakistani papers.

I represented a few MTV presenters, but there wasn't much I could do for them. MTV had its own special brand which was never going to cross over into mainstream television. Brent Hansen even asked me if I could help his wife, a presenter on his station, get work in one of the major companies. I tried but failed. MTV's presenters just didn't cut it for terrestrial broadcasters.

I'd always been attracted to Dan. A lot of men were! She'd stood by me through some of the worst times of my life. The children liked her a lot and, since Pearl died, we'd all seen a lot each other. She was becoming part of our lives. We started a relationship but kept it secret from my family and our friends. We wanted to see where it would lead before telling anyone. Dan often went overseas on trips for her advertising awards company to drum up business all over the world. November and early December were her busiest times and she would be away for nearly a month.

She'd been gone for just over two weeks and was in Brazil when Elie, then fourteen, came into my bedroom and slumped herself on the bed for a chat. She began asking questions about Dan. I was soon to discover that you couldn't hide anything from your kids no matter how clever you thought you were. Bottom line was she wanted to know if we were 'seeing' each other. Stupidly I denied it. After she left my bedroom to get ready for school I knew I'd fucked it up. I called Deidre Saunders, the doyen of Fleet Street's agony aunts, a client and friend. I'd often sought her advice about personal stuff and whenever I did I began the conversation with a "Dear Deidre". If it was business, it was just "Deidre".

I told her what I'd said to Ellie and she got straight to the point. 'Jon you're entitled to a life no matter how uncomfortable that might be for your children. Tell the truth! The next time Danielle's name comes up, be honest.' I decided that's exactly what I'd do.

That afternoon I did the school run as usual. I stopped off first to pick up Elie who slid into the passenger seat and then Alex and Tom who sat in the back. We drove back from Sheen in South West London, a couple of miles from where we lived in Chiswick. Alex asked when Dan was coming back. This was it; my loins were ready to be girded.

'Elie you know when we chatting earlier about Dan,' she was thumbing through a book and nodded, 'well I wasn't entirely honest.' I told the boys, now eleven and ten, what we'd been talking about. 'Dan and I are sort of going out. You know, seeing each other.' Alex piped up immediately, 'I thought you loved mummy.' Ouch! It was never going to be easy.

'I do love mummy,' I said, 'I'll always love mummy. But that doesn't mean you can't care for someone else.' The car became very quiet. 'So what do you think?' I asked no one in particular. I looked in the rear view mirror and saw that Alex was giving my question a lot of thought. Tom, as usual was drawing away, his big passion. I glanced at Elie who was now staring rigidly at her book. Finally Alex leaned forward and rubbed what was left of my hair, 'As long as you're happy dad,' he said. 'Tom?' He didn't look up from his drawing book and merely said, 'Ok!'

I turned to look at Elie, she said nothing. In fact she didn't speak to me for over a day. Gideon was working by then, having decided studying wasn't his thing and being older, seventeen, with his own seventeen year old problems, didn't seem to mind one way or the other.

A couple of months later Dan moved in. The dynamics changed. Whereas before she was like Cookie, a close family friend, now she was 'competition' for Elie and a new imagined authority figure for the others. Dan had absolutely no intention of replacing their mum or exerting any rules. She was just there for them as she had always been and our lives moved on. Some years later Elie told me that they'd known all along that I'd been seeing Dan for months!

It had been decided by Network Centre that as *The Cook Report* was achieving such great ratings, the next series should be extended from seven programmes to thirteen. It was 1994. Consequently a new contract needed to be negotiated. I was asked to a meeting by Martin Baker, Head of Contracts at Central Television to discuss a new deal. We had had a difficult relationship in the past. When John Willcocks left the Agency, Roger's old contract had not been finalised. The outstanding issue revolved around the sum of just five hundred pounds. Central had been arguing about it for four months. When I took it on I wasn't happy with any of the deal and decided that I'd start again. I called Martin and suggested we meet. He reminded me of a junior bank manager. Slim, diminutive and very neatly dressed. He came to my office under the impression, I think, that we'd probably sort out the five hundred pounds one way or another in five minutes and then get on with our lives.

'Martin, I'll be frank with you, for what Roger risks in making his programmes he's seriously underpaid.' His face revealed he hadn't registered what I was saying. 'He's worth another ten thousand.' I leant back in my chair.

'I'm sorry!' He leaned forward in his. 'But we've nearly closed the deal. I don't understand.'

'Martin, that's the point. The deal isn't closed and Central has had four months in which to do it.'

'Are you being serious? Because if you are my people will be furious.'

'It is serious and your people aren't my problem. It's difficult to make The Cook Report without Roger.'

We met in the middle and he never forgave me. Now we meet again.

I had to travel to Central's Birmingham studios for the mini conference which was held in the office of the programme's editor, Mike Townson. Attending were Martin Baker, Mike Townson, John Edwards the Controller of Current Affairs and me. I'd known John for many years. I did the 'Stones On The Road' deal with him over a decade ago. They were all in a hearty mood.

After all, seven more shows was an excellent revenue earner.

'Thanks for coming up Jon,' John kicked off the meeting.

'I'm sure you'll make it worthwhile,' I smiled. They smiled. We were all smiling.

'What we've got in mind is a further fifteen thousand on his current contract,' said Martin looking pleased with himself.

'Sorry?' I said, the smile having left for pastures new.

'We think it's a fair offer bearing in mind what he's currently on.' Martin said quickly. Perhaps a reference to our previous meeting. I stood up. I always seem to stand up at some point when I'm negotiating.

'I'm confused. Roger makes seven more programmes and you're offering,' I made great play by counting on my fingers, 'just over two thousand pounds a programme.' I really believe they hadn't thought it through. Unbelievable as it sounds they just hadn't done the number crunching. 'Call me old fashioned, but doubling the programmes means doubling the money.' I knew that wasn't strictly true but it sounded the right thing to say at that moment. They decided to call a time out.

'If you're ok with it Jon, we'll go to another office and discuss it further,' John said getting to his feet, 'Use the phone if you want to.' They left me alone. I hadn't come all the way to Birmingham to use their phone. The funny thing was I wasn't remotely surprised. TV is a strange business. Roger Cook risks his life on innumerable occasions while some chat show host or comedian with nothing like his ratings or profile is paid five times as much. The same of course could be said for some foreign correspondents.

They returned twenty minutes later and immediately upped their offer by another forty thousand pounds. I stood up (there I go again); 'It's taken you less than half an hour to come up with another forty grand. I wished we'd had this conversation on the phone and I could have saved a lot of time. No thanks, it's not even close.' I walked out and took the train back to Euston.

After a couple of weeks of talks we did get pretty close to doubling his existing contract.

CHAPTER FIFTY TWO
MAGIC, MICHAEL PORTILLO AND ELENA'S L'ETOILE

After my last experience at playing at promoter it was just common sense not to try again. But common sense and Roseman are strange bedfellows. I've always been a great fan of magic. Woody Allen, also a big fan, said it was the way Jews in particular used it to get over their shyness to speak to girls. I'd met Simon Drake through mutual friends and he'd enjoyed huge success in the early 1990's with two Channel 4 series, called *The Secret Cabaret Of Simon Drake*. It was a late night series because when this guy cut you in half more blood gushed out than in the opening of *Saving Private Ryan*. This man was one of the world's finest illusionists. We had a few lunches and became good friends and he in turn taught me a lot about magic.

I wanted him to do more television but he had a traumatic experience working with the producers of *The Secret Cabaret* and decided instead to buy an old early Victorian pub in Kennington near the Oval Cricket Ground and convert it to a venue where he could entertain the public. It is a fantastic place and includes a house of horrors in its cavernous cellar. If he wouldn't do telly, then I persuaded him instead to do a small tour. He tried to dissuade me, knowing the pitfalls of such a venture, but I didn't listen. In all we did about twenty two gigs and I lost a bundle! After he'd won the prestigious Perrier Award, but before he was famous, we used Lee Evans as one of the warm up acts. His rendition of Queen's *Bohemian Rhapsody* brought the house down. That is when we played to a house big enough to bring down.

Like all comedians Lee needed to try out new material which didn't always work. It was when that material came to make up fifty percent of that act that I had to intervene. As the promoter, the guy picking up the bills, I didn't have any option. In retrospect it did seem a little churlish as he was only paid one hundred pounds a night. This might be a little less than he takes home today!

At about this time Michael Portillo memorably lost his Enfield Southgate seat in the 1997 General Election. He decided on a broadcasting career. He asked Kelvin McKenzie, who had by this time left The Sun, and had embarked on a broadcasting career himself, though as an executive, who he'd recommend as an agent. My name came up. He called me and we arranged to meet for coffee at midday at Elena's L'Etoile in Charlotte Street.

Elena's restaurant was my real London office. I'd known her since 1973. She is a remarkable and wonderful woman who's still working at ninety. I first met her when she ran a restaurant in Soho called *Bianchi's*. She'd been there for over thirty years. Her husband, Aldo, also worked there. It was on the second floor and access was up two flights of steep winding stairs. She had garnered a clientele of everyone and anyone in the media, film and stage. She moved on to *L'Escargot* in Greek Street, having been enticed by the restaurateur Roy Ackerman and then finally in 1998 to *L'Etoile* in Charlotte Street. The name was immediately changed *to Elena's L'Etoile* to cash in on her reputation. If she ever retired, I suspect the place would suffer. The stardust would have gone.

I arrived a little early and chatted to her. When I told her who I was seeing, she shook her head and told me he'd been very rude to her when she was running her floor at *L'Escargot*. Lots of people had told me he was arrogant and could be deeply unpleasant. In over thirty years I'd never heard her utter a single negative word about anyone other than Michael Portillo. Michael, accompanied by a young attractive assistant, arrived just after twelve. The restaurant was empty and we sat at my usual table. After the normal preamble we got to the nitty gritty.

'Michael I don't mean to be rude but you have a terrible reputation. A lot of people in the business say you can be, how shall I put it, ungracious and a little arrogant.' I thought his secretary was going to pass out with shock. She turned puce and studied her finger nails with the intensity normally reserved for a surgeon performing the most delicate incision. His expression however didn't change. Years on the political hustings had inured him to any criticism. 'When I told Elena we were having coffee even she remembered you being rude to her some years back at *L'Escargot*. There's a lot of difficult people working in television but it also provides the opportunity to change people's perception'.

I wasn't sure if I was getting through to him. If he wanted me to represent him and I took the job, I didn't want to deal with some arrogant possibly embittered ex-politico on a day-to-day basis. That was a T-shirt I already had. Similarly if he wasn't going to take my advice it would be a waste of time for both of us. 'The point I'm making is that whatever unpleasant view anyone has of you, you will be in a position to change it. I have listened to you on *Any Questions* and other programmes and I know you'll make a brilliant broadcaster. It's up to you, if you feel I'm making any sense.' He listened carefully but I was under the distinct impression that no one had read him his rights before and he found my bluntness very uncomfortable. I wasn't surprised to receive a fax two days later thanking me for my time but declining to pursue things any further. Since then he's become a very popular broadcaster, but only because he has exorcised the old Portillo.

CHAPTER FIFTY THREE
JILL DANDO, THE BBC A NEW DEAL, THE HALF CENTURY

When I lived in Chiswick I often gave dinner parties for clients, journalists and TV execs. Usually we had sixteen round the table and this was followed up by another thirty or so who would join us for drinks around ten o'clock. I hated these parties with an extraordinary vehemence. I don't like large gatherings of human beings. I'm just not a people person. I rarely go to parties, award ceremonies or dinner parties. What few friends I have stopped inviting me to parties years ago, as they knew I wouldn't show up, much to Dan's chagrin. Dan had her own circle of close friends so at least she had a life outside of us. I once attended an old friend's birthday dinner in Camden Town. At just after ten thirty a mutual friend of ours turned up unexpectedly and he was genuinely astonished to see me. 'What's *he* doing here?' he said pointing at me, 'Roseman doesn't do going out!'

I was in the middle of negotiating Jill Dando's BBC contract, and as she was due at my house for dinner, I arranged for her to drop by early so we could go through the major points. She was delayed and we didn't get the opportunity. The evening, as usual, went brilliantly, mainly due to Dan's cooking and general attention to detail. I was useless and sat around most of the time wondering if I could be somewhere else.

Media people like to drink and as they drifted away around three o'clock in the morning I took Jill to her minicab. It was, to use Snoopy's words, "*a dark and stormy night*". As I led a rather inebriated Jill toward the car she suddenly turned and said, 'We haven't gone through the contract!' The rain is gushing down and I half expected to see Noah's Ark float down the road. She opened her handbag and produced the fax I'd sent her. It was one of the old style faxes and unrolled like an ancient parchment. We're both standing by the cab, rain soaking us and the fax and I'm trying gently to persuade her into the car. But the alcohol was making her more insistent that we should be studying the document despite the time and rain. I finally managed to make her understand that this wasn't the time or the place and finally manoeuvred her into the back seat of the cab.

Dan and her helpers were tidying up when I nipped into the lounge for a glass of something for the road. I wish I hadn't bothered. Seeing one of my gay clients on his knees, performing, what the tabloids would call a sex act on a journalist was taking good relations with the press a tad too far I thought.

We finally got to talk about the contract some days later. I was very unhappy with the proposals from the BBC. Jill at that time was contracted to do the 'Holiday' programme, fifty six days of news presentation and *Crimewatch*. *Holiday* took her out of the mix for over seven months. We'd decided that the time had come to ditch the series and move on. Oddly, in all her time at the BBC, she'd never actually launched a new programme. She had always taken over from another presenter. The next step was going to be a major career move.

Earlier that year, under the new boss, Tony Hall, the *Six o'clock News* was to be revamped. The search was on for a new presenter. Lots of people were in the frame including Jill and Anna Ford. What I couldn't let happen, if Jill wasn't offered the job, was for it to appear she'd been passed over. It would have sent out all the wrong signals.

I met Peter Salmon, then Controller of BBC1 and one of the few bosses I had a genuine respect for. He agreed that if she didn't get the job, he'd let me know some months before, so I would have the time to make it appear she wasn't interested. As it was, the search went on for over seven months. Anna Ford was furious with the length of time it was taking and said so publicly.

Tony Hall felt that Jill's time on 'Holiday' had diluted her credibility as a newscaster and consequently she was never seriously considered. Peter was very disappointed but had little power over the news division unlike his opposite number, David Liddement the Director of Programmes at ITV.

We withdrew from the 'race' citing the absurdly long time they were taking and the plethora of offers that were coming Jill's way. There was no plethora. Steve Anderson, then Controller of News and Current Affairs at ITV, called to tell me that when he and Liddement heard Jill was no longer in the running, they cracked open a bottle of champagne.

The time had come to discuss Jill's future with the BBC. A meeting was arranged at the late lamented Halycon Hotel in Holland Park with the BBC's Head of Factual, Anne Morrison and Jane Lush, Controller of Daytime. We sat around a table in the corner of the bar and were presented with a sheet of paper containing the BBC's thoughts. They may as well have written their 'ideas' on the back of a used envelope.

Among them were four royal documentaries. I asked if the Palace had given their permission for the films to be made. I stared at blank faces. 'Well if you haven't any agreement to film them, then they are purely speculative,' I noted, 'I'll just cross them off.' They tried to object but there was no arguing on the wholly hypothetical nature of the proposal. Another idea sounded interesting and I asked to see a treatment for it. There wasn't one. There had to be something I said. I was told that it was at the 'idea stage' whatever bollocks that meant. I put a red line through that one as well. They'd had five months to prepare for this meeting. I've heard afterthoughts more coherently presented.

Jill drove me back to Chiswick.

'I thought you were a little hard on them Jon,' she said. I knew that Jane Lush was a close friend of hers but that meeting had nothing to do with friendship. This was the first day of the rest of her career. I explained that to her. 'Someone has to watch your back and that's what you pay me to do. You don't pay me to be nice!'

I didn't hear anything from the BBC for a few weeks. I decided that I should approach ITV. I called Steve Anderson.

'Are you serious,' he wanted to know. 'You're not just using us to up the ante?'

'I haven't got an ante to up,' I said. 'I'll be straight with you. I haven't spoken to Jill about this. Before I do, I need to know if there's a very serious interest from your lot.' He said he'd speak to David Liddement. Twenty four hours later he confirmed ITV's interest but warned me that I'd better not be messing them about or they'd have my balls.

I mulled it over with Jill. She wasn't keen at all. The BBC had been her natural home for a long time. She was about to make some life changing decisions, getting married and moving home. A switch to ITV might well be a step too far. She also expressed her concern for the calibre of ITV's factual programmes. I appreciated everything she said but the real problem was that the BBC hadn't come up with anything, and worse than that, they didn't seem to have given it much thought. I told her we'd have nothing to lose from a meeting and everything to gain. She finally agreed.

The meeting needed to be held in some secrecy so we met in an anonymous hotel near Gray's Inn Road, where ITV Network Centre was based. Steve Anderson, Grant Mansfield, Head of Factual Programmes and David Liddement all greeted us when we arrived. There wasn't anything sumptuous about the hotel room but then we weren't there for sumptuous.

David tried to get an immediate handle on how serious Jill was. I'd been totally honest with Steve and had told him in advance the reservations Jill had. As an agent I was in a precarious position. I could piss off the BBC and ITV in one moment of folly, so honesty, at least with ITV, seemed the sensible route. Jill wanted to know if there were any opportunities in News. David said there were. 'But what about Dermot Monyhan?' she asked, 'I heard he's now Trevor's official stand-in.'

He fixed Jill with a steely eye, 'I run ITV and I say who presents what!' No problem there then. 'Jon says you've issues over the quality of our factual programming. I think we do a good job but I'm quite prepared for you to sit next to me as I sift through the proposals. You can have first choice on anything that interests you.' They really wanted Jill. Of that there could now be no doubt.

They left after an hour and their body language told me they'd done the best they could but had little or no hope of landing her. When we were alone I asked her how she felt. I didn't need a doctorate in psychology to tell that her heart wasn't in it.

Back to the BBC.

Peter Salmon, Controller of BBC1, suggested we all had dinner. The 'all' being Jill, Jane Lush and Anne Morrison, me and of course Peter. The time seven o'clock, the place The Criterion in Piccadilly. I drove in with Jill and we talked over her concerns. I told her all I wanted was for the BBC to offer her carefully considered options for one of their most talented and famous faces, not some half baked ideas that would have been more suited to the likes of Anthea Turner but Jill was never comfortable with anything remotely confrontational.

Peter was nearly an hour late, so we demolished a bottle or two of Chablis. I could tell that I wasn't Mr Popular with our friends from the Beeb. I'm sure they'd rather I wasn't there or preferably didn't exist at all. That way Jill could be persuaded to participate in just about anything. Jill wasn't anybody's fool but she dreaded these kinds of meetings. Whilst she had firm ideas about her career, in my view, she also had far too much faith in her current employers.

After Peter arrived we ate and chatted about everything other than why we were there. I personally don't do that kind of chat *per se* but for once I let the evening play out. The dinner over, we attended to the business in hand. Peter launched into a presentation of the projects I'd thought were buried at the last meeting. He is a skilled executive and made them appear fresh and exciting. I still wasn't buying the pitch. It was when he turned to Jill and asked her what she thought about radio, that I nearly brought up my sea bass.

'I think I want to say something Peter, but I need to think very carefully before I do. If nobody minds, I'd like to nip out for a few minutes and have a quick cigarette.'

'Jon, you can say anything you like, you know that. After all we've all known each other a very long time.' Not nearly long enough I thought. Outside Piccadilly was busy as usual. Tourist bodies covered Eros as I paced up and down wondering what I should say so as not to embarrass Jill too much.

When I returned to the table they all stopped talking and looked at me expectantly.

'I'll be straight with you Peter. When you asked Jill, had she thought about radio, I was very disappointed.'

'Come on Jon there's nothing wrong with radio,' Jane Lush said with a distinct edge to her voice.

'I'm not saying there is. But we're here to talk about Jill's TV career.'

'Lot's of our prime talent does radio,' she went on. 'Jonathan Ross, Michael Parkinson.....' I watched Peter lean forward and pick up a bottle of Perrier, for a second I thought he was going to wallop me with it.

'I'm not here for Ross or Parkinson. I know none of you have any great allegiance to radio so why on earth would you want to bring it up. You've had months to consider Jill's career and now you bring up radio, I'm very confused.' Dropping pins comes to mind. Their silence enveloped me. After a minute or two Jill and Jane went to the loo, leaving me with the Controller of BBC1 and the Head of Factual Programmes. They turned to each other and discussed the fucking weather for all I could tell. One thing was an absolute certainty, they had no wish to talk to me either then or for the rest of eternity!

Jane and Jill returned, the bill was paid, and the evening was over. On the way back, our conversation was muted at best.

'I'm sorry if you felt I said anything inappropriate, but as I said, they've had months to prepare and throwing radio into the mix really pissed me off!' She thought for a moment and turned to me,' Jon, I know you're right, and I wasn't happy either, but you know how I get...'

We left it at that. Some weeks later she signed off on a new contract (which didn't include radio). I could only hope that the fine programme makers at the BBC, who did exist by the way, would deliver the goods.

It was 1998 - the year of my fiftieth birthday, January sixth. I'm not good with birthday parties or, as I've said, any parties at all. Dan asked me in early December if I wanted to do something special and I dismissed the idea out of hand. As the clock ticked closer to the day, I had a change of mind. Dan contacted Simon Drake and we used his amazing venue, The House Of Magic, for the party.

As most of my clients were coming I'd contacted *OK!* magazine and invited them to cover the 'event'. Since Pearl died I had been a regular donator to the Marsden and I asked them, by way of a fee, to make a contribution to the hospital. It was my way of sharing my fiftieth with her.

The party by all accounts was a big success. Simon performed a forty five minute routine which was greeted with a standing ovation and his house of horrors scared the living shit out of the guests who'd decided to give it a test drive. There was a good turnout of clients, including Penny Smith who Simon decapitated on stage, Roger Cook, Kate Garraway and Jill Dando.

CHAPTER FIFTY FOUR
TANIA BRYER AND RICHARD DESMOND

I represented Tania Bryer for some years. She was always very pleasant and it was obvious she came from 'good stock'. She began her TV career as a weather presenter which is never a good starting point. There's an old joke where a couple who'd lost their way in Ireland ask a local for directions and are told, 'well I wouldn't have started from here.' The same can be said of weather presenting. Young female presenters, in those days, see it as a way into the business, but no matter what talent they posses, they will be forever branded as a weather girl.

Tania was very bright and had a good range of contacts, and was always seen at the right parties. This proved to be of some help. She came to the attention of *OK*'s then editor who thought she was just the right person to be an occasional contributor. The magazine was only a few years old and was fighting a fierce circulation war with *Hello* to establish itself. Richard Desmond, the owner and publisher, had chosen a tough marketplace to compete in.

The editor, Tania and I had lunch at Joe Allen's, a fashionable theatreland burger restaurant in Covent Garden. It was *OK!*'s choice, as I've never been remotely fashionable. The editor and Tania got on very well so I decided to try another pitch.

'I'm the first to admit I know nothing about the magazine business, but your rivalry with *Hello* is not exactly a secret. And, while I don't want to appear contentious, *OK!* is viewed as rather low rent.' I waited to see if she'd either throw a condiment at me or waltz out, never to be seen again. She just looked at me expectantly. 'So rather than just offer Tania the occasional column why not utilise her fabulous contacts and let her be a sort of ambassador for the magazine. What more upmarket presence could you want? She goes to all the right places and she can wave the *OK!* banner wherever she goes.'

'Jon that's a brilliant idea. I'll see what Richard says.' Her boss had to agree everything and had a fearsome reputation for detail.

We spoke the next day and negotiated a deal which had to be run by the man upstairs. They agreed to pay a hundred and fifty thousand pounds for one year. I couldn't believe I had the chutzpah even to ask for that amount, let alone have Richard Desmond sign off on it. But I didn't know Richard. After three months the money was cut to one hundred and twenty thousand: a month or two later it went down to one hundred thousand. None of this by discussion. The first I heard about the reductions was when the money came in. When I enquired why it had been cut back, I was told 'cause Richard said so'. I certainly wasn't going to argue with him, I was amazed he'd agreed the money in the first place. Finally after six months the money settled at eighty thousand and I think, for what she was doing, that was a fair figure.

Some years later I went to see Richard at his old offices off Blackfriars Bridge. I'd rung him up and suggested coffee. We'd spoken many times over the years but had never met. Reception announced my arrival and I was shown up to his office by his butler in full livery. When I arrived, he was having a noisy discussion with one of his marketing people. Apparently *OK!* had been offered around one hundred and fifty thousand pounds to carry a chocolate bar on its cover. The marketing man was saying newsagents hated these kind of promotions as the magazines became difficult to stack; Richard on the other hand liked the cash.

His butler quietly interrupted the two men to introduce me to Richard. He took a long look at my diamond stud earring and said,' You a poof then?'

'Actually I am.' I replied. His face froze. I was carrying a rolled up copy of the *Evening Standard* and as I playfully smote him across his buttocks with the paper said, 'I'm only joking Richard.'

He turned to me and asked, 'So what would you do Jon, annoy the newsagents or take the money?'

'Take the money!'

'That's what we'll do then.' He dismissed the man from marketing and we went inside his office. It wasn't palatial as such, but big enough to allow him to have his drum kit in a corner! His butler brought in the coffee and we sat down and talked about our mothers. He offered me a large Cohiba from the biggest humidor I'd seen outside of Harrods and we both lit up. I found him amiable and enjoyed his company, but then again I didn't have to work for him.

Martin Townsend and Peter Hill, editors of the *Sunday* and *Daily Express* respectively, are both friends of mine and they are strongly protective of their boss and honestly admire him. It's no secret that so-called "newspaper people" feel he is the anti-Christ of publishing. Then there are others who don't think so highly of him!

CHAPTER FIFTY FIVE
MURDER AND GOOD MEN DIE LIKE DOGS

I was sitting in my office in The Power House in Chiswick mulling over a contract, it was eleven thirty.

It was the 26th April, 1999 .My phone rings. It's the news desk at *The Mirror*. They've had a tip off that Jill Dando's been hurt in an accident, had I heard anything? No I hadn't. Two minutes later I get a call from *The Daily Mail*, they've had a report that Jill may have been assaulted near her home. I had no comment to make having nothing to comment on. Then a call from *The Sun*. They had a tip off that Jill had been stabbed. One call could mean anything, two could mean something, three certainly meant that there was a problem.

I called her fiancé, Dr. Alan Farthing. I told him I'd had a couple of calls to say Jill may have been in an accident and that I wasn't in a position to check it out, but as he was both a doctor and her fiancé he was best placed to make a call. I had already been on-line to get the number of Fulham police which I passed onto him.

Then I heard the scream. It was from my senior agent Allisonne (Ally) Lewis. 'Jill's been shot!' It had just been announced on *Sky News*. I fumbled for the TV remote and turned on my television, went straight to *Sky News* and there it was. I stared at the pictures not really taking any of it in. I couldn't believe it. I didn't believe it.

I rushed downstairs from my office, the staff were crying and I did what I could to calm things down. I knew the phones were going to start ringing off the hook and I wanted us to be able to reflect some semblance of professionalism under extraordinary circumstances.

The first call I took was from Alan. He told me he was with the police at the back of Charing Cross hospital where Jill had been taken, in order to avoid the press hordes now camped outside the front entrance. Later I learned that that she'd been murdered, and contravening all police procedure, they'd allowed Alan to see her body. It was a wretched time for him, her family and friends. The press and television coverage was immense.

Over the next few months everyone who knew Jill was interviewed, some, like myself on many occasions. It was not difficult to tell that the police were struggling with the investigation. Apart from all the calls they received with information that had to be followed up, they couldn't establish a motive. The nature of the murder seemed to many observers to scream out 'professional hit'. Various things disturbed me about the BBC and the police at this time.

ITV wanted to make a programme about the murder in an attempt to jog people's memories in case they had something to offer the investigation. I was asked if Ally would take part. She was probably the last person to speak to Jill, since Jill had rung the office minutes before she was killed for a catch up.

She and Ally were very close. Jill had told her she was on her way back to her house in Gowan Avenue in Fulham to pick up some faxes, as, by this time, she was living with Alan in Chiswick. We all wanted to do our bit to help catch Jill's killer, but I had to be mindful of the fact that ITV weren't being entirely altruistic in their request. It was obviously going to make good TV as well.

I asked Ally if she wanted to do the programme and she readily agreed. In order that the police investigation wouldn't be compromised, I suggested she call them to check that they were ok with it. They were happy. The BBC was furious.

The day after the programme went out, Jane Lush, the BBC's Controller of Daytime, rang Ally and accused of her screwing 'everything' up by participating in the ITV film and left her in no doubt that she'd made a serious error of judgment. Ally was in tears when she came to my office and told me what Jane had said. I was not a happy man. I called her. Before I could get a word in she was off.

'Jon, how could you allow Ally to do an interview for ITV?' She was a very angry lady.

'I'm sorry I'm not sure I understand you.' I said.

'You know what I'm saying,' the tone notching up to anger mark five. 'She's one of *ours* for god's sake.'

'Surely you're not saying that any help we could give to find Jill's murderer should be the exclusive preserve of the Beeb?'

'That's exactly what I'm saying. We've got a special Crimewatch programme coming up and this has caused us a lot of problems.' I'd known Jane for many years and always found her a clever executive with sound judgment but this was absurd. 'The police have given their full co-operation in the making of *our* programme and all ITV have done is to try to get one over on us.' She was now shouting. It was completely out of character.

'This is ridiculous. Whatever anyone can do to help solve Jill's murder should be done. I don't care whether it's the Beeb, ITV, Sky News or Al Jazeera. Do you think we didn't check with the police to see if they wanted Ally to do it, to find out if it would be the right thing to do?' Jane had heard enough and hung up.

What I found disturbing about the *Crimewatch* programme was the way the BBC promoted it. They claimed to have an exclusive identikit picture of the man the police were looking for. The public had to wait several days after the initial promo before the programme was broadcast to get a glimpse of the most wanted man in Britain! Now call me old fashioned, but if you had a picture of the possible killer, why would you take your time before putting it into the public domain; the trail was already getting decidedly chilly.

Nick Ross, who I'd once represented, has a good heart. I'd witnessed it on several occasions. When Pearl was very ill we'd had lunch and he asked me if I needed anything, anything at all. Was I all right for money and did I need a private nurse to help look after her? I knew him as a kind, caring man, but somehow he'd suddenly become Jill's fiancé's best friend and 'official' spokesman for the family as well as the BBC. Though they co-presented Crimewatch together for four years, it was only one day a month and I was uncomfortable that he was giving the impression that he was one of her closest friends.

I had long held the belief that Jill was murdered by a professional hit man and gave an interview to a national newspaper explaining my thoughts. I went to great pains to point out that I had no special skills or knowledge but it seemed to fit the facts as I knew them at the time. My theory was simple: Jill had made a recent television appeal for the Kosovan Albanian refugees. It was a high profile event. It would have angered the likes of the mass murderer Radovan Karadzic and his more fanatical supporters. When NATO bombed the television station in Belgrade a few weeks later, the Bosnian-Serb culture would have called for an eye for an eye. There was a lot of talk of 'you kill our journalists, we'll kill yours'.

With men like Arkan, the Bosnian-Serb warlord leader on your payroll, revenge would have been no problem.

Jill was murdered on her doorstep with one bullet. No one, least of all Jill herself, knew she would be dropping by her house at that time and on that day. Jill was on her way to lunch with a friend and after doing a little shopping decided at the last minute to stop by her house and pick up some faxes. We know she wasn't followed, the CTTV footage we've all seen confirms that.

What's perhaps difficult to understand is that if a professional hit man was responsible, he would have done a great deal of preparation. He'd have followed her, found out where she lived, which wasn't at Gowan Avenue, studied her day-to-day movements and would want to ensure a good escape plan. Allan lived in a private enclave in Chiswick. No passing cars or people other than a few neighbours. He would have observed that Alan left at regular times for the hospital where he worked leaving Jill alone in the house. What better place to conduct such a terrible deed? Alan leaves, the door bell is rung, Jill answers door, the murder is committed, close the door and make good your escape to Heathrow which is less than a thirty minute drive away.

So why on earth would a professional take the huge risk of killing her on her own doorstep in daylight in the middle of Fulham? I suggested that if it was a hit ordered by Radovan Karadzic, it would have had to be done within days of the Belgrade TV station being bombed which was a Friday. There was evidence to suggest that his wife had some ownership of the TV station. The funerals for the victims of the bombing were to be held on the following Monday. This day would provide a perfect platform for symbolic retribution. There would have been no time to make any serious preparations. My guess is that they flew someone into London over the weekend who met a sympathetic Serb who would have provided the weapon and cartridges. The evidence confirmed that the gun was a re-commissioned one and the bullet that was fired had been tampered with in order to suppress the sound as it left the barrel.

A professional would have no problem re-commissioning the weapon or 'fixing' the bullet. The only address they probably had available was her Gowan Avenue home. He'd certainly have had a photo of Jill and must have waited around Gowan Avenue for her to turn up. The fact that she did was the assassin's good luck and her devastating misfortune.

We're told by so-called 'professional' hit men that waiting for her to get to her front door instead of doing the deed as she gets out of her car is not the work of an experienced killer. I suggested that while any member of the public would recognise Jill from fifty yards a visiting Serb would only have a photo and her address. He may have recognised her as she left her car but for complete certainty he'd wait till she walked up the small path to her front door. This would account for the inconsistencies that the so-called 'experts' found difficult to accept.

I never believed Barry George could have committed such a well planned murder and said so many times. This brought me into conflict with Nick Ross in particular. Sometime back I did an interview where I expressed some regret at ever having gone public with my thoughts. I'd become a sort of first stop for every reporter writing a story on Jill and this was making me very uncomfortable. Nick misunderstood the reasons behind what I'd meant in the interview and emailed me believing that I regretted saying George was not guilty. He was wrong.

A few months before all this horror came into my life I'd finished my first book. It was a comic thriller about a good looking Jewish agent (!) whose clients are murdered alphabetically under mysterious circumstances. I called the book '*Good Men Die Like Dogs*'. The title came from the late Hunter S. Thompson. *The TV business is a cruel and shallow money trench, a long plastic hallway where thieves and pimps run free and good men die like dogs.* I'd spent the last six months revising it when Jill was murdered. I mentioned the content of the book in passing to a friend on *The Daily Telegraph* and he asked me if I'd told the police about it. I hadn't. I asked him what possible relevance it had to their investigation. He pointed out that if they did make an arrest and it went to court and my book surfaced it might complicate matters. I wasn't buying into this nonsense but I called Ian Bloom and sought his advice. He came straight to the point, 'Did the agent do it?' I told him 'No,' 'Well that's alright then,' he said. I was beginning to think someone had slipped me a magic mushroom. This was getting all too surreal for me.

I called them anyway. I'd been interviewed on about five occasions all by the same officer, let's call him Paul, but often with a different colleague. They met me at my office in Chiswick one Saturday morning. As they sipped coffee I pulled out the manuscript from my desk drawer and put it on my lap.

'This might sound ridiculous but a journalist friend advised me that I should tell you about a novel I've written.' I stood up and handed the bundle of papers to Paul. 'It's a thriller I finished last year about an agent whose clients are murdered.' I looked at them and felt like a total idiot. If there was an offence for being a dickhead, they'd have cuffed me and taken me away.

'How long was there between the first murder and the second one?' Paul asked. He couldn't be serious. I looked at him. He was.

'Two weeks.' I said feeling that I'd stepped into the *Twilight Zone*. We talked for twenty minutes and they left taking my manuscript with them. I hadn't thought about the book let alone worked on it since Jill's death. I took another copy from my desk and idly flipped through it. It occurred to me that I must have been one of the few would be thriller writers around who could measure the accuracy of what they'd written by events that were happening in real life. I re-read some of it and the interviews the main character had with the police were remarkably similar to my own with Paul. There was one omission. He had, in our very first meeting, asked me if I insured the lives of my clients. I didn't. But it wasn't a question the fictional police had asked in the book. They should have. There was no way I could have attempted to get the book published as it would have been potentially interpreted as cashing in on Jill's death. Now, ten years on, I'm revising it...

Paul came to see me again two weeks later and observed that, though he hadn't finished reading it, I didn't appear to like the police very much. He was referring to their first introduction in the book where I'd written, *the police from the land of fuck you entered my office.* I told him that if he'd finish it he'd find they were the heroes in the end.

He finally returned it a few weeks later. 'I really enjoyed it,' he said with a wry smile, 'it's very good!' I had this vision that I'd be going on vacation via Gatwick Airport and there would be on sale at the South Terminal bookshops my book, '*Good Men Die Like Dogs*', and highlighted across the cover, *A great read, The Met!*

CHAPTER FIFTY SIX
WEDDING BELLS, ANTHEA AND LIP GLOSS AND THE MERINGUE INCIDENT

After the terrible events of the previous couple of months Dan and I were invited to a friend's wedding in Padua in northern Italy. Liam Hamilton, a dour Scot, had held various senior executive positions in ITV from Editor of *This Morning*, Managing Director of LWT and Controller of Daytime for The Network Centre. He'd met and fallen in love with a beautiful Italian actress, Ilaria. All his friends knew she was way out of his league, but she wouldn't listen!

We all headed off to Padua, the setting for Shakespeare's *The Taming Of The Shrew*. A beautiful place standing on the Bacchiglione River. The guests included, David Liddement, Controller of ITV, Peter McHugh, then Head of GMTV, Anthea Turner and estranged hubbie Peter Powell and the late, lovely Caron Keating.

The wedding party was held at a sumptuous villa on the outskirts of Padua. As a tribute to Liam's Scottish ancestry many of us wore kilts. I'd taken some advice the night before the nuptials while drinking in the piazza with some of his Glaswegian friends as to the mystery of what a man wears under the kilt. By common consent the answer was nothing. The lying bastards! The temperature was in the nineties and as the day wore on the roughness of the kilt and the continual outpouring of sweat made me incredibly sore around all points south. I made no secret of my discomfort. I have no pride!

The villa's dining area had been laid with forty tables all tastefully decorated with the most beautiful orchids, the starched white tablecloths moving gently with the occasional welcome gust of wind. I noticed Dan had a tube of lip balm which I assumed contained Vaseline. I announced to the table that I was off to the men's room with said lip balm to alleviate the growing soreness in my nether regions. I rubbed it on to my fingers and then applied accordingly. I was pretty certain the instructions for its use didn't state, *in case of soreness in the area of genitals due to wearing a kilt in hot climates apply liberally.*

Back at the table I was suddenly overcome with the most overwhelming pain from down below. I told Dan who thought for a second and began laughing.

'It's got menthol in it,' she said. It took ten minutes for the pain to subside. I was glad to see the entire table took huge amusement in my agony.

Anthea Turner and Caron Keating were table hopping and stopped by to say 'hi'. Anthea, seeing the lip balm lying next to Dan's handbag, picked it up.

'You don't mind Danielle,' she said applying it to her lips. Everyone at the table stared at her believing, wrongly, that I'd just rubbed it on my dick and balls. Laugh? I thought they'd pass out. It wasn't till some weeks later that I got a call from *The Sun* asking if it was true that Anthea had used a tube of lip balm that I had, only minutes earlier been intimate with. I expressed plausible deniability. Two days later I read the story: At a wedding in Padua, Italy, top London Jewish (I think this was a reference to being circumcised) agent Jon Roseman finding himself in some pain from wearing a kilt with no underwear applied his partner's lip balm to his private parts to obtain some relief. Someone, *not*, Anthea Turner, then in full view of everyone at the table applied it directly to her lips.

I bumped in to her a few weeks later and she wiggled her finger at me and smiled. She was alright was our Anthea.

I rarely went to weddings since, as I have pointed out repeatedly, I'm not very good in the company of more than a dozen people. However when one of Dan's best friend's, Yara Karmiloff, got married she was asked to be one of the bridesmaids. I had no way out. Oddly this was another wedding held in Italy. It managed to cough up one further catastrophe for me. The event has gone down in our family history as The Great Meringue Incident.

The wedding and reception took place in a beautiful villa in Ca Vendri just outside Verona, and belonged to the family of Serena Melloni, an old friend of the bride's. It was magnificent. I'd always had an ambition to live out my old age in such a place. Now, I'd be lucky to get a job cleaning it. There were long steep steps from the veranda down to the sun drenched olive groves below which spread out over several acres. Seated on the bottom steps were a young couple smoking and chatting. I asked Serena who the couple were. They turned out to be relatives of hers. I noticed a huge ornate plate full of small meringues. Feeling in a playful mood I picked one up and casually asked her what they'd do if I tossed it down the steps and it actually connected with one of them. She just laughed and said, 'Do it Jon, it's ok. It's only a meringue.' I launched the missile.

Unbelievably, it hit the girl on the top of her head and exploded in a wisp of white mist. They both stood up immediately and ran up the steps, stopping only momentarily in front of me to utter some curses in Italian, the girl in tears, and then fled into the villa. I turned to Serena in disbelief.

'What was all that about, it was only a meringue for god's sake?'

'Oh! I remember now,' said Serena remembering. 'She was in a very bad car accident last year. She had to have a metal plate put inside her head and was in a coma for five days.'

'What part of *is it ok* didn't you understand?' I said. 'How could you possibly forget that she had a metal plate in her fucking head?' To make matters worse, if that was possible, the boy came from the Sicilian part of the family. I have no problem in admitting I hid in our rented car for most of the afternoon.

CHAPTER FIFTY SEVEN
NICK FERRARI AND DAVID BANKS AND KELVIN McKENZIE

I represented Nick Ferrari and David Banks when they were asked to join Kelvin MacKenzie's *Talk Radio* in 1998. Nick had worked for the *Sunday* and *Daily Mirror* as well as the News Of The World and went way back with Kelvin. Banksy had been a journalist since recorded history and had edited the Daily Mirror.

Kelvin called me to cut the deal. It was a very lucrative fixed two year contract for both of them. I asked Kelvin for something in writing but he was far too busy, so I faxed over a couple of paragraphs which he signed and returned. They hit the air waves running as a unique double act called The *Big Boy's Breakfast.* At the time, they both made William Perry, aka "The Refrigerator", the Chicago Bears NFL player, look undernourished.

I was very careful to make a provision that if the contract was terminated for whatever reason the entire fees would fall due immediately taking no account of accelerated payment or obligations on them to mitigate. Often if a contract is ended early and there's, say, eight months remaining, then rather than pay the full amount, the paying party would be able to negotiate payment for a shorter period on the grounds that the payment had been 'accelerated' i.e. paid well before the due date, and in any event, the presenters should find other work anyway.

After a year Kelvin decided to reformat the station and change its name to *Talksport*. Banksy and Ferrari were out of a job. I wrote to Kelvin asking for the full amount on both contracts, over half a million pounds. He was not best pleased. In fact he was furious. He had intended to pay off the contracts but on a monthly basis. I sent him a copy of the fax he'd signed a year before and in typical Kelvin fashion he told them, through me, to go fuck themselves.

Hello Ian Bloom! The four of us had lunch at Elena's to discuss a strategy. Both journalists liked a few drinks and despite the serious nature of the matter at hand, a few bottles were despatched. Ian said there was no defence and advised serving two statutory demands on *Talksport*. He said, short as it was, the contract was clear. My mobile rang, it was Kelvin. I left the three of them to another bottle of claret and went outside into Charlotte Street to speak to him. It was a brief conversation. In case I was in any doubt (I wasn't), he wanted to make himself clear. There was no way he was going to pay the full amount in one lump sum and they could go fuck themselves. It had become his mantra. I tried to explain that legally he had a major problem but he wasn't in the mood to listen. I was going to suggest he paid it off in two stages, as I was certain, when he refinanced the station, he hadn't allowed in his cash flow for such a significant sum to vanish from the company's bank account all at once.

I rejoined the boys who were eager to know what Kelvin had wanted. I told them. It was time to press buttons. Ian served the necessary paperwork allowing *Talksport* 21 days to pay, challenge or be wound-up. Every day the money remained outstanding it was accruing interest, not a lot of interest but on five hundred and sixty thousand pounds at 8%, it would pay for several cases of claret. Finally Kelvin caved in and the day before a winding-up petition could be issued a cheque was biked round for the outstanding money plus costs and interest. It was two hundred and ninety pounds short. We let it go.

CHAPTER FIFTY EIGHT
NATASHA KAPLINSKY THE EARLY YEARS

L ife can be full of regrets and mine in particular has long overflowed with them. Which brings me to Natasha Kaplinsky. It all started when Clive Jones, Chief Executive of Carlton Television, called me. One of his myriad responsibilities was *London Tonight*. He and the editor had their eye on a local presenter working at Meridian TV. He explained that her agent didn't think a move from down South to London was career enhancing and would I be interested in representing her. I told Clive, who I'd known for twenty years, that I didn't poach clients from other agents but if she wanted to come and see me that was her call.

Kaplinsky came to see me a week or so later. Personally I didn't understand what the fuss was about. Her track record as a journalist was zero and she wore more make up than a clown. I told her that in my view a move to London was crucial if she wanted to progress. She was having such a great time with Fred Dinenage that she really didn't want to move. I understood because I'd briefly represented him and he was a lovely bloke, but then, so was Alistair Stewart. I told her I'd be delighted to represent her if she committed to *London Tonight* as it was the right move. If she didn't accept my advice, then it was a waste of time me being her agent.

She moved to *London Tonight*.

She bonded brilliantly with Alistair and the move was a great success. As she lived less than a half a mile away from me I saw more of her than I usually would most clients. Her boyfriend, Mike Barnard, was a fantastic guy. I'd tell anyone who'd listen that if you could pick a best mate it would be him. He liked a good glass of wine, loved his rugby and was extremely clever, sensitive and well read. If I'd been gay and unattached and thirty years younger I'd have married him!

What did impress me about Natasha was the way she hid her ambition. Her initial refusal to move from Meridian was an example of this. As an agent you never want to get involved in a client's personal life provided it doesn't affect their on-screen or public persona. I'd picked up some rumours which I was careful not to bring up with her. The London News Network (LNN) who she was now contracted with was very pleased with the pairing of her and Alistair and things ticked on well for some months.

I often discussed with her what I felt would be a barrier to her success which was her lack of journalism. I always remembered that great anchor for Sky News, Jeremy Thompson, saying to me. 'You're not a journalist till you've been either shot or shot at!' Personally I think that may be a step too far but his underlying point is you've got to put in the air miles.

One of the problems she had to contend with was her surname; people had suggested that she should change it. She came to see me and asked for my advice. My advice was simple, don't! As the months rolled by I seemed to be spending more and more time with her. One of my GMTV clients told me there were rumours going around about an affair! God forbid!

Towards the end of her first year in 2000 at LNN, I started to call a couple of friends in News to see if there was anything suitable to help her increase her journalistic credibility. I soon discovered she didn't have many supporters out there, particularly women and women journalists at that. She did have one big fan though, Sky's boss, Mark Sharman. Lunch was arranged.

Over a glass or two of Amarone, we batted around the idea of a move to Sky News for Kaplinsky. From my point of view it was perfect. Sky News, under the stewardship of Nick Pollard, would provide a master class in presentation skills, as well as honing her wafer thin journalistic abilities. Since Mark had taken over at Sky, he'd been pressing Nick to take on a couple more 'sexy' presenters. He felt that the presentation line up needed to be turned up a few notches. Nick didn't take well to interference in his operation and could point to a fistful of awards to confirm that the train was on the right track. We left it that Mark would have a word with him. I didn't tell Kaplinsky what I was up to as I knew she wouldn't want to move to a satellite broadcaster with a tiny audience, let alone be based in Osterley, West London, even though it was only a thirty minute drive from her home.

A couple of days passed and Nick Pollard called me. He wasn't a happy bunny. Since we were good friends he felt able to come straight to the point. There was no way in this lifetime he was going to hire her! That didn't leave me much room to manoeuvre. I pulled the old Roseman trick, lunch. I took him to La Trompette, one of the best restaurants in London and based in Chiswick, so he didn't have too far to travel. I wanted him relaxed, drunk actually. I wasn't remotely confident I could shift his position but I prayed a bottle or two might loosen him enough to at least agree to meet her. After a few hours he finally said yes.

Next I had to tell Natasha. I sat her down outside a little patisserie we often had coffee at in Turnham Green Terrace in Chiswick, which was equidistant from where we both lived. She was appalled. She was as vehement about not going to Sky as Nick was in not wanting her. I spied a little conundrum here! What to do? What to do? I had to get at least one of them onside before we met, otherwise it was going to turn out to be a car crash.

I did my best to persuade Natasha that it was a great move and would provide the much needed journalistic experience she was sorely lacking. Obviously I wasn't going to mention that Nick didn't want her as much as she didn't want to go. She agreed that she needed more experience, but wasn't there somewhere other than Sky she could get it? I'd already tried. The best shot I had was Steve Anderson, Head of News and Current Affairs at the Network Centre. He'd already told me there was nothing doing. The BBC were completely indifferent to her. Finally she agreed to the meeting. A date was set for a week's time.

285

One of the problems all agents have to deal with is that their clients are either married, have a boy/girl friend, often a 'best' friend or all of the above. They canvas views concerning their careers from everyone. Success or failure can hinge on the comment of well-meaning friends or family. Natasha rang me daily to gnaw at the Sky News bone. Oddly, after a week, she seemed to grow more positive about it. She appeared more convinced that it might be a genuinely useful move. I knew she'd mentioned it to Alistair Stewart, who really didn't want to lose his co-presenter, but I could tell someone else, with a lot of news experience, had been endorsing the move. I was to find out later who that was, when the shit hit the fan.

The three off us met in a hotel bar, Nick's choice of venue, and we settled down to talk at a corner table. There would have been more understanding and flexibility at a Middle East summit than there was round that table. When she asked Nick how long she'd get the script before she went on air his whole posture drooped. There are no scripts. You sit behind the desk and it all unfolds in front of you. For better or worse whatever happens you're expected to deal with it. She took a loo break and Nick just shook his head forlornly, 'This isn't going to work Jon. I really can't see how it can work.'

The following morning he rang me and his mood hadn't changed. I fell back in to that often used agent speak, 'Trust me on this one.' Finally he agreed. Natasha was still only sixty-forty for the idea but I went ahead with the contract anyway. We lunched at Elena's to sign off on the deal. She was in tears. "Isn't there anywhere else?' While she dabbed away, Steve Anderson who was lunching there popped over to the table. Seeing the state she was in, I think he instantly regretted coming over.

'Hi Natasha,' he managed to say. She wasted no time launching in to him,' I don't want to go to Sky' speech. 'Isn't there anything at Network Centre for me?' Steve shifted uncomfortably and would have liked to call Scotty but he had nowhere to go. He went on executive auto-pilot.

'I'll see what I can do,' from the man who'd already told me there was nothing he could do. I reminded him of this. He feigned a memory lapse, nodded, made his excuses and left.

It was the only tear-stained signed contract I ever saw in thirty five years of being an agent.

For the first few months she rang me every day, sometimes twice a day, actually three times a day, telling me how much she hated it. They, in turn, weren't that happy with her. Jeremy Thomson, who she co-presented with, felt only contempt for her and saw her merely as 'telly totty.'

Kay Birley, the reigning queen of Sky News, viewed her appointment with suspicion. I am very fond of Kay. I used to represent her in the late eighties and early nineties but she can act strangely on occasions. Some years back I was having drinks with Steve Kutner and Lucian Grange both of whom I knew from my pop video days. Steve is now a soccer agent with clients like Frank Lampard and Lucian won the jackpot and is now Universal Music Group Chairman and one of the most powerful people in the music business. I mentioned to them I was having a client party at the Groucho Club. Once or twice a year we threw a party so clients could meet TV and corporate executives. When Steve found that Kay was going to be there, his salivary glands went into overdrive. 'I'd love to shag that,' he groaned. I pointed out to him we weren't that kind of agency, but invited them both anyway.

The party was nearly full when Kay arrived. I took her straight over to meet Steve who was having a drink with Lucian. 'Kay, this is Steve Kutner. He'd love to shag you!' I left them to it. I found out later that she rather liked Lucian, but Steve wasn't the kind of guy who gives up and they soon became an item. Kay had been down to my house in Sussex and had met Pearl and knew how ill she was. She was fantastic with her. Kay, when she wants to be, can be one of the funniest and most incisive people you could meet. Pearl loved her visits.

One morning Kay called me to say she and Steve were going on holiday and that on their return they were going to throw a huge party. I suggested that marriage was on the agenda. She laughed and gave me the date of the party. Two days before the said party Pearl had to go back into hospital. I left a message on Kay's answering machine to tell her I why I couldn't make it. She didn't speak to me for fourteen years.

I was at a loss to understand why. I asked Jill Dando and Penny Smith, who had both known her for years, and asked what they thought of my sudden dismissal from her life. They both expressed the same, albeit fond view. 'That's just how she is!'

When Natasha joined Sky, Kay had no intention of relinquishing her hard fought status. One morning, prior to going on air, Natasha was emailing a friend at LNN and mentioned in passing Kay's alleged cosmetic surgery. Unfortunately she didn't log out, and when she took her place in the studio Kay took her place at the computer and went through all her emails! It was then I received my first communication from Kay in nearly ten years. She wrote me a letter saying how highly we regarded each other's integrity and that she would like to meet me to discuss a matter of some urgency. It was by now common knowledge in the news room what had happened. Natasha was furious, and rightly so, that Kay had gone through her emails and Kay was equally furious, wrongly so, at what she had written about her. I called Kay but she'd left for a holiday and by the time she called me I'd left for mine. It would be some years before we'd actually speak face to face.

Dealing with a breaking story is the most rewarding and challenging time for a Sky News presenter. It's all hands to the pump when pictures start coming in from anywhere and everywhere. Kate Garraway, when she briefly worked there, told me that on one major international story she was told, via her earpiece that they would be going to an interview in ten seconds. What she wasn't told was who she was about to interview, where that person might be and what they had to do with the story anyway. When the picture came up on her monitor her first thought was, 'can I identify the city?' which may have given her a clue to the interviewee.

Natasha was four months into the job when a breaking news story fell in to one of her shifts. She handled it very well - much to a lot of people's surprise. It was just what she needed. Having now been bloodied, her confidence level increased accordingly. She was slowly beginning to be grudgingly accepted by her colleagues. As a result her phone calls to me were less intense. Though after ten months she came to see me wearing her, *I've really had enough* face. The friendly, butter-wouldn't-melt-in-my-mouth persona had long since passed. I was now dealing with the real Natasha Kaplinsky.

'You said I'd only have to work there a year.' She accused me.

'I don't think so.'

'You promised.' One of the first lessons you learn as an agent is *never* promise a client anything. Unless you have some uncanny ability to see in to the future you'll shoot yourself every time, in both feet.

'Natasha, I never promised you anything. Ok?'

'That's not true. You *did* promise.' Petulance reared its head. I'd endured countless phone calls from her over the preceding months, most of them full of vitriol for her colleagues and I'd had enough. I wasn't prepared for her to sit in my office and call me a liar.

'Natasha, that is just not true and you know it. How could I promise anything? I'm not actually God. If you're not happy with my advice than I suggest that it may be time for us to part company.' Out came the tears. She apologised profusely, saying she was under great stress at the moment and would do the best she could. In turn I told her she was doing very well and it would only be a question of time before her hard work would be recognised.

Dumping your agent is a whole other world. When a client gives you notice they want to leave it's usually done in one of two ways. Oscar Wilde wrote in *The Ballad of Reading Gaol*, and I paraphrase, 'the coward does it with an email, the brave man over a coffee.'

Most do it with an email. No need for confrontation. Davina McCall fired her agent this way. Others do it with a letter or a phone call. Rarely is it done face to face. Uniquely, for one of our clients, Laura Green, it was done by her brother-in-law, the ex DJ, Mike Smith.

Laura Green was the sister of the much more successful Sarah Green. When she was taken on she wasn't doing much, but one of the company's agents felt she had potential. To be frank apart from one or two people I signed, I was a lousy judge of who would make it and who wouldn't.

Simon Drake delights in telling the story (again and again!) of when he tried to get me to watch a showreel of an unknown Davina McCall. I never seemed to make time to view it and even if I had I probably would have passed.

I've always maintained that most presenters shouldn't be allowed to own a television set let alone appear on one. If you were to place five presenters in a room with a bunch of TV execs none of them would agree on who had that special factor. Jill Dando would probably have been the only exception. As William Goldman memorably wrote in his *Adventures of the Screen Trade* about movie-making, "nobody knows anything." It applies to TV too.

In early 2001 we'd been contacted by the National Geographic Channel in America. They were interested in Kate Garraway presenting a series for them. By then we'd represented her for quite some time. Kate flew out for an audition, but despite their interest she didn't feel able to move her life over there. They asked us for other suggestions and we came up with a few names, one of whom was Laura Green. We sent them her showreel and they liked her enough to ask her over for an audition. She's offered the job!

Are we all happy? No. I get a visit from Mike Smith who tells me that that Laura is deeply unhappy with the Agency and that we nearly ruined her opportunity of getting the job by suggesting Kate Garraway! We never treated her with the respect she deserved and that we hadn't even arranged a limo to both take and collect her from the airport! Consequently she's leaving the Agency for the job in America and we're not entitled to any commission; though she is prepared to pay the Agency two thousand pounds for a year if we agree to keep up her profile in the UK while she's away.

The deal she's offered by National Geographic is worth two hundred and fifty thousand dollars a year with an option for a second year. I suggest to Mike that perhaps his sister-in-law might like to reconsider her position. He tells me it's a done deal and we're not getting a penny.

It's time to unleash the lawyers. I don't actually enjoy litigation having been involved in so much of it. The cliché that the lawyers are the only winners is not a cliché - it's the absolute truth, the whole truth and nothing but the truth. With the strong dollar exchange rate at that time, it means we're probably owed around sixty thousand pounds in commission, assuming they renew her contract for the second year.

Now the long suffering Ian Bloom is involved, we're talking real money as far as costs are concerned. After a few months I write to Mike Smith and suggest the company will accept twenty thousand pounds in full and final settlement. He says no. He hasn't lived. Before he knows it that sum will merely represent his *own* lawyer's costs. The case drags on for months, like cases always do.

We have a court date set and we were within ten days of it when Laura calls me. It's the first time we've spoken in over a year. She wants to settle. How about twenty five thousand pounds? I try to explain to her that my legal costs are nearly that much. She doesn't believe me, she reckons her own costs are around five thousand pounds. Sweet really.

We go to court. After one day of the trial, they agree to settle. I'd be amazed if it cost Mike Smith less than a hundred thousand pounds. Whether Laura made any contribution will be one of life's mysteries.

CHAPTER FIFTY NINE
ROGER COOK AND LIBEL

Roger Cook had led a charmed life. He could have been shot, stabbed, eaten by lions or blown up over the course of thirty years as a pretty fearless investigative reporter. A man long overdue a gong or two. But he'd survived. However pain comes in different forms. Break a leg and after the initial agony you're merely uncomfortable for a few weeks. If a newspaper writes libellous diatribes about you, and you sue, the pain, and it's a very real pain, can last for years.

Roger and his programme, *The Cook Report*, were attacked first early in January 2000 by *The Sunday Times* and then on three separate occasions in February and April 2000 by their sister paper *The News Of The World* (*NOTW*). The articles consisted of accusations mostly of fakery. Having been round the libel block myself, I knew what Roger must be going through. It didn't help that Carlton TV, the broadcaster, initially did nothing to defend him, the programmes or indeed their own integrity. The *NOTW* got away with those three front page articles before Carlton lifted a finger. I wrote to Carlton after the initial article on Roger's behalf demanding they take action but nobody wanted to know. Roger decided to pursue the matter unilaterally and as a result Lord Waheed Alli, then master of all he surveyed at Carlton TV, summoned me to a meeting at the House of Lords.

I arrived for the meeting and was told he was running late as he was making a speech and would I like to sit in the press gallery? I'm always up for the occasional new experience so after I was lent a tie I took my seat to witness the proceedings. The debate was on Portugal and I had no idea why. I counted a dozen people in the great chamber. At least four were asleep and perhaps two or three were dead. It was difficult to tell.

Waheed, who'd made his name as a backer of *The Big Breakfast*, was a dapper little man. I'd always admired his achievements and his elevation to the House Of Lords, was in my humble opinion, well deserved. I followed him to the Tea Room where we sat opposite each other and had tea. The room reminded me of one of those old fashioned tea rooms that are still dotted around tiny villages full of elderly couples talking about the weather and other trivialities. The simile was pretty close actually.

'Waheed I just don't get it, 'I began, 'Exactly how many libellous articles are Carlton going to put up with before you decide to do anything?'

'Jon, you don't understand our strategy.' Perhaps it included destroying my client's career. 'We know exactly what we're doing here.'

'If you aren't going to take immediate action, then as you know, Roger will, with or without your help.' I seemed to have triggered his 'fuck you' button.

'If Roger proceeds on his own, then he'll get absolutely no co-operation from us. In fact it could quite easily go the other way.' I gazed round the room looking for the Mad Hatter or at the very least an occasional dormouse.

'Please tell me Waheed, what you're waiting for, because all I can see is you're letting a man who's won the station numerous awards and often risked his life drown in a welter of lies and innuendo.'

He scratched his chin, his eyes darted from side to side checking out who may be listening and leaned forward in full confidential mode. The voice sotto now. ' Rupert Murdoch is after a terrestrial broadcast licence,' he spoke, as though if overheard, death would be the only outcome, 'If his papers proceed on their current course against Carlton and Roger there's no way he'll ever be granted a licence.' This was it! Unbelievable! 'So you see Jon he has to back down and instruct his papers to apologise.'

I'd found the Mad Hatter.

My only course of action was either to thank him for his time or have him sectioned under the Mental Health Act. I thanked him for his time. Back at the office I told Roger and Ian Bloom what had happened and they proceeded with preparing a claim against News International. I had promised Waheed that if Roger was going to issue a writ I'd give him an hour's notice before the writ was issued. The following day around eleven o'clock I called him.

'Glad you called Jon. We've decided to sue! Tell Roger's lawyer to call our people and we'll be picking up all his costs.' Michael Jackson's life made more sense. Why the sudden about-turn? I called Steve Hewlett, Programme Controller of Carlton. He told me he was with Waheed when I called him and could offer no explanation. I called Clive Jones, Head of Television at Carlton and, he too, had no idea. I never did find out why.

Writs were issued and vigorously defended. Apart from Carlton and Roger a bunch of other producers from the programme also sued News International. It became a real legal *cause celebre*. The costs became ridiculous. With a few months to go before the trial was scheduled to begin (it would have tied up Judge David Eady for several weeks), I attended a meeting with Roger and Carlton's legal teams. There must have been ten people round the table including Roger, Steve Hewlett, Ian Bloom, Carlton's in-house legal team, Carlton's solicitors/barristers and a miscellaneous support cast.

I was glad they'd not been involved in my libel action. Carlton had no idea what they wanted either by way of an apology or damages. Having spent hundreds of thousands of pounds, not one of them had the common sense to contact the other side to see if a settlement could be worked out. I mentioned that Stuart Kuttner, the then Managing Editor of the *NOTW*, was a friend of mine and perhaps it might be worth a shot if I called him. After all what did they have to lose?

My suggestion was met with a stony rebuke from the assembled lawyers. What did I know about libel? Any interference by such an amateur would be a disaster. I was told emphatically to stay out of it. My views and opinions were not required. All I could see was a bunch of money grabbing lawyers who didn't want the wheels to come off their gravy train.

I went back to my office and called Stuart Kuttner. After exchanging the normal pleasantries I asked him if he was up to speed on the libel action.

'Not really,' he told me, ' The last time I gave it any thought was when we had lunch a couple of months ago.'

'Well I've just sat with Carlton's lawyers for three hours and I can't believe a bunch of grown ups can't figure out an acceptable solution.'

'Let me call Tom Crone and get back to you.' Tom Crone, the doyen of in-house libel lawyers. He had worked with News International since the early 1980's. He was one tough mother. I admired him. Stuart called me back in thirty minutes.

'I've spoken to Tom. He suggests we meet for lunch tomorrow to see if we can find a way through this mess.'

'Ok but I need to know there's an apology on the agenda. At the very least there must be an apology and I mean from *you* guys!'

'That's agreed.'

I called Ian Bloom and told him of the lunch. He in turn called Carlton's 'people'. Steve Hewlett than called me.

'Which part of 'stay out of' it didn't you understand.' He was in a mean mood.

'Your point being........?'

'You were told not to call Stuart Kuttner.'

'I don't work for you guys. My only interest is Roger and him I do represent.'

An hour later Ian calls me to say that Carlton want to have their lawyers at the lunch. I tell him I'll check it out with Stuart Kuttner. Stuart speaks to Tom Crone. Tom says no. The lunch was going to be just the three of us. I persuade him to let Ian and Steve Hewlett attend. We're on!

I have to attend a meeting before the lunch with Ian and Carlton's lawyers at their offices. They were living on another planet. Ian was instructed to ask for damages, costs, an apology and his bus fare. They were trying to win the impossible. I said nothing while Ian wrote copious notes.

The lunch takes place at my regular haunt, *Elena's L'Etoile* in one of their private dining rooms upstairs. The table reminds me of King Arthur's, it almost fills the room. Tom announces at the start that he's picking up the tab and this is greeted with muted amusement. Ian than decides to get stuck in immediately. Unfortunately every time he gets into his stride he's interrupted by waiters asking about wine, filling glasses with water or wanting to know what we'd like to eat. Finally he thinks he's on track and gets away with two uninterrupted minutes. Tom is fidgeting with his glass of wine and staring straight ahead into no man's land. When Ian gets to the question of damages, Tom can contain himself no longer.

'Ian I don't mean to be rude but we're not going to pay a penny in damages.' Ian turns to look at Tom and instinctively brings up the matter of costs. Tom has had enough. 'We're not paying a fucking penny of your costs.' Steve Hewlett decides it's time for him to make his play.

'We're not going to walk away from this Tom. We *will* go through with it.' Tom responds instantly.

'We've spent over nine hundred thousand pounds to date and our insurance kicks in at a million. So be assured we will defend the action vigorously.' I was mortified by the costs. That's a shit load of kidney machines.

'Well we've just lost four hundred million with ITV Digital,' Steve waves his willy too, 'so be assured we're up for it.'

These guys were involved in the lives of hundreds of people, had jobs that affected millions of viewers or readers and they were acting like kids in the playground. No one spoke. Cutlery was moved unconsciously around plates and eye contact was scarce to say the least.

Finally I broke the silence. 'Tom, what about the apology?'

'I'm not minded to discuss that Jon.'

I looked over at Stuart Kuttner. 'Stuart this whole meeting was predicated on an apology.'

'He's right Tom.' Stuart agreed. The News International lawyer smiled. He'd won the stand off.

'Ok,' I said, 'I believe Ian has five points he wants to make with respect to the apology.'

Later that afternoon Ian, as the only legal representative of Carlton at the lunch, had to provide them with notes of the meeting. One small section read, *then Jon Roseman told Tom Crone that I had five points to make with respect to the apology. As we had never discussed even one point........'*

Since his note was dictated on a mobile phone to his secretary while he rushed to an airport and he never saw the note for a week, he did very well under the circumstances.

Steve Hewlett called me the next day to tell me I was persona non grata with Carlton and to have nothing further to do with the entire matter. Apparently even though my attempts had helped speed everything up, they were seriously pissed off with me. I had no problem with that. At least the children were talking.

A week went by, then Tom Crone called me.

'Have you seen the apology they want us to agree to?'

'No Tom. I've been told by Carlton to fuck off and mind my own business.'

'Well I can't deal with these people, but I can with you.'

'Send me the apology,' I said.

I read it and it didn't seem that onerous. I called Tom and asked him which bits he didn't like. All of it was his response. I suggested he adapted it and send me a version he could agree with.

An hour later I'm reading his preferred version. It might just as well have said, 'We Carlton TV and Roger Cook apologise unreservedly for putting News International to so much trouble.'

I called Tom. 'Have you spoken to Roger about this?'

'What do you mean?'

'It's exactly the version Roger would want, because Carlton would reject it out of hand and he'd get his day in court. Why don't we just go through the original version line by line and see if we can work something out.' We proceeded to do just that.

The document consisted of three pages. The first page was fine, most of the second page was ok and we made a few minor adjustments. The last page, after an hour, began to look insurmountable. The sticking point was the word 'apologise.' I had two thesauruses on my desk and there weren't many alternatives for the word 'apologise'. Let's face it, that was what it was all about! After a couple of hours we were down to six words that he wasn't happy with. I'd had enough and told Tom to argue the rest out with Carlton's lawyers.

Steve Hewlett phoned me the following afternoon in self-congratulatory mood.

'You won't believe this Jon but they've nearly agreed to all our demands. I'm actually amazed, I never thought Tom Crone would have gone along with it.'

'So pleased,' I said.

It was settled. Both sides paid their own costs, nearly three million pounds, and Roger did pretty well financially too, though I can't reveal how much. It was an even bigger success for the lawyers.

CHAPTER SIXTY
MONTY DON AND BUCKINGHAM PALACE

There is an old French saying, 'the customer is always wrong.' Most agents apply this aphorism to their clients and no doubt it is returned in spades by the client. You can't win them all; the secret is winning most of them. Jonathan Shalit who came into the public eye with his supreme management of Charlotte Church's career decided to extend his business by representing TV presenters. We met when I found out that he was trying to seduce away one of my clients. In the old days I would have called him and threatened all kinds of mayhem but when you hit your late fifties your approach tends to be less confrontational. Instead we had lunch and became friends.

He would often call me to exploit my thirty five years worth of knowledge of the business. On one occasion he asked me what I thought of his client, Mylene Klass, participating in *I'm A Celebrity Get Me Out Of Here*. My advice was that reality TV is a dangerous game, and that show in particular is full of Z list celebs well past their sell by date. As Mylene was seriously riding up the ladder, why take such a risk? He ignored my advice. She was pictured all over the national press taking a shower in a white bikini and, as a result, a star was born. The experienced agent, me, was wrong. It happens!

To have any long term success as an agent you must have the ability to sublimate any pretence to an ego. Your daily dealings are with clients whose own egos are mostly out of control and who are equally splattered with large amounts of insecurity and TV execs whose egos are largely out of control and are also equally splattered with large amounts of insecurity! Most agents I know complain that TV execs rarely return their phone calls. As Woody Allen once said, 'the business is not about dog eating dog, but dog not returning other dog's phone calls.'

An agent spends his life walking a tightrope. After a time it is inevitable that you'll slip occasionally. You can lose a deal, lose a client or offend some senior TV exec who has the power to try and blacklist you and your agency. None of these elements need necessarily destroy you, provided you always take the blame, whether it's yours to take or not, and you always remember who you're working for i.e. *everyone*. If, like me, you're not prepared to do any or all of the above then it's sayonara. My own slide into the chasm began around 2002. Rule one of Agenting is hold on to your key clients no matter what they put you through. These clients are your living, breathing, pension fund. No matter how much they may humiliate you, don't let them go. When you hear, as you often will, that one of your biggest clients is lunching with another agent with a view to dumping you, just take a deep breath, smile and whistle a happy tune. What are you going to do? Challenge them? Try it.

'I heard you had lunch with Mary from ILM yesterday.'

'No I didn't!' Ok then!

Or...

'I heard you had lunch with Mary from ILM yesterday.'

'We were at Uni together. We were just catching up.' Yeah right!

Denial and lies come as easily to most clients as it does to a good agent!

Once the process has started you have to acknowledge they are going to leave you. Worse they're sending out a signal to everyone in the business that you're not good enough. Worse still, they are sending *you* a signal that you're not good enough. Egos are fragile little buggers and losing your first client is very painful and it doesn't get any easier. What agents aren't in a position to do is pre-empt their clients by being the dumpee. Get in first. Dump them before it gets around that you're a useless piece of crap! It doesn't work like that. You hold onto their flesh as though your life depends on it and often it appears that it does.

There is only so much humiliation that you can deal with and when you can take it no more then time to get out. Hire someone who can replace you and who has the capacity to bear endless amounts of abuse. Without knowing that my mindset had radically changed, I continued on a reckless course. I wasn't prepared to be whipped anymore. I was to do what an agent should only *think* of doing.

Monty Don, a client of some years standing and a talented gardening writer for the *Observer* and a natural presenter was offered a series by Channel 4, *Don Roaming*. This was a massive break for him. I explained that as the series was intended to be such a long-running one, he should consider setting up his own production company. Channel 4 would not contract such a high cost series to a new production company and told him he needed to find an existing production company Channel 4 would be comfortable with.

Cutting a deal shouldn't be a problem. Monty was in the driving seat and he could choose who he wanted, and agree terms accordingly. By advising him to pursue this route, I was effectively cutting myself out of the action. But this was the right move for Monty and as an agent you must look beyond immediate gain and consider the client's future.

Months later, as he was filming the series, I received an email from his new secretary. It queried the commission we were taking on a ten minute radio insert he did providing gardening tips for a commercial station. He would phone it in and was paid seventy five pounds a week. We were taking our normal broadcast commission of fifteen percent. Monty apparently felt it should be ten percent. Having just advised him on a deal that would make him tens of thousands of pounds and lost any ongoing commission for the Agency I felt him querying the sum of three pounds seventy-five pence was a tad churlish. I emailed him telling him I couldn't afford to take the loss and suggested he find a more reasonable agent!

Not a clever move, dumping a client over a couple of quid. I should have let it go....but the worm had turned. Stupid bloody worm!

Not all clients were insecure, ego fuelled cases. For some years we'd represented Dickie Arbiter who had worked for the Buckingham Palace press office for fourteen years. He'd had specific responsibilities to the Queen, and Charles and Diana's media relations were included in his portfolio. We used to have the occasional dinners and he was fascinating company. Unfortunately he was the most discreet man I'd ever met. Getting information out of a Mossad agent about dodgy passports would have been easier. If he liked a drink maybe I'd have stood a chance, but he only ever sipped diet cokes. I did ask him who his favourite Royal was and he made me guess. Like everyone I started with the Queen Mother. He shook his head and made it clear she wouldn't have even been on the list. Apparently she was one of life's battleaxes. It was in fact Prince Phillip. What Dickie liked about him was that he called it as he saw it and you knew where you stood with the man.

On leaving his post the Queen graciously gave him a private ten minute audience. I thought that a bit mean after fourteen years of loyal service but then I've never understood that whole royal thing. The Palace threw him a leaving party which he kindly invited me to. As I've mentioned, I don't do parties. But this was a must. I mean it was pretty unlikely that I'd ever have another chance of being invited to Buckingham Palace.

The party was at seven o'clock one winter's evening. It was a lousy night. Rain teamed down, I had no coat or umbrella. I drove there early as the police had recently put up a large number of concrete bollards for additional security. Finding your way through them to get to the entrance wasn't easy. I drove round a few times to get the lay of the land and finally parked next to the police box at the entrance. A very polite policeman asked if he could help me and I told him I was there for Dickie's party. He took my name and went inside to check.

'Sorry sir but we don't appear to have your name on the list.' Part of me was disappointed but as I'm not a party animal it was no big deal.

'I guess you could check one more time?' He left and returned a minute later.

'I do apologise sir, I found your name.'

'Excellent. Where do I park?'

'You can't park in the Palace sir you need a special pass.'

'Pleease,' I begged, the rain now hurtling down. 'Dickie said it would be ok.' He thought about it for a second and pointed over to a space beside a few 4x4's to the west of the Palace. I drove there, got out of the car and legged it over to the entrance and rapped on the door. A flunky opened the door dressed in full regalia. I'd got the wrong entrance and was redirected to a large arch with sentry boxes either side. I ran over to it just in time to bump into a long file of what I think were Life Guards, all metal helmeted with soggy white plumes and red uniforms. They were marching right past the entrance I needed. I wasn't going to wait for them to pass by as I'd have been soaked through to the proverbial underwear, so I charged through them. No doubt highly inappropriate.

The front of the Palace that mere mortals can't see is covered in red tarmac. *Very* royal! Once inside I was greeted by Dickie and his lovely wife Rosemary and found out I was the first to arrive. As we walked up the stairs towards the room where the party was being held, I couldn't help noticing five *chaise longues* stretching down a long corridor parked against a wall. Each *chaise longue* must have been fifteen feet long. Who the hell makes fifteen foot *chaise longues*?

The room started to fill up and I, naturally, went looking around for a 'souvenir'. The ashtrays didn't have ER embossed on them, so nicking one would provide no proof whatsoever that I'd visited the place! I did spy a paper knife on a bureau but I figured if I got caught slipping it in my pocket it wouldn't do my relationship with Dickie a power of good.

I needed to visit the men's room. What I found was a high tech, stainless steel facility that wouldn't have looked out of place on a space station. One of the guests told me it had been designed by Prince Charles.

I began chatting with a lovely man who turned out to be the Queen's chaplain. He wore a tailored dark suit and was impeccably groomed, with short grey hair and a face that had seen much and no doubt had heard more secrets than Max Clifford.

'I'm so glad you told me who you are, as I swear rather a lot and that could prove very embarrassing. Don't chaplains have some to wear some kind of..er..uniform?'

'Usually I wear a dog-collar but I'm going out for dinner tonight and it's not necessary.' We were joined then by a large man in a bad suit. His jacket buttons losing the fight against a mighty stomach. The chaplain knew him and introduced me with the immortal line, 'Frank Stevens, head of CBS Television, Jon Roseman, Dickie's agent, he swears a lot!'

After a few glasses of wine I left, souvenir less, and drove back to Chiswick. As I turned in to the Brompton Road in Knightsbridge I realised I'd left before Dickie's farewell speech. I really am crap at parties!

CHAPTER SIXTY ONE
GMTV, PENNY SMITH, ESTHER McVEY AND TOYAH

My association with GMTV goes right back to its inception. The station first started transmission some months after *The Big Breakfast* and struggled in its early years. Fortunately for them there was little competition from the BBC.

Peter McHugh, GMTV's Director of Programmes, now retired, had a simple, though autocratic, style of running GMTV. He took the view that all presenters, with few exceptions, were lucky to work at all. That they should do as they were told and if they had any complaints, they could stick them where the sun don't shine. While this approach might not be conducive to most people, at least you knew where you stood with him. No one joining the company was under any illusion about what to expect. If you didn't like the philosophy, don't join.

GMTV held a unique place in the ITV network. It was then owned 75% by ITV Plc and 25% by Disney. Now it's wholly owned by ITV. It was never going to be a bastion of journalism, but then it lacked the resources of the BBC and had no tie up with ITN. Peter set his stall out from day one. It was no more or less than a tabloid TV show. For example, straight after a live studio interview with, say, the Prime Minister, the presenter would turn to camera and announce, 'Next the daily quiz. To win a holiday in Spain answer the following question; what is the capital of France? a) London b) a chair or c) Paris.' As has been well covered by the media, these quizzes nearly brought the company down.

The daily programmes were glued together with, how I lost weight by only eating glass fibre models of

Michaelangelo, a story about a shop in Grimsby that sells only used matches, or, a big hit this one, keep fit by doing our daily workout with Yuri the one legged Siberian dwarf. All mostly good fun. The advertisers liked it and the company managed to survive almost anything that was thrown at them.

Notwithstanding Peter's stringent running of the company, the newsroom, like all news rooms, was a hive of resentment and vitriolic gossip. Shortly before Kate Garraway joined in 2000 (of which more later), the Editor had been replaced by Martin Frizzell, himself now gone following ITV's purge in 2010. Martin had been a GMTV correspondent for some years but had no experience in an executive capacity. That in itself made it a rather odd appointment. Add that to the fact that he's married to one of the station's main presenters, and it becomes a little bizarre. It would place the show's producers and presenters in an invidious position.

If a presenter is performing below par by, say, not doing their homework or too many late nights, producers need to be able to discuss this with their bosses. Presenters need to work in some kind of comfort zone, and there are occasions, where rivalries need to be addressed. It's a brave or stupid presenter or producer who is going to take any issues involving Fiona Philips to her husband.

Paul Corley, who was appointed as MD after Martin was in place, confided to me over lunch, after a year in to the job, that he would never have made such an appointment. No sensible executive would. Not that Martin didn't do a good job. It merely reflects that GMTV doesn't operate within the normal parameters or practices of the marketplace.

In the early days Penny Smith found it difficult to forge a good working relationship with John Stapleton. I'd been Penny's agent for a long time and twenty years before had represented John. McHugh was a close friend of 'Stapes', as he is fondly known, and asked me to take the pair of them out for lunch to try and sort out their problems. Unfortunately the day of the lunch coincided with me having some major flu bug that resulted in profuse sweating and absolutely no appetite.

My only contribution to the conversation was a murmur or two and shaky, sweaty palms.

Penny came away not convinced and complaining about the way Staples drank. Apparently when placing glass to mouth his tongue popped out!! Everybody has their own predilections and presenters are no different. Now of course they are the best of friends.

Not long after Anthea joined the station, Penny made it quite clear she wasn't her biggest fan. She called her, among other things, a knicker flasher! It got so bad that Peter McHugh asked me to arrange a dinner party at my house for Anthea, her husband and manager Peter Powell and Penny to try and affect a rapprochement. Why he thought I possessed these Kissengeresque skills he never made clear. The dinner never happened.

In the early years of looking after Penny we would lunch about once every six weeks. She would always pick the newest places and sometimes I felt she was surreptitiously writing restaurant reviews, financed by me, for some nameless publication.

Negotiating contracts at GMTV could often be wonderfully bizarre. Some years later my mate Jonathan Shalit rang me in the middle of dealing with GMTV on behalf of his new client, Emma Crosby, to express huge dismay and puzzlement as to how they did business. What could I say? I was used to dealing with the bizarre, like Roger Cook's Central deal, but that doesn't come close to our friends running breakfast telly. Once I lunched with Peter McHugh and we talked through a new contract for Penny. We settled on a number and when I got back to my office I confirmed it by email. A month passed before Peter called me.

'I'm sorry Jon, but the Board won't sanction Penny's money.'

'But we agreed it.' I said rather lamely. I knew I wasn't going to sue them for breach of contract even though we'd probably have won. And anyway how many swimming pools can Ian Bloom find room for?!

'I know. I did my best but they wouldn't agree to it.' He told me what they would pay and it was short by around twelve thousand pounds. 'She can have the difference in lunches,' he said. He wasn't joking.

There have been very few times in my life as an agent where a conflict of interest rises to bite you on your backside. Agencies tend to specialise in particular kinds of talent. There are agents for comedians, actors, extras, presenters, etc. It's not rocket science that, if you're a comedian, you don't sign up to a presenter's agency.

Over the years when people came to see me about representation we'd chat and they'd sometimes observe that, 'aren't I too similar to client A or B?' Meaning that they would be in competition for the same job. The answer is yes. But then, whether they were clients of mine or not, they'd still be up against them. It's not my call who gets the job. All I can do is try and put the right clients in the frame and pray a lot. When the pushing and shoving is over, I don't care who gets the gig as long as it's one of mine.

One rule I always had was no poaching. If you try and poach a client from another agent, you place yourself in a difficult position. You tell them that their agent isn't up to it, that they are killing your career and that you, and only you, have the secret of the Holy Grail. Then you make them absurd promises and many months later you can't deliver and they leave. If potential clients come to you on recommendation, and you take them on, and things don't work out, they can never point their finger at you and utter that immortal Kaplinskyesque line, 'but you promised!'

We once represented Esther McVey. She was a very attractive and clever Liverpudlian presenter but many people found her strong accent irritating. Fiona Phillips was about to take time off for maternity leave and GMTV needed a replacement. After much discussion with Peter McHugh, and the requisite large consumption of alcohol, it was agreed that Penny would be her stand in.

On the Friday before she was due to join Eamonn Holmes on the sofa, Peter called to say 'they' had had a change of mind and wanted Esther instead. As agent for both of them, bearing in mind my old axiom that, 'as long as it's one of mine', it shouldn't have been a problem. Wrong! I was very fond of Penny and this late change was deeply hurtful and unethical. Though ethics and GMTV are not necessary mutual bedfellows.

Peter offered to tell her himself but I somehow felt it was something I should do. By coincidence I was having dinner with her the following night. As we sat down, and before we'd even looked at the menu, I told her. She burst in to tears and I nearly followed her. I said that I would cease to act for Esther as I felt so uncomfortable about the situation. But Penny wouldn't hear of it. She quickly recovered her composure, we had our dinner and we discussed the best and most painful way to kill McHugh!

Esther spent six months co-presenting but she didn't receive a single offer of other work. By this time she was going out with Mal Young, then head of BBC drama, who told her she needed my personal attention otherwise her career would stall. But there was nothing I or anyone could have done for her. She just didn't appeal to any other broadcaster. It wasn't long before she left television for a career in politics.

A similar situation arose with the delightful Sam Norman, daughter of the king of film critics, Barry. Sam was in my top three all time favourite clients. Apart from being very sexy and talented, she possessed a huge heart. My daughter, Elie, adored her. She worked as a VJ for VH1 at the time. She had to take time out for maternity leave and Frances Naylor, a good friend, and head of VH1, asked me if I had any suggestions for a replacement. We represented Toyah Willcox so I put her name in the frame. Frances met her, liked her and she was offered a six month contract while Sam was away.

Many months later Dan and I were on a boat off the coast of Tenerife watching dolphins skipping above the waves when Frances called me. Why I had taken my mobile with me to such a beautiful location is beyond stupid. She told me they liked Toyah so much that they wouldn't be having Sam back. I was profoundly shocked and upset. Frances knew how very fond I was of Sam and offered to make the call. And, as with Peter before, I told her it was something I needed to do myself. I felt that somehow I was to blame even though sheer logic told me it hadn't been my call and even if I hadn't suggested Toyah they may well have got there themselves.

I called Sam and she was very hurt, but she let me know that she felt no blame whatsoever attached itself to me. Four months later she left me for another agent. She'd never been a big earner for the Agency, but that wasn't even the remotest consideration, I felt I'd damaged our special friendship. A year later she came back and all was forgotten.

I'd met Toyah through Dan and her boyfriend, Simon, in 1993. We'd driven down to Brighton where she was appearing in *A Midsummer Night's Dream* at the Theatre Royal. We all went out for dinner afterwards and suddenly I ended up representing her. Toyah has handled her career brilliantly. She's reinvented herself more times than Madonna. Singer, film and stage actress, TV presenter and writer, she could turn her hand to anything. To achieve what she has you have to be a real toughie. She married King Crimson's Robert Fripp, a fabulously talented performer and an altogether great guy.

Dan and I would often have dinner with them and when the bill came we always went Dutch. That included Toyah *and* Robert as well! They paid on separate credit cards. Toyah told me that on their wedding night they sat in their hotel room and divvied up the cost of the reception!

Toyah had been close friends with Dan for many years before we took her on which made what she did some years later incredibly hurtful. Apparently she'd heard that Dan had financial problems and was going to declare herself bankrupt. Now this was untrue, but Toyah called my office and told one of the staff what she'd heard and said she wanted to make sure her money was ok. Dan's financial situation had nothing whatsoever to do with the Agency. Toyah must have known that.

When I heard why she'd called and what she had said I phoned her immediately. I told her that her behaviour was totally inappropriate. I explained that whatever she'd heard, if she was a friend of Dan's, the first thing a friend does, if they'd heard bad news, is call and ask if their friend is ok and offer support - not run for the lifeboat. I told her she was no longer a client. She rang Dan some time later to apologise. Maybe now, if I'm more charitable and time has passed, I suppose you can't achieve what she has if you're not constantly looking over your shoulder and being wary of every flickering shadow. And then again, given what was to come, she was right to look after herself. But the way she did it, still rankles. Perhaps I could have handled the situation differently. Rather than ask her to leave the Agency maybe I should have dismissed the incident and kept her on - after all she provided a reasonable income stream. But after Monty Don and Laura Green, I wasn't in the mood to consider another kicking. Most other agents would probably just have taken the grief and thought of the money.

It's an old maxim of mine that if your client needed a kidney and you gave them one of your own don't be surprised if they dump you three months later. There are exceptions, very rare exceptions, and not many of them.

I liked Claudia Winkleman and her departure from the Agency was both odd and sad. She was intelligent and bubbly and reminded me a little of Paula Yates when she first started out. She is the daughter of Eve Pollard, ex-editor of the Sunday Express and step-daughter of Sir Nicholas Lloyd who once edited *The News Of The World, The People* and *The Daily Express*. She grew up steeped in journalism. We had an extremely successful relationship for two years. She was popular with the broadcasters and made four network series in the short time we looked after her. Her background gave her an edge over the rest of the pack. She had real potential. But it wasn't enough for her. She left to join another agent and within a few weeks left the new agent to join yet another one. She's probably the only presenter I can recall who had three agents in as many weeks.

Notwithstanding all her success with us, she had a major problem. She confided to me that whenever she went to premieres or to the openings of various clubs and restaurants the press never took her picture, while the likes of Davina McCall or Denise van Outen were blinded by flash guns. I pointed out that it would come, if that's what she wanted, but it wasn't a prerequisite to a glorious TV career. I think she could have achieved so much more in the realm of serious programmes, if she wasn't so preoccupied with the thrill of the flashlight. I bumped in to her at an awards ceremony some years after she'd moved on and she was accompanied by her PR.

What is it about girls and PR? I sat next to Fearne Cotton some time back at yet another awards ceremony and she was with her 'PR person.' I must admit, at the time, I'd never heard of her. While we're on the question of 'what is it about?' what is it about Ms Cotton? She was discovered on a talent show and presented *The Disney Club.* She's best known, as the press would put, it 'for a string of celebrity boyfriends,' or as I would put it, 'shagging B listers to get tabloid press exposure.' In my view an iguana has a higher IQ. Let's not forget her 'best friend' Holly Willoughby. What a pair. And I don't mean Holly's double frontage.

CHAPTER SIXTY TWO
MORE KAPLINSKY, BRENDAN COLE AND STRICTLY

Three months into 2002 the BBC offered Natasha Kaplinsky a job co-presenting their breakfast show with Dermot Moynahan. Had she not gone to Sky and picked up a few vital shreds of journalistic credibility, she'd still be presenting local news programmes. All her angst over the previous year evaporated. Now I'm the hero!

In typical Kaplinsky style, she sent me flowers and a note. Later we would exchange wreaths! When I opened the note, a load of tiny hearts fell out. As the months rolled by, she received even more terrible press. Women just didn't take to her and men just wanted to give her one! I was forever fighting battles to dilute the anti-Kaplinsky stories in the tabloids. She made few friends at the BBC. She came across as cold, aloof and clinically ambitious. It would have a taken a fleet of Max Cliffords to remove even a minor dent in the damage she was bringing on herself.

The call I'd somehow been expecting came on a Friday early in November 2003. An hysterical Natasha. Could I come over to her house straight away? Something terrible had happened. On the short drive over there, I tried to guess what it was to make her so upset. Sitting in her small living room in her house in Hammersmith she shared with her boyfriend Mike, she told me.

The People newspaper was going to run a story about her affair with Lloyd Bracey, her old Meridian boss. It was the first time I'd heard his name. I asked her if it was true. It was. What have they got? I needed to know. She was too upset to give me the kind of details I needed before I could advise her on her options. I called the editor, Mark Thomas. It appeared they'd got pictures of Natasha and Lloyd strolling hand-in-hand in Brighton, shots of them leaving their hotel room together, everything apart from colour pictures of what they ate for breakfast. He said he'd fax me over what they were going to print, to allow Natasha to comment on it. Madness! It was only Friday.

I asked her where her boyfriend Mike Bernard was and if she'd spoken to him? Paris and no. Had she tried to reach him? Yes and left a message.

'Natasha you have only three alternatives. Say nothing, give them an interview or do a spoiler. What you can't do is go on record denying it.' A spoiler is simply an interview with a journalist you trust from another paper to ruin the scoop and attempt to take the sting out of the story. None of the options are necessarily right or wrong. All are painful.

'What do you think I should do?' The million dollar question.

'Let's go through the options. You say nothing. If they've given you the opportunity to comment and you don't, that doesn't necessarily imply it's true. On the other hand, they've got so much stuff that a denial would be absurd in this case. It would be naïve in the extreme to ignore the fact that every other tabloid is going to be all over you like a very nasty rash. Therefore no comment allows no mitigation. Giving them an interview is not on. It gives them a bigger story and they'll never give you copy approval, so you're just committing suicide.'

'A spoiler can be dangerous. But provided you know what the other paper has, and you are careful, you can mitigate the damage to a certain extent, provided you have copy approval. In this case *The People* have made a huge error of judgement and I can't understand why. Only an idiot calls up on a Friday morning to tell you they've got a big story coming out on Sunday. It makes the spoiler more effective. You can pre-empt them by a day. They lose the exclusive and will probably put it further back in the paper and edit it down.'

'So you think I should do the spoiler?'

'Natasha, it has to be your decision.'

'But your advice is to do a spoiler?'

'My advice would have been not to have put yourself in this position in the first place. But it has to be your choice. I've given you the options and now my advice is to speak to Mike and certainly to your parents, then see how you feel.'

The phone rang. It was Mike. I left her and went outside for a cigarette. I kept asking myself who this Lloyd Bracey was. How long had she been seeing him? I guessed all would be revealed when I read the fax from *The People*. I was just lighting my third cigarette when she came out to tell me she'd finished the call and had spoken to her father. She looked pale and tears were flowing down her face.

I sat back down and said nothing. She walked up and down her little front room clenching and unclenching her hands. After two or three minutes she said, 'If we do a spoiler, who do you suggest I should talk to?'

'Alison Boshoff. She writes for *The Daily Mail* and she's a good friend.'

'Can you call her and see what she says?' I called her and told her what we needed which included full copy approval. She had to speak to the editor and would call me back. We sat in silence. I wanted to ask a bunch of questions, like what did Mike say? Who is this guy Bracey? How did your father take it? I sat still. It was Natasha's problem and I really didn't want to know any more than she wanted to tell me.

Finally Bosh called back and said if we wanted to do it, we were on. I said I'd call her back.

'We'll have to tell the BBC you know. We can't just let them read it in the papers.' Her face went even paler if that were possible and she put her hand to her mouth and just gulped. I think with the shock of the last few hours, telling her boss hadn't been on her emotional agenda. She sat down and put her head in her hands and sobbed. I guess I should have sat next to her and offered her a comforting arm but I just couldn't. This feeling had nothing to do with any ethical considerations. It was just who she was or what she'd become. Any fondness I'd had for her had long since passed. I saw before me a spoilt, ruthless woman. I suddenly realised not only didn't I like her, I positively disliked her.

She gave the interview to Bosh and, because we had the fax from *The People*, we were able to deal with the parts of the story that were the most damaging. It appeared in the following day's issue of *The Daily Mail*. I heard later that Mark Thomas, *The People's* Editor, went ballistic, probably because his bosses told him he was an idiot for calling us on a Friday.

Going back to work on Monday morning must have been a real trial for her. Newsrooms could be very cruel. She rang me later that afternoon.

'My Editor said it was a mistake doing the spoiler.' She implied it was my decision and therefore my advice was flawed.

'I don't agree. You have the fax from *The People*. Compare it to what they printed. It's been cut back by at least thirty percent.'

'He said I shouldn't have done it. There were other ways of handling it.' He's right about one thing. She shouldn't have been screwing the guy. If she hadn't, none of this would have happened.

'What other ways?'

'That's all he said.'

'I'm going to call him.' I said.

'No, don't do that he's very angry.'

'I'm going to call him.' I said again and hung up. I dialled the Beeb and we spoke.

'I understand from Natasha you felt she shouldn't have done the spoiler.'

'That's right.' Talkative guy.

'She said you told her 'there were other ways." No response. 'Perhaps you could enlighten me and tell me what those other ways are?' Nothing. 'Ok just help me out with *one* other way.'

'She shouldn't have done it, that's all.' I hung up. Whether he'd been referring to the spoiler or her sex life I had no idea.

The months following the story were very painful for all of us. She would regularly bring up the spoiler as though I had in some way made her expose intimate details of her private life to the masses. The fact that Mike stood by her amazed me. Love as they say is blind - or at the very least half cut most of the time. Then weirdly, Lloyd Bracey started to call me. He wanted me to act as a go-between for him with Natasha. He'd tell me very emotionally down the phone that he'd sacrificed his wife and family for her and desperately wanted to 'win' her back. I told Natasha about the calls and she was furious. How dare he call you she ranted. I said I didn't know and perhaps she'd like to call him and put him out of his misery. After a couple of months his calls stopped.

Less than a year later along came *Strictly Come Dancing*.

Jane Lush was then Head of Entertainment at the BBC. She called me to see if I could get Natasha to do the show. The Dando row had long since been buried between us. After all, we were both over twenty one and this was business not personal. We met and she described the show to me. It's always difficult to predict how a series will turn out from a pitch. Often things change as it develops and sometimes it ends up completely different from what was originally envisaged. Reality shows are normally low rent and I would usually reject them out of hand.

I'd worked very hard on Natasha's career and one bad judgement call could either set it back or even kill it. I needed to be certain that if we went with it, the decision would be the right one. Her career had become an academic exercise for me now. I had absolutely no regard for her. It had become solely about testing my abilities as an agent.

In principle I liked it. In theory it had a lot going for it. It had class. I respected the people who were making it. It was Saturday night. I thought it may have a chance of changing people's perception of her which was becoming more important bearing in mind the lousy press she was getting even before the Lloyd Bracey incident. Natasha rejected it out of hand. I'm a serious news presenter on the BBC now, she told me. One year on Sky, another two years on *BBC Breakfast* and now she's 'a serious news presenter.' Jeremy Thompson was right. They should have sent her to a war zone to see what a serious journalist does for a living!

I called Jane and told her the problem. She was very disappointed and suggested that it may help if Natasha dropped by for a chat. I agreed. They had a chat, but Natasha still thought she was up there with Barbara Walters. Finally I got a call from Lorraine Heggessey, Controller BBC1, one of the better controllers. She too was very keen on Natasha doing the show, she wanted to know if she could help smooth the path. I explained that while I was onside, I didn't think even the Controller of BBC1 could make a difference. I suggested that what might help would be her boss at *BBC News* getting behind it. I asked Lorraine to check him out. I figured if he had no objection and positively endorsed it, that might shift her position.

He didn't take much persuasion and as a result Natasha was invited for tea by Lorraine. Apparently she nearly won her over, but it didn't help that when she left Lorraine's office she bumped in to Alison Sharman, Controller of Daytime, who, too, asked her in for tea. She asked Alison's advice which was, don't do it, the show's going to be a disaster and you'll go down with the ship.

When Natasha told me about all her little chats, I began to wonder how the BBC ever got any of its programmes on air. I called Lorraine and asked her why her own executives would undermine her in this way. Life was hard enough without this kind of 'support'.

It was probably her News boss who finally convinced her. He felt that prime-time network exposure of one of his presenters could only benefit his own ratings. She was paired with Brendan Cole.

They set about a rigorous rehearsal schedule and began an affair. Rumours leaked out and now the ladies of Fleet Street had something else juicy to write about; add to that the recent split with her boyfriend Mike, and she was starring in her own soap. My whole *raison d'être* for her doing the show was to improve her image. I couldn't win with her.

Throughout her progress on the show our relationship thawed a little. She and Brendan came down to our house in Sussex for the occasional Sunday lunch. They were obviously in a relationship and she seemed a different person in his company. A forthright New Zealander, he called it as he saw it. He's had some terrible press, none of it deserved, in my view. He was one of the best clients I ever represented.

She was driving with Brendan down to Sussex one weekend and called me from her car.

'I think I'm pregnant,' she told me laughing. I could hear Brendan in the background. 'Is that going to be a problem?' she added. More laughter from both of them. With Brendan around she was less painful to deal with and he didn't take any nonsense from her. I suspect the previous men in her life let her walk all over them but this wasn't in the DNA of a Kiwi. When I mentioned this conversation a week or so later, she denied it ever took place. She had happily cocooned herself in her own make-believe world.

The show was a huge success and she was a sensation. Her win catapulted her into the front row of TV presenters. The fact that most of the press despised her and continue to do so, made her triumph all the more infuriating for them. In our society we are influenced strongly by what we read. The press can make you and they sure as hell can break you. I can only think of one other 'celebrity' who managed to defy the odds, Robbie Williams. He came back, notwithstanding a concerted campaign against him by *The Sun.*

Natasha had by now outgrown the world as we know it. No one in my office wanted to deal with her. She had reversed the process of metamorphosis. The butterfly had turned back into the caterpillar. Late in December 2004 she rang the office.

'I've got a corporate this afternoon and I can't do it,' she declared. 'I've a lunch and then I'm supposed to rehearse with Brendan for the Christmas show.'

'But it's been in the diary for six months,' she was told.

'Can't you get someone else to do it?'

'That's not the point. We have a contract with them and they booked you.'

'Well just get someone else. What about Daisy Sampson?' She was a client of ours working with ITN.

'I'll have to speak to Jon about this.'

'He's such a pain. I know what he's going to say.' The office phoned me. I was so angry with her sheer lack of professionalism that I couldn't summon the strength to call her because I knew I'd say something I might regret. One of the other agents who had heard the exchange between the office and Natasha was asked to make the call.

'I'm told you won't do the corporate this afternoon.' the agent said,

'I didn't say that,' Natasha protests.

'Didn't you ask if Daisy could do it instead?'

'No!'

'Are you saying you'll do it?'

'Yes.'

Ten minutes later Daisy calls to say she's had a call from Natasha about a corporate. Enough was way more than enough. The office tell me she's out of control and becoming an embarrassment. I decide there and then to terminate our agreement. As it's nearly Christmas I make the decision to leave it till January. The day before my birthday, on the fifth, I asked her to a meeting in one of Elena's private rooms above the main restaurant.

I came straight to the point. 'We can no longer represent you. You're a lying, conniving bitch.' It was way too late for niceties.

'I'm not a liar,' she protested. Apparently the rest of the description was fair comment!

'You told the office that you hadn't spoken to Daisy and denied you weren't going to do the corporate.'

'I did not!' I stood up.

'I can't deal with this. We live in different worlds.'

'Go on tell me a lie I've told you.'

'I just have.'

I'm not a liar,' she insisted.

'You denied telling me you were pregnant.'

'I was only joking.'

'So you did tell me.'

'Yes!'

'Natasha your problem is that you lie about lying.' I walked out of the room. That afternoon we sent a letter round to her house by messenger terminating our agreement.

She found a new agent who I heard advised her against continuing her relationship with Brendan. She dumped him soon after. To his eternal credit, despite being offered large sums of money, he never even contemplated doing a kiss and tell. Another high earning client bites the dust.

If I'm giving the impression that an agent's life is all about pain and suffering and not parties, fancy dinners and posh award ceremonies, I could be misleading you. Some agents enjoy engaging in such activities but I had long since given up on all of it. My sell by date had expired. I felt like a boxer who should have retired years ago. I couldn't roll with the punches any more. Recovery from each fight took longer and longer. I was now haemorrhaging money. Losing significant clients, whether by choice or 'natural' wastage, would prove to be a disaster. I'd become too confrontational. It was like the old days when I made stupid decisions when affected by drugs. Now it was having to deal with a never ending stream of Industry and personal egos. As each year went by more grief came my way. Most of it, perhaps, self-inflicted. Most agents would have stood back and taken the slings and arrows. I couldn't do that anymore.

CHAPTER SIXTY THREE
MIKE SMITH AND REVENGE

More grief followed in the form of Mike Smith. It was 2003 and he was still smarting from losing up to a hundred grand on his sister-in-law's ill-conceived litigation with the Agency a couple of years back in 2001. He hadn't given up in the revenge stakes. He made a complaint to the Department of Trade and Industry (DTI), claiming I was acting as a director of a company after being disqualified from doing so after JRA was put in to administration in 1997. As a result I was interviewed by the DTI, under caution, with my solicitor Ian Bloom present. I had been exceedingly careful not to act in any executive role in the new company. I was not a cheque signatory, nor was I involved in any of the accounting procedures of the Company. Dan, who was for a few years, the sole director, had a very tight grip on all things corporate. I was happy not to be involved, as every time I was, it went wrong.

A small agency, one that employs very few people, tends to run on a democratic basis. If clients are taken on without the full agreement of the other agents, this can be a recipe for disaster. In a company of three or four people everybody answers the phone and deals with any enquiries. Mike Smith claimed I "ran" the Company and consequently broke the law. As responsible grown ups, who loved what they were doing, we all just got on with our jobs. Obviously, as the most experienced agent, my advice was sought on occasions by the others but that was only to be expected. In fact I spent 80% of my time at home. I came to town once or twice a week to lunch with clients and media folk at

Elena's and visited the office for perhaps an hour a week at most.

After nine months, much to Ian Bloom's surprise, the DTI decided they were going to prosecute me. By this time I had so many T-shirts that I was pretty inured to yet more grief - not that I wasn't taking it very seriously.

Ian hired a specialist barrister to defend me, Professor Mark Watson-Gandy. The most likely outcome I was advised was a fine, and a not inconsiderable one at that, although they warned me that the judge had the discretion and the power to hand down a custodial sentence. I asked him why they'd decided to proceed against me and he explained, having worked for and against the DTI, that they liked high profile cases, particularly ones that had a celebrity factor. He also added that they choose them very carefully because losing cannot be an option. That set the old diseased heart racing!

So on June 14th 2004 at ten in the morning I found myself in the dock in Isleworth Crown Court, near Brentford, standing before a Judge and Jury. Mike Smith arrived with wife Sarah and her sister Laura. It was a regular Smith family picnic. The DTI were relying totally on their evidence. As my barrister put it, *the only evidence that Mr Roseman has been managing a company contrary to his disqualification as a company director comes from a discredited former client of the Company whose personal animus to Mr Roseman and the hostility of her brother-in-law ought to mean the Court should give no credence to their evidence.*

Laura certainly played her part well. She was very cool under questioning from my barrister but couldn't provide any plausible evidence of any wrongdoing. Watson-Gandy's questioning was pedantic and nothing like the drama we see in the movies. But he wasn't there to win an Oscar; he wanted to prove that the DTI had no credible evidence and they were clearly struggling to come up with anything close.

Mike Smith took to the witness box like a man on a mission. Smug doesn't come close. He made great play of my description on the Company's web site as 'the

Don'. To him that was conclusive evidence that I was running the Company. My barrister suggested to him that the description was suppose to be 'jokey', a suggestion he didn't agree with. Pressing home the point he asked whether the descriptions of the other members of staff were to be taken as seriously as mine. The others being variously described as a failed Polish pole-vaulter, an expert cherry jam maker and an Atlantic naked swimming champion. He offered no comment.

Things seemed to be going well until an affidavit I'd provided at Laura Green's trial was introduced by the DTI. An error with respect to the dates of my disqualification as a director seven years earlier was pointed out and the Judge, who was not overly fond of me, grasped it with both hands. It was fairly obvious that he wanted the jury to convict me and now he felt he had the necessary ammunition.

It was an honest error by Ian Bloom who was mortified that it was going to be used against me. At the end of the day he hastily returned to his office to prepare an affidavit that would explain to the judge that it was a mistake on his part and not a lie on mine. The judge dismissed it, telling the jury in his own inimitable style, that I was obviously an evil, corrupt and thoroughly disreputable human being and hanging would be too good for me. Three out of three I guess. Now things weren't looking so good. I felt that I was no longer staring at a substantial fine if found guilty but a prison sentence.

Dan was called as a witness and under severe cross - examination by the DTI's barrister stood firm in my defence and impressed the jury with her calm, qualified responses. Ian later said it was solely her evidence that saved me from *Madame la Guillotine.*

When the court adjourned for lunch I set about making plans for my possible incarceration. My legal 'team' while offering me succour, weren't exactly discouraging me from making plans for any eventuality. I called one of my most trusted friends, Caroline Righton, and told her what page I was on. I asked her if it was possible for her to take charge of things if I ended up sharing a room with a violent axe murderer from Willesden. Of course she would. She is a woman of great personal integrity and someone who offers friendship unconditionally.

As I walked into court I felt numb. We had been moved from the small court to one that was reminiscent of Judge John Deed's place of business. I sat in the dock and listened to the judge's summing up to the jury. He made great play of 'the Don' reference and even greater play of the inaccurate affidavit. I was definitely sitting on a knife edge with the blade grazing my balls when the jury went out to consider the rest of my life.

We waited in the canteen while deliberations took place. After half an hour we were told to return to the court. I again sat in the dock to hear the foreman ask the judge if he'd accept a majority verdict. He agreed to a majority of ten. We all left the court again, the jury to their special room, us back to the canteen.

Dan was, as always, strong and determined and convinced that everything would be all right. As for me, well, I was already making plans how to fend off unwanted advances in the shower. As Ian Bloom pointed out later, when I told him of my dark thoughts, you're not such a great catch even to an elderly prisoner, who's blind and hasn't had sex for a couple of decades. Even sex starved truckers apparently would find me unacceptable!

Finally after a further fifteen minutes we were ushered back in to court for the verdict.

Not guilty!

The judge was really annoyed. When my barrister asked for costs he fought it with all his might but the law was against him. We left the court and adjourned for a celebratory glass of champagne. I heard later that Mike Smith was attempting, vainly, to shove his own champagne cork back in to his bottle, no doubt to keep it fizzy for another day.

CHAPTER SIXTY FOUR
COUNTRY LIFE AND NANCY DELL'OLIO

Dan, who had been in charge of the Soho office for the London International Advertising Awards (LIAA) when the great and the good came once a year to a London hotel to receive accolades for being the best of the best, had the last of her many run-ins with her boss, Barbara Levy.

She left LIAA, after eighteen years. It meant, to me at least, that we no longer had to live in London. Dan hated the idea of moving out of the city. She would miss Soho and its energy, but she surprised herself after a few months and started to enjoy country life.

In April 2004 we rented a house in Crowborough, the home of Conan Doyle, near Tunbridge Wells, and settled into a quieter, calmer life; fed a lot of birds and the occasional fox cubs and watched the deer munch their way through the flower beds. I fed the fish in the pond and laid careful, but unfulfilled plans, to destroy the herons that made early morning commando raids on the fish in my pond.

The company was now working from an office in Queen Anne Street close to Harley Street and Geraldine Woods had her hand on the talent tiller bringing in her own people. Geraldine was an ex- executive with LWT after serving a twelve year sentence on This Morning. A woman very highly regarded and with fantastic contacts within ITV. She was the epitome of elegance and possesses a very sharp mind and has the potential to be one of the best agents in London.

2005 began with Nancy Dell'Olio and finished with the end of my relationship with Fern Britton. Nancy Dell'Olio is a prime example of tabloid invention over substance. I represented her for three months. In that time she enjoyed innumerable photo spreads in a bunch of tabloids and magazines, none of it anything to do with me. All of the pictures were set up and the photographic agencies shared the fees with her. You can't blame her. How else is a 'girl' going to make a living? She was determined to carve out a niche for herself using whatever talents she didn't have.

I asked Sean O'Brien to come on board as I needed an experienced tabloid journalist to try and control her excesses. Sean had been with the *News of the World* and had been show biz reporter on *The People*. Without him I think I'd have been locked up for a string of violent offences. Her relationship with Sven allowed her to hold court at Claridges Hotel in London's West End which had become her second home. She had her own table and was treated like royalty. I had so many meetings there with her that the doorman knew my name!

Sean and I did a lot of hustling to find her work, but by then she'd been around for so many years that the boat had sailed. The waters had been muddied to such an extent that any career in the media was impossible. She did hold out the carrot of her 'book', giving the impression it would tell the real blockbuster story of her life with the England coach. It was never to be.

We managed to scrape the bottom of the barrel and persuaded her to present six shows on MTV called *Footballers Cribs*. The shows were all recorded in one day and involved her doing links to camera and reading off an autocue.

It was a disaster.

Sean worked his butt off, rewriting links that he hoped she would be able to pronounce in a way that normal folk would understand. The title of the show had to be mentioned constantly. No big deal you might think. It wouldn't have been if she could pronounce it. It came out constantly as *footaballaz crisps*! As there were six shows she had to deliver the title thirty six times. It was a nightmare for the producer. Hours were spent trying to get her to deliver the two words in an accent that was understandable in the UK. It wasn't just her accent that made the whole thing a disaster. She didn't look that great either. Ian Hyland, *The Sunday Mirror* TV critic, said she looked like the late American actor Roy Schneider!

The end came one weekend when Sven was all over Saturday's *Sun* yet again shagging for Sweden. Nancy had already been, in my opinion, demeaned by a bunch of previous revelations about Sven's sexual activities with a harem's worth of women. I never really understood why so many ladies of Fleet Street defended her decision to stick by him. Some of them saw it as a sign of a liberated, brave woman, I saw it, no doubt in common with much of the rest of Britain, as the story of a sad woman of a certain age who was riding the gravy train and didn't want the Bisto to run out.

She was on her normal seven week holiday in Italy when the story broke. She rang me perhaps thirty times as I dealt with a barrage of press enquiries. I didn't know at the time she had just signed to another agent! Sven, bless his libido, hadn't bothered to call her about the article even though he knew about it the previous day. In fact he never called her at all, and they didn't speak till she flew back late Sunday night. He's such an old romantic in the Silvio Berlusconi tradition.

I volunteered to pick her up from Gatwick and offer her refuge from the press hordes. She declined my offer. When I, in turn, picked up the morning papers I discovered that her new agent had collected her. That's how Sean and I found out our relationship with her was at an end.

We spoke briefly on Monday morning, and I mentioned in passing that I was little put out to read in a national newspaper that I was no longer representing her. I think the 'c' word may have come up.

CHAPTER SIXTY FIVE
FERN, THIS MORNING, POLICE AND THE PHOTOGRAPHS

One of our many trips to Cornwall to visit Fern on her regular family caravan holidays ended our relationship in the most terribly bizarre way. It was the summer of 2005.

I'd represented her for some years having been introduced by her then husband Clive Jones. In those days she was successful but not overly busy. She began standing in as a one day a week presenter on *This Morning* on Fridays. The viewers loved her and so did the TV crews. After they'd spent the week with Richard and Judy, Fern was a breath of fresh air.

After she met and married Phil Vickery, Dan and I used to enjoy regular dinners at their home and we all grew very fond of each other. She was soon to take over the programme presenting with John Leslie. They made a good team, John with his 'Jack the lad' persona and Fern with her 'mumsy' but sexy image.

When John was turned over by the press the search went out for a new co-presenter. Philip Schofield got the nod. I was called by the editor and told about his appointment. I, in turn, called Fern. She was furious. She didn't like Philip and thought he was the wrong man for the job. We were both a little irritated that ITV hadn't even sought her input, though they had no contractual obligation to do so. But the decision was made and she had to make the best of it.

As the months rolled by, she became increasingly more irritated with his penchant for taking things over. At that time she was not the kind of presenter who protested, provided that she could see suggested 'improvements' were in the best interests of the programme. Philip was forever trying to adapt the programme to the way he thought it should be. He would sit in on editorial meetings, something Fern rarely did. It all came to a head after she called to tell me she'd had enough of Philip since he was always sticking his finger in the programme pie. I conveyed this in the most diplomatic way possible to the Editor and things calmed down for a while.

Time passed, but Philip wasn't the kind of man who would play second fiddle to a woman and tensions were never far from the surface. At that time Fern was earning considerably more than Philip and that, I think, helped to take the edge off things, at least for a while.

Personally I'd always disliked him, though I only had cause to meet him on a few occasions. The man was too smug for me and his view of himself would have shamed Narcissus.

Fern has always had a much publicised problem with her weight. Her husband, Phil, was concerned about the problem too. I sat with him in the coffee bar at Marylebone station, as he waited for a train back to their home in High Wycombe. He asked me if ITV were worried enough about her weight not to renew her contract. I told him that while I doubted it very much, I had been advised by Diane Nelmes, Head of Daytime for Granada, that concerns were being expressed. I suggested I mention it to Fern next time I had dinner with them. He in turn said he didn't want to be there when I did.

I have always had the highest regard for Phil. I've seen him with Fern's children from her marriage to Clive and he is an exceptional step-dad. He loves his football and a glass or two, and like Natasha's ex-boyfriend, Mike, he was great company.

I arrived at their home one evening and they'd decided to have a Chinese take away. Even professional chefs like Phil need some time away from the Aga. I drove with Fern to pick up the food and decided that it might be a good time to bring up the highly sensitive subject of her weight. She listened very carefully and I could tell she was deeply hurt and upset. But I knew I wasn't telling her anything she wasn't already aware of.

She began to cry and told me why she thought the whole weight issue had started. As with all such problems you have to go back to childhood. With her it was her mother showing more warmth and love for her sister. She has never shown any fear in talking about the darker side of her life either privately or in print.

We returned to the house and managed to talk it through more calmly. Her size never affected her fitness and she was remarkably flexible being able to exercise in a way only a practising Yoga teacher could manage.

When they asked me to be godfather to their daughter Winnie, I thought I'd have to revise my old axiom about clients' relationships with agents. The Fern I knew then went on to change into quite a different person. My daughter Elie used to say if she could choose a mum it would be Fern. I guess a lot of kids may have felt the same way. She was big, cuddly and safe and full of worldly advice.

I was always the barrier between her and her bosses and if there were problems to sort out I had on occasions played Mr Nasty. She was paid very well for her work on *This Morning*. We were watching '*Who Wants To Be A Millionaire*' in her living room one evening. One of the contestants reached thirty two thousand pounds. I casually remarked that was what she took home in less than a fortnight. She said, 'that's your fault!' But money was extremely important to her. Her early career was spent on the breadline and it was a time she never wanted to revisit.

Back on that fateful day on the beach in Cornwall, unknown to any of us, someone had taken pictures of her in her black bikini. The beach was private and belonged exclusively to the caravan park. But the pictures were soon splashed over the tabloids and, although the captions were not vindictive, it none the less caused her great pain.

She blamed Dan and I for taking the pictures. How or why she could have reached a conclusion is inexplicable and bizarre in the extreme. Dan believes it may have been because she'd confided to Fern on the beach that day that the company's book-keeper had failed to advise either her or her accountant about what the tax people define as 'benefits in kind' that she received from the Agency for a period of seven years. This resulted in Dan owing the taxman nearly fifty thousand pounds! Dan felt that Fern had concluded that the money from the sale of the pictures would have covered her liability to the taxman. Dan was distraught by Fern's accusation and left a tearful voice mail offering to send her the memory card from her camera by the way of proof, if proof were needed, that she hadn't taken the pictures. Fern never responded. I'm not sure I totally agree with Dan and feel other unknown forces were at work. She left the Agency and we've not spoken since. When she repeated the allegation to a client of mine, I was forced to send her a lawyer's letter explaining that the accusation was slanderous. The pictures were circulated by a large photographic agency, Big Pictures. I called the owner, Darryn Lyons, but he couldn't tell me who he'd bought them from because of the Data Protection Act, but did write my lawyers a letter confirming that neither Dan nor I were involved in any way. We copied the letter on to Fern. She never replied.

The fact she could believe Dan and I were involved is inexplicable.

Fern experienced two major setbacks that began to alter both the public's and her bosses' perception of her. She became involved in a range of clothing without consulting ITV. They were furious at what, potentially, could be a serious breach of the guidelines on impartiality. Endorsing a product without approval could bring about a conflict of interest. By now she was being represented by Phil's agent who, perhaps, wasn't as familiar as I was with the vagaries of the workings of ITV. She, in turn, was angry by what she saw as unnecessary interference by the powers that be in her private affairs. Harsh words were said by both sides and the clothing range never appeared.

The gastric band incident was a PR disaster. Her apparent inability to understand, or want to understand, that you couldn't claim that weight loss was down to exercise and a healthy diet when the reality clearly pointed to 'cosmetic' surgery was odd.

This, with her appearing in the Ryvita commercials, seemed a clear betrayal of the public's trust. Her performance on the programme after the tabloids' revelations was very sad. Her change from the Fern I knew was complete. Some people who had known her well for many years told me that the 'new' Fern had always been simmering beneath the surface. If that was true, I'd never seen it.

It was certainly the end of the love affair that she had enjoyed up till then with the tabloids. The old axiom of 'they build you up only to tear you down' had never been so true. Seeing it from afar I thought it was all eminently avoidable. I don't know who, if anyone, was advising her. It had long since ceased to matter to me. Nevertheless she went on to accuse me of all sorts of business malpractice which resulted in the police knocking at my front door. The CPS saw no reason to proceed.

And so it was that another high profile client bit the dust.

CHAPTER SIXTY SIX
KATE GARRAWAY, DEREK DRAPER, A WEDDING AND LIBEL

I've always felt very paternal toward Kate Garraway. I'd represented her for nearly ten years and we'd travelled a long path together; from Meridian TV through Sky News and finally GMTV. Before we represented her, she'd chosen a difficult man to marry and it ended in divorce. We shared much of the turmoil of those later years. I only met him once and that was after the divorce. We'd gone to an awards ceremony together and as we passed between the packed tables we bumped into him. I was introduced briefly and we continued to our table and sat down. She asked me if I was surprised. I think she meant by his somewhat diminutive size and his general appearance. I have to admit, by this time, life rarely threw up many surprises and I'd learnt not to prejudge anyone's relationships. The time I spent with her was mostly business and rarely social, so I had no idea of the kind of men she liked.

Anyone who works for GMTV is in an invidious position regarding how they're viewed by the rest of the business. This perception could well have coloured the broadcasting fraternity's view of Esther McVey. Oddly this perception wasn't reflected by newspaper Editors. Eamonn, Fiona, Lorraine, Penny and Kate have all had newspaper columns at one time or another. Since the station was launched in 1993 only three GMTV presenters have ever moved on to achieve any real success elsewhere, namely Anthea Turner and Eamonn Holmes and, to a lesser extent, Lorraine Kelly.

Anthea moved from Blue Peter to GMTV and won the biggest media prize in the history of British TV. She became the face of the National Lottery. In those days though, if my spaniel was the face of the Lottery, he'd have made millions too. Wherever you looked, there was Anthea smiling away. On the covers of magazines or daily papers, in the financial sections if there were articles on Camelot, on the sports pages if the Lottery were funding a sportsman or woman, even on the inside pages if they'd funded some good cause. She probably had more column inches in the first year of the Lottery than Princess Diana. None of this was down to GMTV.

Eamonn's work outside the station reflected his popularity and professionalism. What about Ben Shepherd? Well there's always been a shortage of male presenters between the ages of twenty six and thirty five. I look at him as a vacuum filler, someone with little substance and personality. I'm sorry, a man with a second class degree in Dance and Drama who names his son after Jack Bauer, the lead character in the TV series *24*, just doesn't cut it for me.

Broadcasters have never been overly fond of GMTV presenters. Some years back they (GMTV) conducted a very expensive confidential survey on their presenters which just happened to fall in to my hands. It made for interesting reading.

Lorraine Kelly came out tops followed by Eamonn. Fiona didn't do so well but Kate was thought to have star quality. She was a good journalist, and an excellent presenter, who could switch from interviewing a senior political figure, to a man who kept pet ants, in the flicker of an eye. She was attractive, women didn't find her threatening and men had their secret, and not so secret, fantasies about her. Just google her name and you'll see what I mean. But offers of work were scarce. That's not to say she was bereft of offers. It was that the work on offer was low profile and short-lived.

Penny Smith came out worst in the research particularly from punters north of Watford. They just didn't get her. Strangely when she appeared on the BBC's Just *The Two Of Us*, 'singing' with Curtis Stigers in 2006, she came fourth. Those same people north of Watford kept her in the competition and should have proved to producers what a special talent she possessed. In fact with her increased profile she was offered a brief spate of work but it didn't last for more than six months. People write about the curse of Hello, but GMTV's curse is much more mysterious. For my money, Penny Smith has been the most under-rated presenter on mainstream British television for the last 10 years and was let go in the aforementioned ITV purge.

I've already mentioned that clients often canvas friends and family for career advice and it's something an agent has to live with. Sometimes, though, that advice can be so off kilter that it's comparable to a back seat driver insisting that they know the way, even though it's via the top of a cliff.

Enter Derek Draper.

Kate and Derek's marriage in 2005 was covered by *OK* magazine. Thankfully it didn't suffer from Anthea's chocolate bar catastrophe. However it did have its interesting moments. Just before the speeches Claire Nasir, one of the station's weather presenters and a close friend of Kate's, came up to me to point out a gatecrasher. A reporter from *The People*. How she got past *OK*'s security guards is a whole different story. Perhaps she'd tunnelled in.

I wandered over to where she was sitting comfortably taking in the proceedings just like any other guest and suggested she accompanied me out of the hotel. She retrieved her jacket and we walked out through the foyer. It was then I asked her what she was doing gate-crashing the wedding particularly as it was common knowledge that *OK* had exclusive rights. Her answer gave me a slight cause for concern. She explained that the *Sunday Mirror* had a front page story the following morning claiming Kate was pregnant. She'd come along to get a quote. You had to admire her *chutzpah*.

I called the *Sunday Mirror* and asked to speak to Tina Weaver who was the editor and a friend. She was on holiday and I was put through to the news editor. It was about seven o'clock. I introduced myself.

'I've been told that you're running a story about Kate being pregnant. Is that right?'

'Yes!'

'Do you know where I can find Tina?'

'She's on holiday.'

'I know, but as a friend of hers I would like the opportunity of a quick chat.'

'She can't be reached. Are you denying the story?' I knew it to be true so I tried a different tack.

'I'm sure you're aware of the Press Complaints Commission (PCC) guidelines that a paper cannot publish a story about any pregnancy if it's less than three months.'

'So you're not denying she's pregnant?' I'd been in the game for over thirty years and wasn't about to get caught out by some *pisher*.

'What I asked is simply whether you were aware of the PCC's guidelines.'

'So you're *not* denying the story?'

'As I'm sure you know I'm actually at Kate's wedding as we speak. I'd like to ask one final time, how you can be so certain that Kate is either pregnant and particularly over three months?'

'So you're not denying it!' He was hardly likely to reveal his source so I disconnected. When Anne Diamond was pregnant with her second child, the press were tipped off by a source at the private hospital where she was having a scan. So anyone, friend, nurse, hospital receptionist could have told the paper. I went back into the wedding reception just in time to miss the speeches. Clare spotted me and came over to ask what was going on. I told her. As one of Kate's best friends she knew the story was true.

'You can't tell her about it now,' she said, 'it'll ruin her day.'

'Clare I don't even know if her mum and dad know. I can't just let them read about it in tomorrow's paper. I think that will certainly ruin *their* day!'

I went off in search of Kate, stopping off briefly to find a glass of brandy. I whispered in her ear that we needed to talk privately and we exited stage left to a stairwell. I lit a cigarette and told her about the *Sunday Mirror* front page.

'Fuck!' she said, and leant against the wall of the stairwell. A more incongruous sight you'd have to wait a lifetime to see. An empty stairwell, a floor that hadn't been cleaned in months and one of the country's most recognisable presenters in her wedding gown pressed against a grubby wall. 'Fuck!' she repeated and grabbed the cigarette from my hand and took a huge drag. Not very PC, bearing in mind her condition, but understandable. 'How did they find out?' I shook my head.

'Who knows? He wasn't the most communicative of mortals.'

'Our parents don't even know.' She said. I stood next to her taking a swig of my brandy. She thought for a moment or two and after another drag said matter of factually, 'Well we'll just have to tell them.' There was nowhere to hide. She ground the cigarette out and we went back to the throng. Bride and groom hastily retrieved respective parents and disappeared in to a private room and explained all. After the initial shock everyone was delighted and it only added to the celebration.

As time rolled by, Derek had several contretemps with the office which usually involved him shouting and swearing. Geraldine Woods, the company's senior agent, seemed to be the recipient of most of these maniacal tirades. She's a toughie and told him bluntly that no-one spoke to her like that and hung up on him.

One Christmas, Kate rang the office to ask for the Agency's email contacts list, so she could post her Christmas cards. This was a list that we weren't too happy to give out as it had taken a very long time to put together and to some extent was confidential. But she pressed them very hard and we gave in. Derek had set up a company to sell media training. He used the contact list to help promote his new company. We were all disappointed with the subterfuge he used. I received dozens of calls from the Agency contacts asking why they'd been emailed with Draper's company's website.

Kate was getting impatient with her lack of career momentum and began asking around about replacing me as her agent. We work in a small community and word got back to me about her search. I'd always taken the view that if a client wants to leave, then whatever you try to do they are not going to change their minds. It just becomes a question of when. I was well aware that Derek wanted me out but then he wanted to excise most of the people who were close to Kate before they met.

On the face of it, her career was hardly flatlining. It was merely the way the station was perceived by other broadcasters. If she had taken the huge, but very risky step, of leaving, it might have only been a matter of time before something special came along. In the two years since her departure from us, that big break has still eluded her. But the world of broadcasting has entered a new era. The world of stringent cut backs. GMTV is currently undergoing major surgery perhaps amputation is a more apposite description. Now it's a question of holding on to whatever job you've got because there's precious little going on anywhere else.

When Kate was selected for *Strictly Come Dancing*, both she and Derek felt that this could be the *big* one. Derek threw himself into it in the same way he no doubt did when he was spinning for Labour. A small PR team was assembled. I've never been a great fan of PR for PR's sake.

Once you try and manipulate the press you leave yourself wide open for the old, we made you and now we'll break you, syndrome. Up until *Strictly*, Kate enjoyed very good press. In my view, Derek's insistence on PR affected her long term relationship with them.

I attended one meeting at their house in Islington with two independent PR's where he'd prepared a schedule of activities that wouldn't have been out of place in his old spin doctoring days. It was very sad. It was as though he, and perhaps she, felt that PR was the Holy Grail to raise her career up to another level. Perhaps there is evidence of the positive use of PR for some presenters' upward mobility. How else can you explain the success of the likes of Johnny Vaughn, Tess Daly, her husband Vernon Kay, Fearne Cotton and Holly Willoughby among others?

The barrage of stories that their 'team' placed with newspapers and magazines was in my view, wholly unnecessary and ultimately destructive. The press love it when you do the leg work for them. They've a lot of column inches to fill and when material is shovelled onto their plates they consume it voraciously. But after all this over-consumption, where are they when you need them? Suddenly the girl next door image is tainted by over-exposure.

I took a call from Tina Weaver, the Editor of the *Sunday Mirror*, one Saturday afternoon which was the beginning of the end of some of the press's love affair with Kate. Taking into account their very hostile view of her husband, Kate had done well to garner the amount of positive press she'd achieved since her marriage. Who can forget Piers Morgan's immortal comment after they announced their engagement, 'If I knew she'd set the bar so low I'd have had a go myself.'

Tina told me they had pictures and video footage which proved Kate was having an affair with Anton du Bek, her dance partner from *Strictly*. Now it wouldn't be the first time a client hadn't confided some indiscretion to me and left me to deal with an aftermath that would have been so much easier to deal with if I'd been forewarned.

Some years back, I'd been called by a tabloid and told they had information that a client's wife was having an affair with a local builder. I called the client and told him a newspaper was asking questions about the state of his marriage. He said the allegation was completely without foundation. I believed him. I called the reporter and gave both a denial and a warning. The warning being, expect a writ for libel if you print the story. I have never lied to the press. I've had clients who've asked me to but it's just not worth it. Once you're caught out in a lie, any further denials are taken with a pinch of salt. My dealings with the press have always been based on the fact that if I say it's untrue then, to the best of my knowledge, that's the case. If it is true, I deliver a 'no comment'. I appreciate that sends out the rather obvious message that it probably is true, but that far outweighs the numerous occasions when my denial is completely accepted without question. And, more, to the point, nothing gets published.

That same day he happened to go home early and found his wife *in flagrante delicto* with the said builder. He called me in tears to tell me, but by then I'd issued the denial, and wasn't about to call the reporter back to tell him I'd been misinformed!

I told Tina that it wasn't in Kate's nature to be unfaithful, it was completely alien to her entire persona. Tina, who'd known Kate for some time, wasn't buying it. She asked me to contact her for a comment. I spent the entire afternoon leaving both her and Derek messages. Finally, around five thirty, I managed to speak to them. Derek started ranting about my ineptitude in dealing with the matter. I explained as patiently as possible that I wanted to send them a lawyer's letter warning of the grave consequences of publishing such a piece but that I wasn't prepared to do that unilaterally. Why, he screamed, did I wait all afternoon before I did anything? Did what? Lie? Tell half truths? I had no intention of blindly going in to bat with fake quotes and some unqualified denial with a national Sunday newspaper. He, of course, called in his PR people totally crossing the lines of communication between myself and Tina. The piece was published and a libel action ensued.

The paper was wrong and, after a few months, had to settle with an apology and pay substantial damages. Unfortunately its sister paper, *The Daily Mirror* had been enjoined in the action. This really angered the editor, Richard Wallace, whose paper had nothing to do with the original libel. That said, the whole matter was deeply upsetting and hurtful for both of them, but having won, you have to be magnanimous. A paper that loses can be very unforgiving, and the winner, in this case a major celebrity, has to be seriously cognisant of ongoing relationships with the losing papers.

It's highly unusual that the victor attends court for the apology. It's usually left to the lawyers to make a carefully worded agreed statement to the press on the steps outside the High Court. To attend, as Derek insisted they should do, and bask in a photo opportunity is rubbing their noses in defeat. To send a text message to the losing Editor, asking her why she's not present is profoundly stupid. Derek sent such a text to Tina Weaver.

Bearing in mind Fiona Phillips is a columnist for the *Daily Mirror*, and taking into account Kate's much publicised rivalry with her, his decision to attend the Court was to prove very uncomfortable for Kate. Soon afterwards I'd ceased to be her agent. When Fiona left GMTV there was considerable press conjecture about her replacement. Both *The Mirror* and *The Sunday Mirror* took their revenge by publishing severely unflattering pieces about Kate and her chances of succeeding to the throne as queen of breakfast TV. Spinning for Blair and Mandleson isn't the same as dealing with the fragile nature of the relationships that exist between on screen talent and the daily press.

I got a call from an old Fleet Street wag around this time. 'Have you heard that Draper's been kidnapped by terrorists and they're demanding a hundred thousand pounds or they will burn him with petrol? Please donate what you can. I have already given five litres.' He was never going to win any popularity contest.

When Emma Crosby's appointment was announced none of the existing presenters were told in advance. They found out about it, like the rest us, from the newspapers. Kate heard on her way into work at four o'clock in the morning and called her boss, Peter McHugh. He wasn't best pleased to be woken up by one of his presenters complaining about GMTV's *modus operandi*, and said so in his normal blunt style. I find it difficult to believe that Kate did this on the spur of the moment and see the Draper hand in the background. Similarly that same hand accompanied by the rest of him must have pushed her into a stormy meeting with Peter later that morning. This time Peter told them both to fuck off. I have a great deal of respect for Kate's abilities, but this business is about relationships and the nurturing of those relationships.

More dust biting. At least losing many more high profile clients was unlikely as I only had a couple left!

CHAPTER SIXTY SEVEN
TV TODAY

Over the years there have been some great BBC controllers. I'd sparred with most of them. Some like Bill Cotton and Paul Fox were exceptional. Others like Alan Yentob and Peter Salmon were clever and approachable, though I thought Alan was far too cerebral for a popular channel.

I don't know where the new breed of BBC executives comes from now - a battery farm in Chiswick or Hampstead perhaps? My dealings with Jay Hunt, the controller of BBC1 revealed a woman with more insecurities than a post natal gerbil. That said I don't believe the elder retirees with all their talent would have been able to solve the problems TV is facing today. The new age of the internet has confounded everyone. There probably isn't an executive in the entire British TV industry that has a grasp of how the future of broadcasting will develop. I'm not sure their American counterparts are any different. Sure there are plenty of seminars and closed door meetings where vast quantities of Buxton are drunk to discuss the future of the business but, to date, no one has any answers. Goldman's aphorism is as relevant as ever. Nobody still knows anything.

I'd been an agent for thirty five years and any positive feelings I'd once had for the job had long since been put out with the garbage. Most dealings agents were now having with TV executives had slipped into farce.

In 2009, when *Watchdog* was being revised, rumours were rife about changes in presenters. The BBC just allowed the rumours to circulate and finally I had to talk to Ms Jay Hunt. She claimed that they were merely taking a look at several programmes and nothing had been seriously discussed let alone agreed. Except, that, notwithstanding great ratings with Nicky Campbell at the helm, she'd decided to replace him. My conversations with her were an object lesson in 'being economical with the truth.'

Both Nicky and I needed to know if he was being replaced at least a couple of months before the decision was announced so, like with Jill Dando, a decade earlier, I could limit any damage to his reputation. Being taken off a highly successful programme much of it down to his powerful skills as a presenter can send out all sorts of signals, none of them particularly beneficial. Hunt agreed that she would ensure this happened. I was no longer an agent when the announcement that Anne Robinson would replace him was made but she ignored our agreement anyway.

The BBC at this time was always on the defensive and worried by the press attacks on them, particularly by *The Daily Mail*. Government scrutiny, concern about the level of the license fee and their involvement in a bunch of scandals all combined to diminish a once great institution. They handled it with all the sensitivity of a Derek Draper blog. They then proceeded to go the whole nine yards with political correctness. How this helped them resolve the intrinsic problems they were facing is beyond me.

They banned any BBC journalist from having their own newspaper columns. They felt the opinions they expressed would invalidate their neutrality. Nicky Campbell was not only a brilliant presenter on both television and radio, but he was a surprisingly good writer. He was filing a very successful weekly sports column for the *Guardian*. I tried to argue with Mark Thompson, the Director General, that a sports column fell way outside such thinking. Let's face it, commenting on the abilities on the batting prowess of Andrew Strauss or picking holes in the England football team's selection process wasn't in the same league as John Humphries writing about Gordon Brown's inability to do simple maths. My argument was dismissed out of hand. This new BBC diktat didn't stop them from permitting the 'occasional' column to be penned. It was typical BBC misdirection. There are some very clever and talented programme makers working at the Beeb but they're swamped by political correctness gone mad; and managers, who in real life, wouldn't be allowed to run a damaged pet shop.

In mid 2007 Moira Stewart came to see me, deeply unhappy with the BBC's treatment of her. She was being unceremoniously shoved out of the mainstream and moved to BBC World. She felt that she was being treated shabbily and I had to agree. The fact that after some twenty five years loyal service as a member of staff, she still was only paid a pittance compared with other lesser talents was deplorable. The press took up the cudgels on her behalf accusing the Beeb of ageism.

We went into battle for her. I involved the well-honed services of Ian Bloom yet again to examine the minutia of her staff contract. As soon as we became involved, the BBC changed their tactics and Moira was offered a more realistic situation. But bizarrely she disappeared from Ian's life and mine as mysteriously as she had arrived. We were never to know the actual outcome of her situation with the Beeb as she didn't return any of our calls!

The BBC also suffered from a string of personal vendettas. If a BBC executive didn't like you than no matter how talented you were you didn't progress.

This is illustrated by Emily Maitlis. Her career had stalled. We had been representing her for a couple of years. She had been presenting the BBC's local London programme, *London News* for some years and was getting a little frustrated. She was bright, attractive and ticked all the BBC boxes except for one. She couldn't overcome Roger Mosey's prejudice against her.

Roger, a corpulent averagely talented BBC veteran, is now titled 'Director of London 2012.' Only the BBC can come up with such an absurd job description. He's in charge of their Olympic coverage - he's not actually running a campaign to be Mayor of London. He doesn't have many fans at the BBC coalface and his promotion seems to me, like many BBC promotions, due more to his length of service rather than any innate ability. I've had several run ins with the man and he's certainly a paid up member of the Jay Hunt School of diplomacy.

When Natasha Kaplinsky and Brendan Cole were asked to make a DVD on ballroom dancing I needed to get clearance from the BBC. Mosey, being her boss, gave it in writing. As the DVD neared its journey to the marketplace he got cold feet as he was being asked awkward questions from his own superiors as to how he could allow one of his news presenters to participate in something that may well undermine the credibility of his department. He began applying pressure on Kaplinsky to back off the project whilst at the same time denying he'd given his complete permission in the first place. Machiavelli - eat your heart out.

Kaplinsky, under pressure from Mosey, broke her contract with the DVD producers and refused to promote the DVD, leaving them to pick up a loss of close to a quarter of a million pounds. They considered suing, but the law as we know, is an expensive pastime.

Mosey's continuing antipathy to Emily prevented any upward movement for her in news and current affairs. At that time Channel 5 were looking for a stand in for Kirsty Young who was going on maternity leave. They were interested in both Kate Garraway and Emily. It would have been a big risk for either of them. At most it was a year's contract with no guarantee of life beyond. They were both in similar situations career-wise. Kate was stuck in a job that she was doing brilliantly but working under the shadow of GMTV, which meant that she was mostly ignored by the rest of the business. Emily, was being ignored by Mosey, and facing major BBC cut backs in local news programmes, which, in turn, could see her fees drastically reduced. At the time her fees were greatly disproportionate to the job she was doing, having been enticed to join in much better times. Working for 5 could potentially help them both. Sometimes leaving a company can send out a signal to your ex-employer that they shouldn't have let you go.

5 wanted either one of them. They both turned it down. I could understand Kate's refusal at the time as there was a distinct possibility that when Fiona left, she could get the plum job. But for Emily, I could see only

gloom on the horizon. We talked about it and I tried to persuade her it was the best option at the time, and with Mosey holding sway, she had nowhere to go. She didn't want to know. I felt that as my advice was being disregarded about something so fundamental then perhaps it was best we part company. Much more of this and I'd be on income support.

The machinations of TV executives never ceased to amaze and amuse me. The TV business really doesn't belong in the real world. What kind of organisation would hire someone to run a worldwide multinational business employing over 25,000 people with an annual budget of over four billion pounds with absolutely no business experience whatsoever? That's what Mark Thompson does as Director General of the BBC. Sir John Harvey Jones would be turning in his grave.

I often used to assist executives in finding work and advise them on their contracts. This activity had to be done covertly. If it became known an agent was involved in the 'transfer' of an executive, then his ability to hire any of that agent's clients could become tainted. If I thought the workings of GMTV odd, companies like the late Carlton Television could give them a run for their money.

Nick Bullen is an excellent producer in a business where there are so few talented people. I was telephoned by a mutual friend who asked me, on Nick's behalf, if I thought Steve Hewlett, then Controller of Programmes at Carlton would be interested in hiring him. By coincidence I was having dinner with Steve that night. Nick Bullen was the editor of *This Morning* working for Granada TV. He was a highly talented man in the field of factual entertainment. Steve jumped at the chance to meet him and a deal was struck. Nick, though, in the fine tradition of a long line of TV execs was merely using Carlton's interest to increase his bargaining power with Granada. To keep him he was appointed Executive Producer of Entertainment.

Steve and Carlton were furious that they had been used in this way, although, given a similar situation, they would have practised such a subterfuge themselves. Steve called me and began to berate me for

Nick two-timing them. I pointed out that it had sod all to do with me as I was merely the conduit and I thought I was just doing everyone a favour. Steve was nonetheless still pissed with me.

Months passed and I was contacted again. Nick was still very unhappy and wanted to know if I'd speak to Steve again to see if there was anything going at Carlton. Unbelievable! If I'd have been Steve and saw Nick crossing the road I'd probably have hit him broadside!

Always up for a laugh and a nervous breakdown I called Steve. He spent five minutes telling me what a shit Nick was and repeated his diatribe of the events of the previous debacle. Then he wanted to know if Nick was serious this time. I pointed out that, like last time, I'd never even spoken to him and was merely the messenger. Television is a wonderful world. After being used and abused Steve made him Controller of Factual Entertainment for Carlton Television.

Back to Emily Maitlis. Nine months later Mosey left his job running news and his replacement, Peter Horrocks, turned out to be a big Emily fan so Newsnight suddenly beckoned and her career path was altered overnight. I had no hard feelings and sent her a bouquet and congratulated her. I liked and respected her a lot. One myth that surrounded her was her ability to speak fluent Mandarin. I asked her about it one day. She smiled and told me it just wasn't true. Another media myth bites the dust!

While I'm on the subject of myths we're all inundated with press revelations of the drug abuse of rock stars, footballers and the occasional rugby player. Throw in your Kerry Katona's and Richard Bacon's and you've got the set. I've rarely witnessed drugs in television. Perhaps in my limited world of presenters it has never been much of an issue.

CHAPTER SIXTY EIGHT
SO, WHAT HAPPENED...?

Despite my imminent demise my family's fortunes were holding firm. My eldest son Gideon studied law at Bristol, got a Master's at Cambridge and now works as a barrister in London.

Elie tried university for a year and didn't like it. She, like her brother Alex, did some voluntary work overseas in Uzbekistan, then came home to carve herself out a great career in sales. Alex did his VSO in Tanzania. When he returned he also decided on a career in sales and has been hugely successful. Tom is studying mathematics at Kings College London. Looking back at what they had all been through, the least of it having *me* as their father, they can all be very proud of what they've achieved. All these good things provided a backcloth to what was becoming my end game.

The last couple of years were unbearable. I kept a brave public face but inside I was totally destroyed. The loss of so many clients meant that I could no longer pay the bills. The TV business was in free fall and was now enjoying its own 'three day week'. The corporate market place, once a great income stream, had dried up. Even if the economic climate hadn't been so terrible, I no longer had the calibre of clients to make up the losses that I was having to come to terms with. My own, by now well documented, inability to deal with financial matters led me to take on the NHI liabilities of two senior staffers drafting them from freelancers to employees. This resulted in a catastrophic increase in the company's costs. I had been warned that the company couldn't afford it but, as usual, history repeated itself. I should have pulled the plug back in 2005 but I didn't. But I still thought something would turn up. And continued to present an image that, as I have said before, I didn't want and couldn't afford.

I had two major life policies, one, a key-man policy with the Company, the other one for my family. The only way to cover the shortfall in my client account and provide for my family was to commit the ultimate act of the desperate.

I planned it very carefully and wrote letters to my family explaining my reasons. I lived with the knowledge of my plan for nearly fifteen months. I was now living from moment to moment.

When I spent time with my family, I found it nearly impossible to completely enjoy their company as I contemplated my terrible, albeit, self inflicted situation. I wanted to do what I thought was the best for all concerned and that meant for me, at the time, cashing in those life policies.

When the day came it was a beautiful late spring morning. I left the house early for what I thought would be my last journey. I was walking down a winding country lane in Eridge, a tiny hamlet about five miles from Tunbridge Wells when I decided to call Ian Bloom. I told him briefly what I felt I had to do and of course he was rightly furious. He told me that I should place the company in administration and that to do what I was contemplating, rather than helping my family, would destroy them.

I wandered around in the warm sunshine watching the rabbits bouncing around the endless fields and came across a dead, decaying deer. It had been hit by a car and its entrails were clearly visible and covered with flies. Everything I'd done in my life had brought me to this narrow lane and this dead deer. I thought about my children, their mother and the love Dan and I had shared over the years we'd been together and finally the wise counsel of Ian.

I turned back.

The company was duly placed into administration and my TV career was finally over. A few clients attended the meeting with the administrator. One of them, Mr Motivator, aka Derek Evans pointed out that I was no better than Bernie Madoff in operating a Ponzi scheme.

Playing catch up, as I perhaps wrongly called it, may well be have been a sort of Ponzi scheme. What I did hurt people, but if there is any difference at all, then it's that I didn't do it to line my own pockets. I didn't buy property, in fact I don't own a home, my car was ten years old, I'd never had any Ferraris, exotic holidays, flash suits or expensive jewellery and no deposits in any off shore accounts. I did entertain a lot and tried to reflect an image that I couldn't afford. This I did in the hope that the longer I stayed in business then, perhaps, the big deal would turn up and I'd manage to cover any outstanding liabilities to the clients. It was wrong and I should have called it a day long before, but sometimes doing the right thing is not as easy as it should be.

This is my story. It's no Greek tragedy, just a tale of ineptitude and stupidity. Having no home I was offered a refuge at a friend's house in Cyprus. Dan and I left our respective families where I hit the keyboard to bring you this account. The emails no longer stuff my in box and my mobile phone might just as well sit in a drawer and rust. No bad thing!

I've had to find a new way to live. I've discovered one thing though, that old maxim that people always roll out after a personal disaster, 'you know who your friends are', is bollocks. You *always* know who your friends are.

AFTERWORD

Christopher Isherwood's *Berlin Stories* in the 1930s inspired a play and a film called *I am a Camera*.

You may think, having got this far, that I could have called this autobiography *I am a Tape Recorder*. In fact I have never taped a conversation in my life. Obviously I would have made a lousy *News of the World* journalist.

You might then wonder at my astonishing powers of recall of discussions held and words spoken, in some cases, over fifty years ago. The truth is that, whilst I have, like I suspect most people, a reasonable memory for certain stand-out events and a hopeless memory for other things (I am not brilliant on dates), the dialogue reproduced in this book represents in virtually all cases the "gist" of what was said, both by me and by others. No one can live their life transcribing everything said to them or said by them to others and, in that respect, and maybe only in that respect, I am quite normal.

However, I have not deliberately fictionalised or made up any dialogue in this book in the sense that the conversations never took place. They did, although the words used are the best approximation to what was said that I can now recall. As an agent for much of my life, I said a lot and I listened a lot. I have tried to reproduce the sense of what was said. Most people, me included, don't speak grammatically or avoid repetition, deviation or hesitation. How boring it would have been to have included every "um" or "er". So I didn't. In that sense, but only in that sense, the conversations have been "improved".

In terms of what I have done with my life to date, you now know the story so far.